Enthusiast!
Essays on Modern American Literature

MANCHESTER
1824

Manchester University Press

Enthusiast!
Essays on Modern American Literature

David Herd

Manchester University Press

Manchester and New York

distributed exclusively in the USA by Palgrave

Published by Manchester University Press
Oxford Road, Manchester M13 9NR, UK
and Room 400, 175 Fifth Avenue, New York, NY 10010, USA
www.manchesteruniversitypress.co.uk

Distributed exclusively in the USA by
Palgrave, 175 Fifth Avenue, New York,
NY 10010, USA

Distributed exclusively in Canada by
UBC Press, University of British Columbia, 2029 West Mall,
Vancouver, BC, Canada V6T 1Z2

British Library Cataloguing-in-Publication Data
A catalogue record for this book is available from the British Library

Library of Congress Cataloging-in-Publication Data applied for

The Collected Poems of Frank O'Hara by Frank O'Hara, edited by Donald Allen, copyright © 1971 Maureen Granville-Smith, Administratix of the Estate of Frank O'Hara. Used by permission of Alfred A. Knopf, a division of Random House, Inc.

ISBN   978 0 7190 7428 8 *hardback*

First published 2007

16 15 14 13 12 11 10 09 08 07   10 9 8 7 6 5 4 3 2 1

Typeset in Caslon 11½/13 pt
by IML Typographers Ltd, Birkenhead, Merseyside
Printed in Great Britain
by Biddles, King's Lynn

For Eli, and Nora

Contents

Introduction: a short essay on enthusiasm

Modern American literature began with a statement of enthusiasm.

> Our age is retrospective. It builds the sepulchres of the fathers. It writes biographies, histories, and criticism. The foregoing generations beheld God and nature face to face; we, through their eyes. Why should not we also enjoy an original relation to the universe? Why should not we have a poetry and philosophy of insight and not of tradition, and a religion by revelation to us, and not the history of theirs? Embosomed for a season in nature, whose floods of life stream around and through us, and invite us by the powers they supply, to action proportioned to nature, why should we grope among the dry bones of the past, or put the living generation into masquerade out of its faded wardrobe? The sun shines to-day also. There is more wool and flax in the fields. There are new lands, new men, new thoughts. Let us demand our own works and laws and worship.[1]

Emerson's intention in writing *Nature*, and in writing its introductory section in particular – with its unanswered questions and its heightened demands – was to issue a provocation. His view was that American writers had not yet (by 1836) established their literature's independence, that they had not yet answered to the fact of a new social and environmental circumstance. His object was to stir his audience, which he knew to consist largely of writers or those who would be writers, to new, more truthful, forms of expression and thought. *Nature* itself set out the elements of a new philosophy, or at least, the newly rearranged elements of existing Transcendental philosophies. But the book's central achievement was rhetorical, Emerson's purpose being to announce a new beginning, and in so doing to raise in his readers new ambitions. *Nature* was a summons. It was a call to creativity. Its object in a modern, recognizable, secular sense – 'The sun shines to-day also' – was to enthuse.

Nature's appeal, the way it construes and relates to its readership, quickly became characteristic of Emerson's early writing. In the addresses and lectures he delivered in the late 1830s and early 1840s – in, for instance, such major documents in American literary history as 'The American

Scholar' and 'The Divinity School Address' – Emerson spoke directly to his listeners and readers, his manifest intention being to produce in them ideas which they would then seek to carry out into the world. He meant for them to leave the auditorium – the library, or the study – intent on continuing and communicating the thoughts they had found there. To inflect a word from Charles Olson, Emerson's intention was that his writing should 'project', that it should act on his readers and listeners in such a way that they might act on others and in the world. Emerson himself had various words for the relationship he was trying to strike up with his audience, for the nature of the transmission he was trying to effect, but one to which he recurred throughout his career was enthusiasm. 'Nothing great', he asserts in 'Circles', an essay on, among other things, influence, 'was ever achieved without enthusiasm. The way of life is wonderful; it is by abandonment.'[2]

'Enthusiasm', in Emerson, is a knowing word. Sometimes its use is as description, invariably approving, of a historic form of religious experience. As when in 'The Over-Soul' he asserts that 'a certain enthusiasm attends the individual's consciousness of that divine presence', and that 'everywhere the history of religion betrays a tendency to enthusiasm'; 'the *experiences*', for instance, 'of the Methodists ... that shudder of awe and delight with which the individual soul always mingles with the universal soul'.[3] I will come to this informed, descriptive use of 'enthusiasm' later. For the moment it is the other use I am interested in, Emerson frequently turning to 'enthusiasm' when he is most keen to inspire – enthusing by raising the prospect and possibility of enthusiasm. Precisely the problem with the English, he wrote in *English Traits*, is that, 'No enthusiasm is permitted except at the opera. ... They require a tone of voice that excites no attention in the room.'[4] This is clearly rhetorical, Emerson defining Englishness in terms of a state of mind he wants to make characteristic of American culture, the force and value of which he outlined in a late essay entitled 'Inspiration'. There Emerson draws on Plato to make his case, Plato observing, 'in his seventh Epistle', that inspiration

> is only accompanied by long familiarity with the objects of intellect, and a life according to the things themselves. 'Then a light, as if leaping from a fire, will on a sudden be enkindled in the soul, and will then itself nourish itself.' He said again, 'The man who is his own master knocks in vain at the doors of poetry.' The artists must be sacrificed to their art. Like bees, they must put their lives into the sting they give. What is a man good for without enthusiasm? and what is enthusiasm but this daring of ruin for its object?[5]

I'll be returning to all this, to the implications and connotations of Emerson's remarks. The point for the moment, however, is to articulate this book's opening claim: that Emerson's central object and achievement as a writer was to inject enthusiasm into American literature; and that since that foundational moment, since the opening paragraph of *Nature*, modern American writing has been decisively shaped by its enthusiasts.

What is Enthusiasm?

To establish what is at stake in this claim, it is necessary to show what the word is being taken to mean. The *OED* defines 'enthusiasm', in its modern sense, as a 'passionate eagerness in any pursuit, proceeding from an intense conviction of the worthiness of the object'. This modern sense will become important, especially when, later, the argument is made for the intrinsic importance of enthusiasm to Modern poetry; it being one of the claims of this book that Modern poetry (American in particular, but not exclusively so) needs to be understood enthusiastically, that enthusiasm throws light on aspects of poetic composition and transmission that tend to go insufficiently noticed by criticism. But the word's much older sense, the sense arrived at through etymology, is crucial also, enthusiasm deriving from the Greek '*enthusiasmos*' meaning to take, or more evocatively, to breathe in the god; *enthusiasmos* being then subsequently translated by the late Latin term 'inspiration', a word which preserves the sense of the inward breath, but which makes the object of the breath not the god, but the spirit – the divine as Emerson would have called it. A third meaning of the term is also important here, being the description of a religious practice – usually Protestant, and usually having its origins in the period of religious ferment which surrounded the English Civil War – in which and through which a person claims a particular closeness to, even an immediate relationship with, God. Martin Madan provided an eighteenth-century definition of this version of enthusiasm: 'To equal the *imaginations of men* to the *holy scripture of God*, and think them as much the *inspiration of God*, as what was dictated as such, to the *holy prophets* and apostles, is strictly and properly *Enthusiasm*.'[6]

To claim that, when Emerson wrote *Nature*, his aim and achievement was to inject enthusiasm into American literature, is to draw on each of these definitions. It is to identify in Emerson, and in his legacy to Modern American writing, a sense, carried through from the Greek, that in the act of composition words enter writing which have to be understood as coming from elsewhere. It is also to identify the thought in Emerson, and this is especially crucial to the particular writers discussed in this book – Thoreau, Melville, Pound, Marianne Moore, Frank O'Hara and James Schuyler – that in the act of composition, understood as an act of enthusiasm, the writer has, or is aiming at, a proximity to what O'Hara, writing about Pasternak, termed the work's 'condition of inspiration'. Finally, as is already indicated, Emerson's sense of enthusiasm was becoming modern, projective even, his object in writing (but also, sometimes, simply in using the term itself) being to create that 'passionate eagerness ... proceeding from an intense conviction of the worthiness of an object' which can, in certain circumstances, drive a person to act.

But if these definitions help, as an initial sketching of the territory, they also get ahead of the argument, because what is needed in order to substantiate the claim that Emerson's object and achievement was to inject enthusiasm into American literature, is a clear sense of the state of the idea at the point at which he took it up at the beginning of the nineteenth century. To arrive at which sense it is necessary to tell a brief history of enthusiasm, as it comes down from the Greeks and enters Anglo-American thinking. The point of such a history is partly to indicate how the term accumulated meanings. But it is partly also, in passing, to gather up a series of values and attitudes connected with the term which have come to inform a certain, highly characteristic strain of American writing; a complex of dispositions which it was Emerson's intention to put to work in the new literature he meant to inaugurate. *Nature* went for the vein. The intention was to pump enthusiasm into the bloodstream of Modern American writing. We need to know what that substance was.

So: Emerson's thinking about enthusiasm, as his essay on 'Inspiration' indicates, begins, quite properly, with Plato – the *Ion*, as commentators observe, being the *locus classicus* of discussions of enthusiasm.[7] In this short early dialogue, Socrates is in discussion with the rhapsode 'Ion'; a rhapsode being a reciter of, chiefly epic, poetry, who in the course of the performance would also sometimes offer commentary upon it. The dialogue centres on the question of enthusiasm, or inspiration, throughout, and is important not least because in it Socrates formulates one of the major tropes of enthusiasm:

> The gift which you possess of speaking excellently about Homer is not an art, but, as I was just saying, an inspiration; there is a divinity moving you, like that contained in the stone which Euripedes calls a magnet, but which is commonly known as the stone of Heraclea. This stone not only attracts iron rings, but also imparts to them a similar power of attracting other rings ... suspended from one another so as to form quite a long chain: and all of them derive their power of suspension from the original stone. In like manner the Muse first of all inspires men herself; and from these inspired persons a chain of other persons is suspended, who take the inspiration. For all good poets, epic as well as lyric, compose their beautiful poems not by art, but because they are inspired and possessed. And as the Corybantian revellers when they dance are not in their right mind, so the lyric poets are not in their right mind

when they are composing their beautiful strains ... For the poet is a light and winged and holy thing, and there is no invention in him until he has been inspired and is out of his senses, and reason is no longer in him; no man, while he retains that faculty, has the oracular gift of poetry.[8]

And so Socrates establishes the lines, or at least the outlines, along which arguments about enthusiasm, and poetry's relation to it, have continued to flow ever since. In the image of the inspired relation as a magnetic stone, he imports into enthusiasm at this outset of its intellectual trajectory, the ideas of communicability, circulation and transmission. To be in the mental state known as enthusiasm is to be ready to receive words, intimations and ideas, but it is also to be in a state to pass them on. The enthusiast, thus understood, is a circulator of thoughts, a person who keeps ideas and values moving. This meaning of enthusiasm, and the image of the enthusiast it throws up, is crucial to this book. Enthusiasm, it will be argued, and more particularly the enthusiast, are integral to the making but also the circulating of literary culture: witness those great American mobilizers Ezra Pound and Frank O'Hara.

It is not, however, the question of enthusiasm's capacity for transmission that most concerns Socrates. What he wants to establish, rather, is the nature of the enthusiast's state of mind. The point of the dialogue is to establish what the rhapsode, and prior to that the poet, knows, or rather doesn't know. By a process of elimination Socrates demonstrates to Ion that he doesn't, in any real sense, know anything about the works he recites – that he isn't, for instance, as well placed as a charioteer to comment on Homeric renderings of charioteering, or as well placed as a fisherman to comment on passages about fish – and that, therefore, either he must concede that in having initially claimed knowledge he was lying, or that, in fact, as Socrates wants to insist, he is inspired. Not that this is a compliment. Poetry, and the performance of poetry, is not, from this Socratic point of view, an art; it does not require technical skill – the form a poem takes is equally a gift of the inspiring agency – but involves, rather, the abandonment of all shaping faculties. In enthusiasm the poet will be 'out of his senses, and reason is no longer in him'. Poets, in other words, are as nothing: 'God himself is the speaker, and ... through them he is addressing us'.[9] The opposition is clear: the mental state known as enthusiasm, the state of poetic composition, is counterposed to reason, and requires that the poet be in some sense 'out of his senses', from which it follows for Plato – as for numerous subsequent commentators on enthusiasm – that the poet, or the enthusiast generally, doesn't know anything, that he or she isn't capable, in that state, of knowledge.

Except, of course, that the poet does know something. He or she does in some sense know the god, the inspiring divinity – in the sense, perhaps, that you might know your lover, or anybody else of whom you could issue a reliable report. The possible implications of this statement are foreclosed by Plato, for the reason that he believes in such an agency – just as seventeenth-century religious critics of and apologists for enthusiasm alike foreclose the argument of enthusiastic religious knowledge because they are confident of the divine. Thus, as the argument runs in Plato, the rhapsodes, and the poets whose work they recite, are in possession of a knowledge of sorts – they know god. But god is god, and he does all the work, and so nothing more needs to be said. The question, however, the question that will emerge for American writers after Emerson, is: what if one does not foreclose the argument between enthusiasm and reason by defaulting to the divine? Enthusiasm, and the idea that composition is enthusiastic – that in some sense, when writing, the poet is outside his or her regular or regulated self – does not disappear with a historic loss of faith in God. The claim becomes less grandiloquent, but as in O'Hara, for instance, the understanding is still that in writing, in the state of composition, one takes a step away. Which means that the question of what the poet might know has to be gone into again, this time without the foreclosing move; that for reasons Plato could not foresee, it is possible to entertain the thought that the poet, in the act of enthusiasm, is in possession of knowledge. To carry Plato forward then, what he claims to prove about enthusiasm, and about writing produced in the enthusiastic state, is that it has a special capacity for communication and transmission. What he also allows for, however, despite himself, is that in enthusiasm resides the possibility of knowledge. It is a possibility, as will be argued chapter by chapter here, that the American writers discussed in this book took extremely seriously.

Plato's flatteringly pejorative view of the poet, and of the state of mind in which the poet's composition is possible – out of reason and without knowledge, but also divinely inspired – marks the earliest discussions of enthusiasm in the British philosophical tradition. Locke's chapter, 'Of Enthusiasm', in *An Essay Concerning Human Understanding* (1689), is consistent with other seventeenth-century reflections on the idea – Meric Casaubon's *A Treatise Concerning Enthusiasm* (1653), Thomas More's *Enthusiasmus Triumphatus* (1656) – in aiming to denigrate a term which had become descriptive of a form of religious worship by which individuals (typically members of radical Protestant sects) claimed (and here a distinction is necessary) a nearness to or an immediate relationship with God. Such modes of worship were born of a dissatisfaction with the progress of the Reformation – with the failure of, in particular, the Church of England fully to discard the apparatus and hierarchy of the Church of Rome – and were characterized, it is worth noting immediately, by ecstatic symptoms or behaviour (depending on one's point of view) from which certain of the sects in question took their names. Thus enthusiasm, the moment of acquaintance with the divine, sometimes presented itself bodily, as with the devotional quaking of the Quakers, but also, in almost all cases, vocally, such that in the state of divine possession the individual emitted sounds or gained a verbal fluency of which, otherwise, they were hardly capable. This was most true of the sect known as the Ranters, but at their inception the subsequently reticent Quakers were also known for their extraordinary verbal outbursts. William Penn noted how the 'meanest of this people' – and this distribution of eloquence was very largely, from all points of view, the issue – gained 'an extraordinary understanding in divine things, and an admirable fluency'.[10] 'The Extasys expressed themselves', as the Earl of Shaftesbury put it, 'outwardly in the Quakings, Tremblings, Tossing of the Head and Limbs, Agitations and Fanatical Throws or Convulsions, extempory Prayer, Prophesy and the like.'[11] (I have in my mind a poetry reading, extempory, agitated: Allen Ginsberg, say, in San Francisco).[12]

Such enthusiasm having spilt so devastatingly into English politics in the middle of the century – the radical democratic claims precipitating the Civil War being continuous with the enthusiastic impulse to unmediated worship – Locke, like Plato, aimed to distinguish between enthusiasm and reason. The enthusiast, in his or her delusion, 'does Violence to his own Faculties, Tyrannizes over his own Mind, and usurps the Prerogative that belongs to Truth alone'.[13] Steering enthusiasm towards the historically related term fanaticism, Locke construes the state of mind as an overpowering – the individual allowing him- or herself, or rather their reason, to be dominated by their 'delusion', and looking in turn to dominate others, 'assuming an Authority of Dictating to others, and a forwardness to prescribe to their Opinions'.[14] The sense of dictation, as Timothy Clark has observed, never goes out of enthusiasm.[15] It is implicit in any claim, however measured, that a person's words, whether in the act of worship, or composition, or conversation, originate somewhere else. Even as he works the idea of dictation to his advantage, however, Locke does not altogether want to deny the logic of enthusiasm, it being incumbent upon him as a Christian to permit the possibility that some people, at some times, have experienced the relationship with the divine that enthusiasm describes. Thus,

> *Reason* is natural *Revelation*, whereby the eternal Father of Light, and Fountain of all Knowledge communicates to Mankind that portion of Truth, which he has laid within the reach of their natural Faculties; *Revelation* is natural *Reason* enlarged by a new set of Discoveries communicated by GOD immediately, which *Reason* vouches the Truth of, by the Testimony and Proofs it gives, that they come from GOD.[16]

Knowledge by Revelation is undeniable by Locke. Otherwise, what of the authority of the Bible? Otherwise, what of the wisdom of the prophets? The question arising from revelation, therefore, is not whether, but when, and to whom? Or as Emerson put it: 'Why should not we have a poetry and philosophy of insight and not of tradition, and a religion by revelation to us, and not the history of theirs?' Religiously speaking, one might think of this as the enthusiast's question, to which Locke's response, like that of numerous subsequent commentators, was to build a third possibility into Plato's original distinction: that there was reason, and that there was revelation, but that there was also enthusiasm, which was a false claim to the latter. It was a form of argument that continued to hold some sway, the pejorative sense enthusiasm acquired during and immediately after the Civil War causing even those who wanted to assert the continued possibility of revelation much more forcefully than Locke to distinguish themselves against the idea of enthusiasm. Well aware of the charges to which Methodism was vulnerable, John Wesley, when he preached on 'The Nature of Enthusiasm' (1755), distinguished his brand of worship from both 'a religion of form, a round of outward duties, performed in a decent manner', and that which 'not only dims but shuts the eyes of the understanding'. His argument, in other words, was with a religion which mistook procedure – form and outward duties – for insight, but his conclusion was a warning: 'Do not imagine you have attained that grace of God which you have not attained.'[17]

Wesley's anxious characterization of it notwithstanding, prominent eighteenth-century commentators on enthusiasm – the Civil War becoming, with time, a less traumatizing memory – sought to rehabilitate the idea, investigating it not primarily for the religious insight it might permit, but as a mode of secularized knowledge and transmission.[18] The Earl of Shaftesbury's 'A Letter Concerning Enthusiasm' (1702) was decisive in this, Shaftesbury looking both to distinguish enthusiasm from its most feverish excesses, for which he introduces the word 'panic', and also to generalize the word's application, reapplying it to poetry, as well as making it an element in all exalted performances: those of 'Heroes, Statesmen, Poets, Orators, Musicians and even Philosophers themselves'. Shaftesbury's argument in his 'Letter', as elsewhere in his writings, is against the hollow formalism and excessive scrutiny that he takes to characterize his age. 'Never was there', he asserts, 'in our Nation a time known, when Folly and Extravagance of every kind were more sharply inspected.' Against this age of inspection he wants to assert the sociability and communication of enthusiasm, from which 'there follows always an Itch of imparting it, and kindling the same fire in other Breasts'. Enthusiasm is aroused, Shaftesbury argues, 'when the Ideas or Images receiv'd are too big for the narrow human vessel to contain'.[19] It is a mode of knowledge and communication, he asserts, that breaches apparatus. (At which point what I have in my mind is a form, asking me to list my aims and objectives, to document the resulting transferable skills ... but we will come to that later.)

Writing 'Of Superstition and Enthusiasm' (1742), Hume argued along similarly proto-libertarian lines to Shaftesbury – if more trenchantly, less inclined to apology. Outlining contrasting religious errors – the first, superstition being 'a gloomy and melancholy disposition' which 'where real objects of terror are wanting ... finds imaginary ones, to whose power and malevolence it sets no limits'; the second, enthusiasm, being 'an unaccountable elevation ... from which arise raptures, transports, and surprising flights of fancy' – Hume is in no question as to which is preferable: 'My first reflection is, that superstition is favourable to priestly power, and enthusiasm not less, or rather more contrary to it, than sound reason and philosophy.' From this it follows that 'superstition is an enemy to civil liberty, and enthusiasm a friend to it' because where 'superstition groans under the dominion of priests ... enthusiasm is destructive of all ecclesiastical power'. The interest of Hume's essay is that while he looks like he is talking about religion, what he actually has on his mind are secular modes of knowledge. Thus it is of little concern to him what claims either the superstitious or enthusiasts make to religious authority – he doesn't believe either is acquainted with God. What matter, rather, are the epistemologies the differing forms of devotion imply. Thus, as enthusiasts freed themselves from 'the yoke of ecclesiastics', so they developed 'a contempt of forms, ceremonies and traditions', thus approaching the divinity 'without any human mediator', from which it has followed historically, he wants to insist, that, 'our sectaries, who were formerly such dangerous bigots, are become very free reasoners; and the Quakers seem to approach the only regular body of Deists in the universe.'[20] Hume's short essay doesn't pursue any further than this the move that was already implicit in *Ion* (though unexplorable by Plato): that it might be possible to regard enthusiasm as a secular mode of knowledge; that it might be possible to think of the state of mind described as enthusiasm outside of a religious framework, and so to reconsider the claims to insight or acquaintance that it made. It required Kant to make that next move. What Hume's essay points towards, even so, is an idea of knowledge unmediated by 'forms, ceremonies and traditions', an idea of knowledge, as it were, untroubled by bureaucracy.

Kant valued enthusiasm. It can look as if he doesn't when he discusses the idea in *The Critique of Judgement*, enthusiasm being contrasted throughout that discussion with reason. He can sound like Plato, in other words, when he introduces enthusiasm as that 'which we call sublime ... in internal nature' as being 'a might of the mind enabling it to overcome this or that hindrance of sensibility by means of moral principles'. As in Plato, then, to be enthusiastic is to be out of one's senses, except that here that description has a positive value, because what it promises is to 'overcome this or that hindrance of sensibility'; the hindrance of sensibility by which the apparatus of human understanding was interposed between the mind and the thing itself being the central problem to emerge from *The Critique of Pure Reason*. Mind, as Kant proposes it there, knows things according to its own forms – the concepts (time and space) of the sensibility, and the categories of the understanding – such that the best that reason could claim was knowledge of things as they appeared. Enthusiasm, from this point of view, as it is presented in the third critique, is not in opposition to reason, but a possible supplement to it. Thus,

> The idea of the good to which affection is superadded is *enthusiasm*. This state of mind appears to be sublime: so much so that there is a common saying that nothing great can be achieved without it. But now every affection is blind either as to the choice of its end, or, supposing this has been furnished by reason, in the way it is effected – for it is that mental movement whereby the exercise of free deliberation upon fundamental principles, with a view to determining oneself accordingly, is rendered impossible. On this account it cannot merit any delight on the part of reason. Yet, from an aesthetic point of view, enthusiasm is sublime, because it is an effort of one's powers called forth by ideas which give to the mind an impetus of far stronger and more enduring efficacy than the stimulus afforded by sensible representations.[21]

We are almost back to Emerson here, almost back to the beginning of *Nature*, almost at the point at which he injected enthusiasm into American writing. Nothing great can be achieved without it, so Kant asserts and as Emerson asserted after him. But more than that, enthusiasm has now been successfully redirected, so that what it has come to offer intimacy with is not God, but the world, giving 'to the mind an impetus of far stronger and more enduring efficacy than the stimulus afforded by sensible representations'. Which means what? Well, it almost means, or almost proposes, something Kant can't bring himself quite to say: that in a state of enthusiasm, when a person is in an enthusiastic relation with things, their relation to those things, to things in general perhaps, is, what? stronger? more enduring? closer? more intimate? more real? than is that afforded by sensible representations. The problem in Kant is mediation, that reason's knowledge is mediated by the mind's operation, by its categories and concepts, so that things, flax and wool for instance, are not known in themselves. What the state of mind known as enthusiasm has always promised, not least because what it names is the condition of being out of one's reason, is immediacy, an acquaintance with its object untroubled by 'forms, ceremonies and traditions'. What if, Kant seems to propose, one were to take seriously an enthusiastic relation with things? What if, in that state, mind was, however momentarily, by whatever mechanism, to go out of itself? This is in some sense what Heidegger wanted to say after Kant, when, in 'The Origin of the Work of Art', he contests that 'Projective saying is poetry', that poetry is 'clearing projection', that '*The work lets the earth be an earth*'.[22]

But Kant doesn't go further. He doesn't go on to propose that in enthusiasm is the prospect of non-alienation, the promise of continuity between humans and things. Emerson, however, does go further, in one of the most famously enthusiastic moments in all literature:

> Crossing a bare common, in snow puddles, at twilight, under a clouded sky, without having in my thoughts any occurrence of special good fortune, I have enjoyed a perfect exhilaration.

In which state, or remembering which state, he finds it possible to assert that

> The greatest delight which the fields and woods minister, is the suggestion of an occult relation between man and the vegetable. I am not alone and unacknowledged. They nod to me and I to them.[23]

In Kant, enthusiasm is not opposed to reason, but overrides it: the enthusiast, in the moment of enthusiasm, is out of his or her senses, but to potentially positive effect. The mechanisms of reason are momentarily suspended, and the effect is an impetus far stronger and more enduring than the stimulus afforded by sensible representations, which in another discourse one might term a revelation, and for Emerson constituted an original, that is to say an unmediated, relation to the universe. Which is not to take Emerson at his word when he says that when he is in the woods the vegetables nod to him. It is, though, to take seriously the idea that after Kant, and after Emerson's Kant, American literature set out to find what it, as opposed to other forms and modes of thought and expression, knew.

But philosophy is only part of the story. The other part of the story, the other aspect of an account of enthusiasm which shows what the term meant at the point at which Emerson established it as a basis for Modern American literature, is more strictly religious. Or to put this another way, fully to understand what enthusiasm meant to Emerson at the point at which he took it up, it is necessary not simply to hear what philosophers have to say about the phenomenon of enthusiasm, but to appreciate it, as it were, as a variety of religious experience. Charged as the term was in the two hundred years prior to Emerson, almost all philosophical commentary on it during that period is shaped by extrinsic, usually political concerns.

What is needed is an account of what, in practice, it means to enthuse. The account I will turn to, in a moment, is William Penn's Preface to *The Journal of George Fox*. Consider, though, before that, the following luminous details.

One: in November 1637 (two hundred years before the publication of *Nature*), charged with prophesying – with claiming to speak as if from God – Anne Hutchinson stood before the Massachusetts General Court, headed by the newly elected governor John Winthrop, as the authorities sought to bring an end to the antinomian crisis. Asked how she knew the spirit had moved her, it is recorded she responded thus:

> Mrs. Hutchinson: How did Abraham know that it was God that bid him offer his son, being a breach of the sixth commandment?
> Deputy Governor: By an immediate voice.
> Mrs. Hutchinson: So to me by an immediate revelation.
> Deputy Governor: How! an immediate revelation.
> Mrs. Hutchinson: By the voice of his own spirit to my soul.

In response to which the 1637 Synod ruled that

> Immediate revelation without concurrence with the word, doth not onely countenance but confirme that opinion of Enthusianisme, justly refused by all the Churches, as being contrary to the perfection of the Scriptures, and perfection of Gods wisdome therein.[24]

Two: in his *Plantation Work*, George Fox described America as 'a peculiar and special work appointed for many in our day'.[25]

Three: in *English Traits*, Emerson stated that:

> In the island, they never let out all the length of all the reins, there is no Berserkir rage, no abandonment or ecstasy of will or intellect … But who would see the uncoiling of that tremendous spring, the explosion of their well-husbanded forces, must follow the swarms which, pouring now for two hundred years from the British islands, have sailed, and rode, and traded, and planted through all climates, mainly following the belt of empire.[26]

Four: in 'Transcendentalism', a *Dial* essay of 1842, written in response to a Quaker correspondent, Emerson observes

> The identity, which the writer of this letter finds between the speculative opinions of serious persons at the present moment, and those entertained by the first Quakers, is indeed so striking as to have drawn a very general attention of late years to the history of that sect. Of course, in proportion to the depth of the experience, will be its independence on time and circumstances, yet one can hardly read George Fox's *Journal*, or Sewel's *History of the Quakers*, without many a rising of joyful surprise at the correspondence of facts and expressions to states of thought and feeling, with

which we are very familiar ... And so we add in regard to these works, that quite apart from the pleasure of reading modern history in old books, the reader will find another reward in the abundant illustration they furnish to the fact, that wherever the religious enthusiasm makes its appearance, it supplies the place of poetry and philosophy and of learned discipline, and inspires by itself the same vastness of thinking; so that in learning the religious experiences of a strong but untaught mind, you seem to have suggested in turn all the sects of the philosophers.[27]

There is a narrative immanent in these details that is best not understood as orthodox history; not, though it could be told this way, as a chronological unfolding of events. It is better understood as something like a mark on the imagination, as an often recurring image or option that, once established, might always be taken up. From the beginning of the colonial period the enthusiast figures in American culture; or, to put it another way, in America, since colonialism, the enthusiast has always been a figure – claiming intimacy with the condition of their inspiration, running into confrontation, challenging the power of the state with their 'extraordinary understanding' and 'admirable fluency', with their 'extemporary Prayer, Prophesy and the like'. More than this, America was the place for it, 'a special work appointed for many in our day'. With the restoration of the monarchy in England, enthusiasts had to look somewhere else, to a social environment where the 'forms, ceremonies and traditions' of state religion might not re-form quite so readily, not to such prompt and devastating effect, hence Emerson's image of the exporting of 'abandonment' and 'ecstasy', the 'uncoiling of that tremendous spring' which accompanied the swarms 'pouring now for two hundred years from the British Islands'. This is, in effect, to present the history of America as a history of the enthusiast – a secret history in which the enthusiast plays the decisive role – which current Emerson enters into as, with 'joyful surprise', he reads *The Journal of George Fox*. Enthusiasm, in other words, as Emerson encounters it and as he passes it on, is a living idea from America's past – the enthusiast, the outline of a figure always waiting to be reinhabited – the meaning of which is best got at through presentations of the religious experience.

William Penn's 'Preface' to *The Journal of George Fox* is a guide to American writing. Penn is valuable here because of his transitional status, articulating as he does the mindset that found it necessary to move from England to America. He is valuable also because he brings to the presentation of enthusiastic devotion a nuance of experience which philosophers, in their secondary literature, driven by cultural political concerns, tended to consider in terms of ranting stereotypes. From the outset, then, Penn's story is complex: man, as he tells it, was originally undone by 'the mediation of ... man's own nature and companion'. It is not the claim to immediacy, as the Massachusetts Synod would have had it, that is sinful, but rather, as Penn sets it out from the beginning, that in mediation is to be located sin. Likewise, the passage in divine history from original sin to redemption is the story of a growing closeness. The Old Testament was characterized by 'an outward priesthood, and external rites and ceremonies', whereas Christ brings in 'a nearer testament and better hope'. That word 'nearer' is worth holding on to. For Stanley Cavell, what defines American literature is a desire for the near and the low, with Thoreau, as he argues in *The Senses of Walden*, getting beyond the Kantian problematic precisely by his extended experiment in and linguistic rendering of 'nearness'. As Penn has it, 'no more at old Jerusalem, nor at the mountain of Samaria, will God be worshipped, above other places ... He will come nearer than of old time, and he will write his law in the heart.' [28]

'Nearness', as a principle and aim of worship, cuts two ways in discussions of enthusiasm. In the first place, for Penn as for Wesley after him, it is a criticism of 'all formality in religion', of the insistence on special sites and conventions of worship. Also, crucially, nearness is not oneness; it is not the assertion of identity with God. Thus there is no question that, in his Preface, Penn defends enthusiasm, and the prophesying – the inspired utterance – that follows from it: Quakerism precisely 'allowed greater liberty to prophesy; for they admitted any member to speak or pray ... even without the distinction of clergy or laity; persons of any trade, be it never so low and mechanical'. At the same time, he wants to distinguish Quakerism from such sects as the Ranters (who forgot their 'humble dependence'), from antinomians and perfectionists who believed that in their worship, and at their moment of enthusiasm, they spoke not because moved by a divinity, but as if they were themselves in fact divine; 'as if Christ came not to take away sin, but that we might sin more freely at his cost'. The distinction is crucial; one can think of it as the distinction Melville draws between Ishmael and Ahab. Antinominans and perfectionists claimed not nearness to God, but divine authority, divinity itself – from which it followed that they were beyond sin.[29] Quakerism, on the other hand, as Penn presents it, though resolutely not formal in its worship, does not claim outright immediacy in its relation to God, but rather, it approaches to nearness through a practice Penn, following Fox, calls – happily – 'experiment':

> So that this people did not only in words more than equally press repentance, conversion, and holiness, but did it knowingly and experimentally ... They reached to the inward state and condition of people, which is an evidence of the virtue of their principle, and of their ministering from it, and not from their own imaginations, glosses, or comments upon Scripture.[30]

The Quaker sense of experimental thought grafts on to the general sense of enthusiasm three ideas that have resonated long and deep in Modern American literature. In the first place, it describes a mode of thought – looking forward we can call it composition – that gains such authority as it has precisely by operating outside convention and form, Quaker worship being an act of waiting for the moment of appropriate and necessary speech, not a performance of established ritual. Second, as Penn implies, experiment as understood by Fox and in Quakerism implies a particular relation to scripture or text. The Bible was to be read not as God's last word, but in conjunction with his latest word, as a guide and help in appreciating spiritual insight. Scripture, in other words, was to be understood not as finished, but as a draft – 'a draft of a draft' as Melville had it – on which spiritual experience could always work and improve. Which position, as David Lovejoy has observed, could, on the one hand, imply radical independence from textual commentators – priestcraft – but which could also topple, at the drop of a hat, into outright anti-intellectualism. The substance of Fox's first 'opening', by which he means revelation, was that 'being bred at Oxford or Cambridge was not enough to fit and qualify men to be ministers of Christ' – hence the fact that he himself would 'get into the orchards, or the fields, with my Bible, by myself'.[31] The gist of this proposition seems unarguable. By the same token, as Lovejoy writes, 'Education and learning were burdens the enthusiasts could do without, for nothing should clutter the path along which the spirit approached'.[32] This too points forward to American poetry, which since Emerson has had, almost as an axiom of its existence, a vexed relation with the authority of the book. More suggestive still, however, in the Quaker sense of experiment, is the temporality of enthusiasm it gives rise to, the necessity of constantly revisiting the truth, of always reacquainting with the spirit. Penn puts it this way:

> Nor is it enough that we have known the Divine gift, and in it have reached to the spirits in prison, and have been the instruments of the convincing of others of the way of God, if we keep not as low and poor in ourselves, and as depending upon the Lord as ever; since no memory, no repetitions of former openings, revelations, or enjoyments, will bring a soul to God.[33]

Which makes enthusiasm, curiously, but suggestively, not so much a claim to authority as a perpetual and necessary revisiting born of uncertainty, a function of the permanent, always fluctuating present. (And what I have in mind now is Frank O'Hara, 'A Step Away From Them': 'A blonde chorus girl clicks: he / smiles and rubs his chin. Everything / suddenly honks: it is 12.40 of / a Thursday'.)

Contra Locke – for whom 'immediate revelation' had become the popular, because the easy, option – Penn presents the enthusiasm of the

Quakers as a most demanding practice, requiring of the individual a constant attention, calling on him or her always to be reacquainting with their condition of inspiration, to which end, towards the conclusion of his Preface, he offers pointers to appropriate worship which read now, in the age of creative writing, like guides to composition; or like answers in a *Paris Review* interview ('When and where do you write?'); or like the concluding section of Emerson's essay on 'Inspiration', where he notes that, 'At home, I remember in my library the wants of the farm … All the conditions must be right for my success, slight as that is.'[34] Thus, as Penn tells it, registering the delicate condition of inspiration, 'Wherefore, brethren, let us be careful neither to out-go our Guide, nor yet loiter behind him; since he that makes haste may miss his way, and he that stays behind, lose his Guide'. As for where to situate yourself to best effect, remember, he says, that, 'Jesus loved and chose solitudes; often going to mountains, to gardens, and sea-sides, to avoid crowds and hurries, to show his disciples it was good to be solitary, and sit loose in the world'.[35] This phrase is irresistible, 'and sit loose in the world': where to sit, how to hold oneself, becoming crucial questions for American writers. Thoreau and O'Hara sat loose in the world, Schuyler looked out of his window. A reading of American literature in terms of enthusiasm is, in part, a study of its composition.

With all the foregoing in mind, there are three things to be said about the way, in his writing, Emerson handled enthusiasm. The first is that in *Nature*, but in the opening paragraph of his anonymously published little book in particular, Emerson provided a quite brilliant summation of the cultural potential of enthusiasm as it was handed down to him through a philosophical tradition culminating with Kant, and through a religious tradition whose richest expression he found in the Quakers. To hear that statement again, but this time with all the underpinning and archaeology in view:

> Our age is retrospective. It builds the sepulchres of the fathers. It writes biographies, histories, and criticism. The foregoing generations beheld God and nature face to face; we, through their eyes. Why should not we also enjoy an original relation to the universe? Why should not we have a poetry and philosophy of insight and not of tradition, and a religion by revelation to us, and not the history of theirs? Embosomed for a season in nature, whose floods of life stream around and through us, and invite us by the powers they supply, to action proportioned to nature, why should we grope among the dry bones of the past, or put the living generation into masquerade out of its faded wardrobe? The sun shines to-day also. There is more wool and flax in the fields. There are new lands, new men, new thoughts. Let us demand our own works and laws and worship.

What is one to call this but a statement of enthusiasm, with its demand for 'our own works and laws and worship', with its call for 'a poetry and philosophy of insight', for 'a religion by revelation to us, and not the history of theirs'? What relation is struck with the world here, if not enthusiastic, when 'God and nature' are to be beheld 'face to face'? What, if not the enthusiastic present, is offered by the image of the sun shining to-day also? In *Nature* Emerson put enthusiasm to work – nothing great, after all, could be achieved without it. He enthused in order to achieve a cultural awakening, an original, which is to say an unmediated relation to the universe; in effect, a new beginning.

But if *Nature* is a great cultural mobilising of the idea of enthusiasm as he inherited it at the beginning of the nineteenth century, it is more than arguable that Emerson himself, in his own writing, did not know where to carry the thought. If anything, in fact, as he crosses the bare common and becomes a transparent eyeball, what he offers up is a weak reading of enthusiasm, an antinomianism of sorts, lacking the nuances of Fox, but more so of William Penn. What Emerson didn't work out, in other words, in his own writing, was how to modernize enthusiasm, how really to investigate its meaning and potential in an increasingly secular age. He sensed that a Modern American literature could not dispense with enthusiasm. What he couldn't determine, as a writer, was what form or forms it should take. Thus for all its goadings and provocations, the late essay 'Inspiration' has reached an impasse, Emerson asking a series of perplexed questions: 'Are these moods in any degree within control?', '…where is the Franklin with kite or rod for this fluid?'[36] There are specific reasons why 'Inspiration' reads like an impasse. Emerson was old and tired when he wrote *Letters and Social Aims*, and hadn't volunteered for the task, but had had it forced on him when the publisher, Routledge, proposed to issue a new volume of his writings unsanctioned. Even so, what 'Inspiration' confirms is what elsewhere his writing shows to be the case: that fully as he was in command of the pre-existing meanings and cultural implications of the idea of enthusiasm, he wasn't equipped himself – as a writer – to make the idea new. And so the third point is this: that when he wrote *Nature* Emerson presented future writers – starting just around the corner with Thoreau – with an immense resource, but also with a problem. He injected enthusiasm into American literature; he also gave few clues as to what an enthusiastic Modern literature might look like. Some answers to that question are the subject of this book.

Our age is bureaucratic

This book is neither a theory nor a history of enthusiasm.[37] What it is, rather, is an exploration of a critical idea: an account of how enthusiasm, as

developed in the histories of philosophy and religion, entered and was altered by American writing. To put it another way, what this book offers is a portrait of the writer as an enthusiast, where the portrait, as will become clear, carries more than a hint of polemic. To sketch in the implications of the critical idea, the history of American literature is barely thinkable without its enthusiasts. There are numerous other writers it would have been appropriate to discuss here, numerous other writers who, for varying reasons, might have been named enthusiasts: Whitman, obviously, Charles Olson, Allen Ginsberg, Robert Creeley, Denise Levertov, Charles Bernstein, Susan Howe, Adrienne Rich. One object in choosing to discuss the figures I have was to present a portrait of the writer as an enthusiast in various aspects, and so to consider quite different writers in quite different circumstances. It will probably be apparent already how Pound and O'Hara might fit the bill. Moore and Schuyler present other, not less valuable, versions of enthusiasm. A linking feature among the writers is the attention they gave to the act of composition: not a truism, I think, but a statement which indicates the fact that they not only contributed decisively to the history and directions of American writing, in its forms, themes, subjects and concerns, but fundamentally altered the way it was done. What this points to is Thoreau at Walden, Marianne Moore among the pamphlets and the guide books, Frank O'Hara at the typewriter in the middle of a party.

This, it seems to me, is one virtue of enthusiasm as a critical idea, that it points criticism back (or forwards) to the making of the work, towards the act of creation, that it obliges one to consider the processes by which writers enabled their work to come into being. Throughout the book what is described is a continuing sense of the writers in question allowing, or enabling, something to come through, where that process is not taken to be mysterious (or is certainly not treated as mysterious), but where the object is, nonetheless, to allow other agents, or other agencies' words, or just language understood as another agency, into the work in progress. Invariably – Plato's slur on poetic craft notwithstanding – the processes in question are technical, but where technique is understood generously, so as to include not just choice of form and metre, but also the situation of the writer, the time and place of writing, the way, in practice, for instance, they incorporate other people's books. This opening of the work to other writers, speakers and their words, is, as Timothy Clark has discussed, something like a definition of the moment of composition itself, and a moment for which 'enthusiasm', and its derivative 'inspiration', remain, long after their divine connotations have dropped away, terms for which writers reach, or which, with little or no forcing, can be used to name the writer's state of mind and practice in the act of composition.[38] 'Opening' was George Fox's word for the operations of the divine spirit upon him, for the moment of enthusiasm. Modern, especially Modernist, compositions – with all their quotes and fragments and aleatory factors, their words coming from elsewhere, sometimes, seemingly, from nowhere at all – constitute hardly less an opening up. And if not an opening, then a clearing, in the manner of Thoreau at Walden Pond, or of that 'state of clarity', as O'Hara observed of Pollock, 'in which there are no secrets'. Where, as O'Hara still wanted to insist in 1958, the 'artist has reached a limitless space of air and light in which the spirit can act freely and with unpremeditated knowledge'.[39]

The great value, however, of enthusiasm as an element in literature, is its dynamic nature. To be enthused is to want to pass things on. Plato put it in terms of magnetic rings, Shaftesbury described it as 'an itch of imparting', of 'kindling the same fire in other breasts'. William Duff, in his essay on genius, described an 'intenseness and vigour of ... sensations ... which as it were hurries the mind out of itself'.[40] Composition as enthusiasm is itself of course communication, an act of passing on, the publication of otherwise unavailable thought. More than that, though, enthusiasm describes a communicative relation with literature. Thus, a further reason for considering the various writers in this book is the great thought and energy they gave to the circulation of other people's work, that they were enthused by it – seized, gripped or inspired by it – and wanted, for no more reason, often, than that they thought it was good, to pass it on. All of the writers here, one way or another, carry this impulse into the writing itself, circulating other works and others' words through their practice of quotation. Pound and O'Hara made enthusiasm integral to their working existences: as editors, critics and curators, but also, more noisily, as boosters and promoters; as galvanisers generally, whose energy was crucial both to the transmission, and in some cases the existence of work they valued. Criticism historically, and understandably enough, has tended to reserve its attention for the end product. A reading of American literature from the point of view of enthusiasm takes seriously the fact that any given book once didn't, but more to the point might have never come to, exist, that literary culture depends for its existence and perpetuation largely on the time and energy of its enthusiasts. The composer Morton Feldman said, with regard to creativity, that what's important is, 'to have someone like Frank [O'Hara] standing behind you. That's what keeps you going.'[41] Hemingway recalled, 'Pound the major poet devoting, say, one fifth of his time to poetry. With the rest he tried to advance the fortunes, both material and artistic, of his friends.'[42]

This is part of Lewis Hyde's point in his brilliant study *The Gift: Imagination and the Erotic Life of Property*, at one point in which he touches on the intersection between the gift and religious and literary enthusiasm. The gift, and gift exchange, as Hyde presents it, is a mode of circulation counter to money, with enthusiasm, in its itch to impart value directly, having an analogy with the gift. Or as he puts it, suggestively, 'Cash exchange is to gift exchange what reason is to enthusiasm'.[43] Enthusiasm, according to this view, is a mode of circulation other than cash exchange according to which values are not displaced and distorted (by the symbols effecting the exchange) but passed on. Not that the argument should be too readily closed off here. The view of enthusiasm Hyde implies is much closer to Hume's cheerful view of it than to Locke's, where what enthusiasm stands for is civil liberty and the free circulation of ideas, as opposed to the desire, in passing ideas on, to overpower another's mind. Which is the difference, as Melville presents it, between Ishmael and Ahab. Which is the difference, perhaps, between O'Hara's enthusiasm and the enthusiasm of the later Pound, where circulation of texts – as I discuss – becomes a much more vexed question. Even so, and especially in Pound's case, a barely stoppable enthusiasm for other people's works was decisive in the renovation of literary culture, enthusiasm being, precisely in the absence of money and significant monetary reward, the best available mode of circulation.

This question of circulation, and distortion by mediation, brings me to the contemporary argument for and of this book, to the British situation in which it is written, and so to its polemical, as opposed to its critical, base. Enthusiasm, historically, is a response to bureaucracy. Quakerism, as Fox conceived it, was a response to both the intermediary nature of the religious practices of the Church of England, and to the sects and sectarianism that evolved against it. Which is not to say that enthusiasm cannot degenerate into sects and bureaucracies of its own – clearly it can – but that in its purest form, the form William Penn presents for instance, enthusiasm, the enthusiastic life, is in revolt against the bureaucratic mindset in all its guises. To put it another way, as religious history testifies literally, and as literary history understands metaphorically (and not to put to fine a point on it), bureaucracy kills enthusiasm. It kills it, or tries to kill it, by its mediations, which is to say by what Hume called its 'conventions' and Penn calls its 'external rites'; by its forms, by its panels of assessment, by its processes of review; by its quality assurance procedures, by its prescriptive languages, by its categories insensitive to specific truth; by its rating mechanisms, by its arbitrary evaluations, by its RAE. What enthusiasm promises is immediacy: between the individual and the divine originally, but subsequently between the creative person and the condition of inspiration, between readers and writers, teachers and readers. Plato's image of magnetic rings to present the effect of enthusiasm is right; what he didn't observe was the solidarity – arising out of shared enthusiasm – which followed from his metaphor, and according to which enthusiasm can be thought of as foundational to ideal communities. Not (to rehearse an anxiety that necessarily runs through any argument for enthusiasm) that the term should be taken here in an untroubled sense – this book does not claim, on behalf of its writers, an immediacy between linguistic work and its subject or situation. What it does argue, however, is that in the compositional act, a knowledge, owing to proximity – one might call it intimacy – with words and things, is made possible. More than this, what the book comes to argue, at various points and in various ways, is that for the writers presented here at least – though one might mention many others – enthusiasm, the enthusiastic state, is literature's way of knowing; that literature, after Kant, and in America after Emerson, has taken seriously the idea that, through its act of composition, it has knowledge, or knowledges, to impart. In this sense the book plots a trajectory, the writers in question refining a developing sense of the knowledge made possible by writing, and in composition. A trajectory which, here anyway, culminates with O'Hara arguing in relation to Fairfield Porter, but also reflexively, that 'composition ... is the personal statement of the insight which observation and insight afford'; and with the claim that what Schuyler arrives at, in his Thoreau-like compositional state, is a writing one can think of as *showing* the world.[44]

And the point about bureaucracy is that it wrecks all of this. In its coercive mediations it constantly forces attention away from the terms writers have arrived at for and through their practice. Literature, in other words, in a British university setting at least, is rendered incapable of making its contribution to the human economy of knowledge because it is forced into forms of thought and expression inappropriate to its insight and understanding. Equally, such bureaucracy intrudes on, and practically shuts down, the enthusiastic circulation that literature depends upon. As relations between writers and critics, teachers and students are more and more mediated by terms alien to the subject, so those parties become alienated from one another: not connected by the enthusiastic impulse – the itch to impart – but sectioned off and compartmentalized by a managerial economy.

A final reason for this book's investment in enthusiasm has to do with Modern poetry, and in particular with the argumentative apparatus that has overlain poetry for at least the past hundred years, and which, in Britain and America, has reduced to a standoff between difficulty and accessibility. In part it was out of sheer weariness with the oscillations of this debate that I began to want to think of a different point of entry into Modern writing, poetry in particular. Enthusiasm is a potentially controversial term in this respect in that, in its seventeenth-century origins at least, it signalled precisely a revolt against the priestcraft which endorsed and thrived on textual difficulty, and which was understood then, by enthusiasts, as a euphemism for class. (On which point, for biographical reasons, I am glad at the implication that, however distantly, George Fox, a man of unremarkable background from southwest Leicestershire, should have had a hand in the origins of American literature; a fact indicating, as Emerson suggests, a trans-Atlantic diversion of English energies, and which I wonder doesn't partly explain my own enthusiasms.) And yet if, in one of its intellectual origins, the idea running through this book is suspicious of claims implicit in the justification of difficulty, the book hardly opts for what might be thought (if it is worth thinking in this way) non-difficult texts. Rather, in its discussion of Modern American writers, it aims to chart a way through the practices and devices that characterize their work – often citational, or allusive, or aleatory – which understands such gestures in that spirit of circulation which, in one sense, constitutes writing's enthusiasm.

There is a fundamental paradox in enthusiasm. On the one hand, what it claims is intimacy, even an immediate relation with, a condition of inspiration. On the other, the way such an inspiration is invariably held to manifest itself in the medium of language – often turned to excess – is as another voice, whether of the divinity, or a muse, or, as in Modern writing, in the quoted words of another book, or as words envisaged as originating elsewhere than the writing self. This book doesn't attempt to make that paradox go away. Rather it acknowledges, from the point of view of the enthusiast, that such a paradox – the ambitions of direct acquaintance with the world, and of speaking in and through others' words – is the true and precarious basis of Modern American writing. The intensification of this paradox has to do with voice, with the fact that, as Clark argues, enthusiasm never completely loses sight of its origin in an oracular tradition, and that as writing turns to enthusiasm certain tensions of concept and expression emerge. Again, these tensions don't go away here. Rather, in their acts of composition, the writers in question are observed refining and complicating our sense of what it means to have a voice, until what we are talking about is not voice as such, but a mode of written utterance it is not improper to think of as voicing.

There is a single argument running through the essays that follow; the argument, to repeat, that when Emerson inaugurated Modern American literature he did so by mobilising what one can call, paradoxically, a tradition of enthusiasm, and that since that moment American writers, some very major ones at least, have sought to answer the question of what it means to be a Modern enthusiast. This said, the answers, as presented here – the answers of Thoreau, Melville, Pound, Moore, O'Hara and Schuyler –

have differed quite radically from one another, and in the spirit of enthusiasm it has been my intention not simply to fit different writing practices to a governing thesis, but to consider what the various writers look like when viewed through their enthusiasm. Nor is it my object in talking up enthusiasm to present it to the exclusion of other aspects of writing. In picturing the writer as an enthusiast I am not, as should become clear, obscuring portraits of the writer as, for instance, reader, reviser, editor and critic. This book, in other words, is not an argument against, but an argument for: *for* enthusiastic engagements with writing, *for* institutions and structures of debate that allow enthusiasms to be passed on.

Notes

1 Ralph Waldo Emerson, *Essays and Lectures*, New York, Library of America, 1983, p. 7
2 Ibid., p. 414.
3 Ibid., pp. 382, 393.
4 Ibid., p. 827.
5 Emerson, *Letters and Social Aims*, London and New York, George Routledge and Sons, 1883, p. 260.
6 M[artin] M[adan], *A Full and Compleat Answer to the Capital Errors, Contained in the Writings of the late Rev. William Law* (1763), cited in Jon Mee, *Romanticism, Enthusiasm, and Regulation: Poetics and the Policing of Culture in the Romantic Period*, Oxford, Oxford University Press, 2003, p. 2.
7 For an extended discussion of Plato's *Ion* see Timothy Clark, *The Theory of Inspiration: Composition as a Crisis of Subjectivity in Romantic and Post-Romantic Writing*, Manchester and New York, Manchester University Press, 1997, pp. 40–60.
8 Plato, *The Dialogues of Plato*, tr. B. Jowett, Oxford, Clarendon Press, 1953, pp. 107–108.
9 Ibid., p. 108.
10 William Penn, 'Preface' to George Fox, *Journal of George Fox*, London, W. and F. G. Cash, 1852, p. 22.
11 Earl of Shaftesbury, *Characteristicks of Men, Manners, Opinions, Times, in Three Volumes, Vol.1*, London, John Darby, 1715, p. 50.
12 The line connecting the outbursts of the Ranters and subsequent poetry has been drawn before. See, for instance, Nigel Smith, *A Collection of Ranter Writings from the Seventeenth Century*, London, Junction Books, 1983.
13 John Locke, *An Essay Concerning Human Understanding*, Oxford, Clarendon Press, 1985, p. 698.
14 Ibid.
15 See, in particular, the chapter on Derrida and Celan, in Clark, *Theory of Inspiration*, pp. 259–84.
16 Locke, *Understanding*, p. 698.

17 John Wesley, *The Works of John Wesley, Volume V*, Grand Rapids, Mich., Zondervan Publishing House, pp. 467, 477.

18 This rehabilitation of the idea of enthusiasm – he discusses it in terms of regulation – is Jon Mee's subject in the first chapter of *Romanticism, Enthusiasm, and Regulation*. See pp. 23–81.

19 Shaftesbury, *Characteristicks*, pp. 54, 9, 51, 54.

20 David Hume, *Essays Moral, Political and Literary*, Oxford, Oxford University Press, 1966, pp. 75, 76, 79, 77, 79.

21 Immanuel Kant, *The Critique of Judgement*, tr. James Creed Meredith, Oxford, Oxford University Press, 1952, p. 124.

22 Martin Heidegger, *Basic Writings*, ed. David Farrell Krell, London, Routledge, 1993, pp. 198, 197, 172.

23 Emerson, *Essays*, pp. 10, 11.

24 David S. Lovejoy, *Religious Enthusiasm in the New World: Heresy to Revolution*, Cambridge, Mass., Harvard University Press, 1985, pp. 75, 76.

25 George Fox and William Loddington, *Plantation Work, The Work of this Generation*, London, 1682, unpaginated.

26 Emerson, *Essays*, p. 931. With this remark Emerson sketches in a continuation of the story Jon Mee tells in *Romanticism, Enthusiasm, and Regulation*. Thus if the argument there is that it was the work of eighteenth-century commentators, and then Romanticism in turn, to regulate enthusiasm, which is to say, to draw it within the confines of polite conversation and society, the implication of Emerson's remark is that for a deregulated enthusiasm one might turn to America, where in religion as well as literature formal constraints have arguably been less successfully imposed.

27 Emerson, *Essays*, pp. 1198–9.

28 Penn, *Preface*, pp. 1, 2.

29 Ibid., pp. 6, 7, 8.

30 Ibid., p. 21.

31 Fox, *Journal*, p. 53.

32 Lovejoy, *Religious Enthusiasm*, p. 41.

33 Penn, *Preface*, p. 39.

34 Emerson, *Letters*, p. 273.

35 Penn, 'Preface', pp. 38, 41.

36 Emerson, *Letters*, p. 259.

37 For a recent theory of enthusiasm readers should go to Timothy Clark's *The Theory of Inspiration*, and for recent histories of enthusiasm one might read Jon Mee's *Romanticism, Enthusiasm, and Regulation* or David Lovejoy's *Religious Enthusiasm in the New World*, from all of which this book has benefited greatly.

38 Clark presents this moment as a crisis of subjectivity (see his chapter 'Orientations: the space of composition', pp. 14–39) from which starting point he stages an investigation into writers and theorists in a European tradition who have dwelt on and intensified the sense of subjectivity in crisis. My interest, in considering composition as a moment of enthusiasm, is in how works are made or come into being, from which it follows that this book is less concerned to

pursue the dissolution of the subject as an effect of enthusiasm, than to consider how, through enthusiasm, works get made.

39 Frank O'Hara, *Art Chronicles 1954–1966*, New York, George Braziller, 1975, pp. 25, 26.

40 Shaftesbury, *Characteristicks*, p51; William Duff, *An Essay on Original Genius and its Various Modes of Exertion in Philosophy and the Fine Arts, Particularly Poetry*, Delmar, New York, Scholars' Facsimiles, pp. 171–2, cited in Clark, *Theory*, p71.

41 Bill Berkson and Joe LeSueur (eds.), *Homage to Frank O'Hara*, Bolinas, Calif., Big Sky, 1978, p. 13.

42 Humphrey Carpenter, *A Serious Character: The Life of Ezra Pound*, London, Faber and Faber, 1988, p. 188.

43 Lewis Hyde, *The Gift: Imagination and the Erotic Life of Property*, London, Vintage, 1999, p. 169.

44 Frank O'Hara, *Standing Still and Walking in New York*, ed. Donald Allen, Bolinas, Calif., Grey Fox Press, 1975, p. 55.

1

Sounding: Henry David Thoreau

We know what Thoreau meant by *Walden*, or at least, we know what he meant for it to do. We know because he told us, on the title page of his book, where by way of an epigraph he quoted himself:

> I do not propose to write an ode to dejection, but to brag as lustily as chanticleer in the morning, standing on his roost, if only to wake my neighbors up.[1]

So that's clear then. In fact, Thoreau could be hardly be clearer. What could be clearer after all, as he amplifies later in the chapter called 'Sounds', than a cockerel crowing

> clear and shrill for miles over the resounding earth, drowning the feebler notes of other birds ... It would put nations on the alert. (W, 116)

Probably nothing could be more clear, in Thoreau's world at any rate, than the cockerel, except perhaps the chanticleer: *chanticleer* being the French for cockerel, and deriving its name precisely from the clarity of its song, its chant clear. So Thoreau is clearer in his statement of intent even than he first seemed to be: he means to issue a clear song. Except that in order to be so clear he has had to make two moves: to a word from another language, and then back, by way of derivation, through that language to the word's origins. Thoreau's epigraph is clear and shrill, if, that is, one listens closely.

Take the opening clause: 'I do not propose to write an ode to dejection'. Coleridge wrote an 'ode to dejection'. Such a form of expression is one of the options available to the writer who – and which writer doesn't? – thinks that all is not as it might be with the world. Formally speaking it is an incongruous choice, the properties of the ode – with its exalted style and enthusiastic tone – being at odds with its subject. Either way, this possible course will not be Thoreau's. He has mentioned it in part to notice that on beginning to write he had faced a choice – it is very much to the point of *Walden* that we acknowledge the choices we make – but also, in acknowledging the Coleridgean option, to clear the way.[2] He means not to praise or indulge low spirits, but by counter definition, to raise them. He does not 'propose to write an ode to dejection'.

In fact, he doesn't *propose* to *write* anything, but instead to 'brag as lustily as a chanticleer', between which two possibilities there is a world of difference. Coleridge, famously, proposed to write things. He proposed to write more of 'Kubla Khan' than he was able to, before the man from Porlock interrupted him, and in *Biographia Literaria* he continually proposes to write something he never quite gets round adequately to expressing – 'Esemplastic', the concept the book trails, being a disappointment when finally it arrives. For all its critical qualities, that is, *Biographia Literaria* has the air of a proposal to write. There is a melancholy in such proposing, a melancholy that comes of alienation, that comes of the distance between stated intention and act. The present book, for instance, was first proposed to its publisher, then, after its publisher's readers responded to the proposal, proposed again. It was then the subject of a proposal to the departmental Research Committee, and following approval there, to the University Personnel Office, and then, in painstaking detail, it was proposed to a funding council, who, in the spirit of scrutiny, wanted to know a good deal about the book that in reality couldn't be told until it was written. It was then subject to two independent assessments, pursuant on which I was offered a right to reply. I barely managed a reply; by that stage I had lost the will to live. To propose anything is to write an ode to dejection.

This said, one way of interpreting Thoreau's epigraph is as a proposal to brag. Actually, though, he doesn't *propose* to brag, he just brags; the verb 'to brag' substituting for the whole over-monitoring phrase 'propose to write'. The word 'brag' changes the epigraph entirely. Firstly, it recasts the activity in hand, shifting it from 'writing' to something more akin to speaking. Writing can brag – Thoreau is about to prove it can – but at very least there is a tone of voice implicit in bragging. Thoreau won't actually speak to us in the book, of course, but his book will have voice, or tones of voice; we will be addressed directly. 'To brag' also introduces an element of risk, with Thoreau's choice of word confronting a problem implicit in his work. If he is to wake his neighbors up, if he is to be heard at all, he has no choice but to raise his voice, and if he does raise his voice somebody, somewhere, will be sure to say that he likes the sound of it. Somebody, inevitably, on encountering the example set by *Walden*, will accuse its author of bragging; so Thoreau gets in first, bragging in order to wake his neighbors up. One of the risks inherent in *Walden*, in other words, is that it will be thought to crow.

But who is crowing? And what are they are crowing about? Judging by the epigraph this isn't absolutely clear, and not least because it isn't absolutely clear from the sentence that it is in fact Thoreau who wakes his neighbors up. Or rather, it isn't clear that it is his voice that does the waking. Does the sentence not allow us to hear it as the chanticleer bragging from his roost, 'if only to wake my neighbours up'? Maybe Thoreau is not making himself plain here, maybe he has not noticed the ambiguity his syntax has opened up; or maybe, through the chanticleer, he is trying to tell us something significant about voice, and more pressingly about voice as it is understood in *Walden*. The chanticleer has a great voice – *cock-a-doodle-dooo* – which, at a certain moment in the day in particular, he cannot help but sound; Thoreau's word 'lustily' (as opposed in the sentence to the bureaucratic constraint of the proposal) making its involuntary nature clear. In effect, what the chanticleer does is sound, or give voice to, the morning; it is as if in some sense its voice comes from somewhere else, as if in sounding it the chanticleer articulates something other than, or more than, itself. The chanticleer crows: it's morning. Perhaps this habit it has of voicing something other than itself is why the cockerel is associated with prophecy. Christ prophesied that Peter would betray him three times before the cock crowed: 'This night before the cock crow, thou shalt deny me thrice' (Matthew 26:34). And, of course, he did.

Thoreau's epigraph is rich. It notes the melancholy effect of certain distancing properties in language, certain abstractions and bureaucratic locutions in particular, and it states the author's intention to raise spirits rather than to endorse or compound low spirits. It establishes the possibility of verbal clarity so long as attention is paid to prior meanings of words. It illustrates, or offers an analogy for, a sense of voice which is both in some sense – 'lustily' – uncontrolled, and in another sense highly meaningful, which can be understood at least in part as issuing from somewhere else, and which when it goes out into the world – which it cannot help but do – results in action; it gets things going. What Thoreau means to do in *Walden*, in other words, in a very full sense of the word, is to enthuse, and what his epigraph gestures towards is the scope and understanding of his enthusiasm.

So far I've drawn on – or alluded to, or borrowed from – the work of two of Thoreau's major modern commentators: Stanley Cavell, who writes brilliantly about prophecy in *The Senses of Walden*, and Lawrence Buell, one of whose importantly responsible questions in *The Environmental Imagination* is (to paraphrase), 'What is it in Thoreau, or in *Walden* in particular, that has secured and stirred so many readers?'[3] What I want to say – it's difficult now to propose it – is that thinking about Thoreau's enthusiasm, and thinking of him as an enthusiast, is a good way of going back to these and other significant issues raised by *Walden* and other of his works, a good way of keeping such issues going. What I don't want to say is that, as he wrote,

Thoreau thought of himself as an enthusiast in the sense that, for a while, Ezra Pound thought of himself as an imagist. Enthusiasm doesn't tend to take writers like that. There's no manifesto, no proposal to write, not least because, if there was, that which it would be proposing to contain would exceed it. What I'm saying instead is that when a writer happens upon enthusiasm as an element of writing, or as a mode of composition, or even, as in Thoreau's case, the possible foundation of a way of life, certain other thoughts tend to follow; and also that because Thoreau was both a wider reader than most writers – he is one of those writers one can be sure of having read what one wants him to have read – and because he was a more rigorous thinker than most writers, one finds in his enthusiasm a very full statement of its possibilities. What Thoreau teaches us, then, is that to approach writing and the world through an idea of enthusiasm has radical implications for thinking about, among other things, economy, epistemology and language. Or to put these categories in terms of the present participles Thoreau preferred (with the grammatical implication, thereby, of action, immediacy and, perhaps most importantly, continuation), Thoreau's enthusiasm has radical things to teach us about 'circulating', 'knowing' and 'deriving'. First, though, 'enthusing' – with what justice is Thoreau called an enthusiast?

Enthusing

Thoreau counts himself an enthusiast, or at least as someone who has enthusiasm, in the opening chapter of *Walden*. 'I do not mean,' one paragraph begins, Thoreau leading us again to what he does mean via the options he has not taken,

> to prescribe rules to strong and valiant natures, who will mind their own affairs whether in heaven or hell … nor to those who find their encouragement and inspiration in precisely the present condition of things, and cherish it with the fondness and enthusiasm of lovers, – and, to some extent, I reckon myself in this number. (W, 16)

There are others to whom Thoreau does not address himself, 'the well employed' for instance, but it is only those who cherish 'precisely the present condition of things … with the fondness and enthusiasm of lovers' whose number he reckons himself among. There are a number of prominent terms in that clause – 'encouragement', 'inspiration', 'cherish', 'lovers' – all of which clearly fit Thoreau, and there is no need to insist that 'enthusiasm' is central. But it is there, defining the number Thoreau identifies himself with. And not only is it there, in this moment of self-definition, but already he is offering us ways of regarding the idea which he will be in the business of unfolding in *Walden*. In one way, then, Thoreau precisely does not cherish the present condition of things, if that were to mean, for instance, the materialism of his society and culture. He does, however, cherish 'the present'; the mental state that is enthusiasm being a means for him whereby the present can precisely be known or cherished. More on this later, as on the opposition toyed with here between enthusiastic cherishing and reckoning: *Walden* being a reckoning of the world which disputes the prevailing calculations, or rather, disputes calculation and the picture of the world it comes up with.

Early in *Walden*, then, Thoreau deftly positions his enthusiasm between ideas of knowing (cherishing) and ideas of measuring and calculating (reckoning). That the term should fall into his argumentation so readily owes to the fact that in the years up to the writing of *Walden* he had been trying out its value, repeatedly, insistently, until it came to mean something important. For instance then – although strictly speaking, no doubt, before the trying-out stage – in an essay written while he was at Harvard, Thoreau notes (without actually troubling to fulfil the requirement of annotation), that as 'some one has justly observed, zeal and enthusiasm are never very accurate calculators'.[4] This was in 1835. Two years later he writes of Paley and his *Natural Philosophy*:

> We may call him a fanatic – an enthusiast – but these are titles of honor, they signify the devotion and entire surrendering of himself to his cause. Where there is sincerity there is truth also. So far as my experience goes, man *never* seriously maintained an objectionable principle, doctrine or theory. (EE, 104)

This is unremarkable, perhaps, except to point out that the term has come to Thoreau, as an undergraduate, freighted with meanings which have, in common parlance anyway, since dropped away. Chaucer, more pointedly – in a lecture on poetry he gave at the Concord Lyceum on 29 November 1843, the text of which he subsequently spliced into *A Week on the Concord and Merrimack Rivers* – is rated less important than Homer and Ossian on the grounds that:

> though it is full of good sense and humanity, it is not transcendent poetry. For picturesque description of persons it is, perhaps, without a parallel in English poetry; yet it is essentially humorous, as the loftiest genius never is. Humor, however broad and genial, takes a narrower view than enthusiasm. (EE, 168)

This is arguable, obviously, as criticism of Chaucer (though equally the sample doesn't represent Thoreau's fully developed view of the poet). It does, though, tell us something of Thoreau's cultural nationalism, enthusiasm being that which, as was implied of the English poet Coleridge, the English poet Chaucer is considered to lack. What does Thoreau mean, one wants to know, as he clears the literary ground, by his word 'enthusiasm'?

Helping with this a little, in his essay on Sir Walter Ralegh, which considers equally the life and the work, and which estimates the work partly in terms of the life, Thoreau associates enthusiasm with action: 'All fair action is the product of enthusiasm, and nature herself does nothing in the prose mood' (EE, 217). This is quite significant for the causation it implies: enthusiasm, previously an element of writing, is now expressly linked to action, an element of the world. Books, this suggests, can be things in the world, can participate quite directly – i.e., not just as proposals – in the world's making. What Thoreau's comment on Ralegh should not be taken to mean, however, is that enthusiasm itself must necessarily be thought of as an active state. Or at least, if Ralegh's enthusiasm is active, Thoreau's isn't, or isn't always, witness the very careful account he gives of it in *A Week on the Concord and Merrimack Rivers*:

> You must be calm before you can utter oracles. What was the excitement of the Delphic priestess compared with the calm wisdom of Socrates? – or whoever it was that was wise. – Enthusiasm is a supernatural serenity.[5]

This is important. Thoreau wrote *A Week on the Concord and Merrimack Rivers* while he was living at Walden Pond, from 1845 to 1847. The enthusiasm proposed here, then – and relative to the immediacy of the later book, *A Week on the Concord and Merrimack Rivers* often reads, in its abstraction and speculation, like a proposal to write – is very much the enthusiasm of *Walden*. There are two ways of substantiating this. First, *Walden* is a prophetic book of sorts – not in the classical sense, perhaps, that it claims to foretell action – but at least in that it is concerned with future actions and future lives. Thoreau means to wake his neighbors up; he means for them to alter their futures. Second, *Walden* is prophetic in that out of the serenity of its enthusiasm, words are uttered which have had, on some, something like an oracular effect. And crucially, and here we are back for a moment with the chanticleer, the words, often, are not Thoreau's own. In one way, of course, they are never Thoreau's own because as Thoreau knows more than most, he doesn't own words. In a more explicit way, however, the words he utters frequently come from somewhere else. He says as much in *A Week*, in a passage on scripture which links readily with his statement on the serenity of enthusiasm:

> The reading which I love best is the scriptures of the several nations ... Give me one of these Bibles and you have silenced me for a while. When I recover the use of my tongue, I am wont to worry my neighbors with the new sentences. (*Week*, 58–9)

This, if ever there was one, is a portrait of the writer as an enthusiast. Thoreau shows himself reading scripture and so all but literally pictures himself breathing in the God, after which, and after a period of silence, he is heard to utter new sentences. We might worry about these new sentences – that when he recovers his tongue Thoreau worries his neighbors by speaking unintelligibly, as if in tongues. In fact, though, his new sentences are old sentences, because what he goes on to do, in the next paragraph, is quote from the New Testament; quotation, the speaking of another's words, being akin to prophecy. Quotation and prophecy are different kinds of speech act, of course, in that to quote is not to make a claim on the future, but there is overlap also, in the sense that in both acts one voice gives itself over to another. Then again, to track prophecy back through its derivations is eventually to find the Greek word simply for speech, as if when it comes down to it speech is quotation, and as if speech properly understood is therefore necessarily enthusiastic.

But this has gone further into Thoreau's enthusiasm, and into *Walden*, than I had meant to at this point. What I wanted to do was to justify calling Thoreau an enthusiast by reference to his increasingly knowing use of the term; and it is clear that Thoreau knew about enthusiasm – that he knew its force, its implications, its history and its values. But then of course he did: Thoreau was steeped in enthusiasm. He was a classicist by his university training, and knew exactly what the idea meant to the Greeks. He was also a student, as were all the transcendentalists, of turn-of-the-century German thought, and of Romanticism, and so he knew that it could be claimed, as Mme De Staël had (from whose *Germany* he copied into his journal) that with regard to this period, 'enthusiasm is the distinguishing characteristic of the German nation'.[6] Equally, when he numbered himself among those who manifested the enthusiasm of lovers, and the prevailing Unitarianism notwithstanding, he was simply numbering himself among his friends. Bronson Alcott, for instance, was, as Robert D. Richardson has noted, 'a talker of shattering, almost apostolic brilliance' who 'wrote inspired, ecstatic gospels' and for whose 'orphic speech' 'Neoplatonism and both German and French Romanticism' afforded the best parallels.[7] More than most, more than anybody perhaps – more, as *Walden* demonstrates, than his mentor Emerson – Thoreau knew what enthusiasm could mean.

Circulating

In turning to think about Thoreau and circulation I take it as read that Thoreau, in the guise of *Walden* at least, has circulated. He only published two books during his lifetime, *A Week on the Concord and Merrimack Rivers* and *Walden*, the former making so slight an impression on the market (from the initial print run of 1,000 copies, 703 were left unsold after 4 years), that he struggled to persuade his Boston publishers, Ticknor and Fields, to publish his second book: a commercial reluctance subsequently justified by further poor sales (by 1880, 26 years after the book's publication, and 18 years after the author's death, total sales of *Walden* stood at 3,695). Since then, however, the circulation of *Walden* has become legion, the book having reached, and influenced, politicians, writers, scholars, so-called ordinary readers, naturalists and eco-activists alike, and there is nothing to be added here to Lawrence Buell's definitive account of the book's reception, marketing, canonization and readership.[8] *Walden*, no question, is a book that has been passed on. What I want to consider instead, in this context of his enthusiasm, are reasons internal to Thoreau's writing that can be thought to have guaranteed its circulation.

The historic success of *Walden* presents a paradox, because one of the most obvious readings of Thoreau – of *Walden* in particular, but of his excursions generally – is of a man out of circulation. As his defining gesture has it: 'I lived alone, in the woods, a mile from any neighbor, in a house which I had built myself, on the shore of Walden Pond'. He received visitors, of course – there is a chapter devoted to them – and he would in turn visit his friends, notably Emerson, notably (sometimes) for dinner. He also records in 'The Village' how he would regularly step back 'to hear some of the gossip which is incessantly going on there, circulating either from mouth to mouth or from newspaper to newspaper' (W, 151). So he wasn't a hermit. Nor though, by a long chalk, is *Walden* a populous book, and socially speaking during his sojourn at Walden Pond Thoreau could hardly be said to have been in circulation. For Emerson, according to his posthumous 'Biographical Sketch' this being out of circulation was the trouble with Thoreau: 'It seemed as if his first instinct on hearing a proposition was to controvert it, so impatient was he of the limitations of our daily thought ... Hence, no equal companion stood in affectionate relations with one so pure and guileless.'[9] This says nothing that would have surprised Thoreau, or even, perhaps, offended him, despite the eulogistic occasion of Emerson's words. In his own essay on friendship, embedded in *A Week on the Concord*, his definition of the relation strictly delimited his circle. 'We do not wish,' he insisted, 'for Friends to feed and clothe our bodies, – neighbors are kind enough for that, – but to do the like office for our spirits. For this few are rich enough' (Week, 217). Delimiting further, 'None,' he is speaking of friends still, 'will pay us the compliment to expect nobleness from us. Though we have gold to give, they demand only copper' (Week, 218).

The question of the proper currency is fundamental to Thoreau, for whom 'Economy' was of the first importance. In the first place, then,

Thoreau took himself out of circulation, to a plot of land he could occupy at minimal cost, and he built his house himself – although, as he later details, with help from some friends – chiefly to avoid the burden of a mortgage. The burden of a mortgage is the way it intrudes on a life. A loan whereby a property acts as the security on the loan taken out to secure the property, and which frequently, as Thoreau is at pains to point out, and as the Old French derivation (dead pledge) indicates, takes the best part of a life to pay back, a mortgage has a relation to living which is equivalent, say, to the relation between a proposal to write and *writing*. As such, as it intrudes on the matter that ought to be in hand – and here one should hear pre-echoes of Ezra Pound, Thoreau's mortgage standing as an equivalent to Pound's usury – the mortgage replicates the effect of money, on which subject Thoreau is a tireless commentator. 'Visitors', for instance, offers a particularly clear definition of money furnished by a friend, probably the Canadian Alex Therien. Quizzing him on many subjects, in order to establish the 'Homeric' quality of person it was possible to encounter in modern North America – to establish the presence of gold not copper – Thoreau brags:

> When I asked him if he could do without money, he showed the convenience of money in such a way as to suggest and coincide with the most philosophical accounts of the origin of this institution, and the very derivation of the word *pecunia*. If an ox were his property, and he wished to get needles and thread at the store, he thought it would be inconvenient and impossible soon to go on mortgaging some portion of the creature each time to get that amount. (W, 135)

Thoreau would seem persuaded, although in passing the definition on, and in his clarifying of the meaning of money through its derivation, he quietly offers counter modes of circulation. Once again he presents a choice.

Elsewhere the questioning of money is more shrill:

> I respect not his labors, his farm where everything has its price; who would carry the landscape, who would carry his God, to market, if he could get anything for him; who goes to market *for* his god as it is … who loves not the beauty of the fruits, whose fruits are not ripe for him till they are turned to dollars. (W, 177)

This turning to dollars is the issue; or rather, the issue, as Thoreau repeatedly makes clear, is that dollars turn everything into themselves. A strong version of this argument is presented in his exacting late essay 'Wild Apples', where again the image is of taking to market: 'There is … about all natural products a certain volatile and ethereal quality which represents their highest value, and which cannot be bought and sold' (Ex, 273). His attention is drawn, then, to the wild apple 'hung so high and sheltered by the tangled branches that our sticks could not dislodge it'. Such 'is a fruit',

Thoreau wants us to believe, or wants himself to believe, 'never carried to market ... quite distinct from the apple of the markets, as from dried apple and cider, – and it is not every winter that produces it in perfection'.

We should appreciate where we are here. We are not only by Walden Pond, not just anyway; not a mile from any neighbor and so to all intents and purposes out of circulation; we are, rather, in the maw of the nineteenth century, that engine room just to the side of which Karl Marx was, at this very moment, setting himself up in his own hut, otherwise known as the British Library. The commodity is king and from the security of his vantage point, Thoreau, like Marx, has entered the factory, only here the factory is a farm, or a landscape, but same difference: same rules, same grid, same demand for production; same process whereby materials become commodities in order that they should be carried to market, whereupon they will be turned, every last one of them (completing the alchemy) into money. One can hardly think of Thoreau without thinking of Marx. One can hardly think, for instance, of those tables pricing up his house – 'Two casks of lime, ... 0 31 That was high' – without thinking of the tabulations by which Marx holds capital to account. In the insistence on detail also: Marx absorbing his from factory inspectors' reports, Thoreau from naturalists' surveys of the altering and denuding of the landscape. Like *Capital*, *Walden* means definitively to get the measure of its moment, to appreciate the forces by which the mid-nineteenth century is being shaped. The difference is that where Marx was engaged in its critique, and so necessarily became enmeshed in the operations of the money economy, Thoreau, who did not 'propose to write an ode to dejection', set out to establish an alternative, to remove himself from circulation. Marx didn't think this possible, witness his criticism of the utopian and model societies of which Brook Farm was an intellectual relation, but he did (with Engels) recognize the impulse, witness the *Manifesto of the Communist Party*, published in 1848, the year after Thoreau left Walden:

> The bourgeoisie, wherever it has got the upper hand, has put an end to all feudal, patriarchal, idyllic relations. It has pitilessly torn asunder the motley feudal ties that bound man to his 'natural superiors,' and has left remaining no other nexus between man and man than naked self-interest, than callous 'cash payment'. It has drowned the most heavenly ecstasies of religious fervour, of chivalrous enthusiasm, of philistine sentimentalism, in the icy water of egotistical calculation.[10]

The phraseology is the same – 'Enthusiasm is never a very accurate calculator' – though as they have no investment in it, Marx and Engels' sense of enthusiasm is a good deal less considered than Thoreau's. Marx and Engels said another thing: 'The need of a constantly expanding market for its products chases the bourgeoisie over the whole surface of the globe.

It must nestle everywhere, settle everywhere.'[11] Thoreau's response to such globalization was to take a step away.

Except that in *Walden*, as in all his mature writing, Thoreau doesn't step out of circulation but into it. (The analogy is with O'Hara apparently stepping 'away from them', but actually, always, stepping into the midst of things.) Thus the problem, to be clear, as Thoreau perceives it, is not circulation, not that things circulate, but that in a money economy, as things circulate, so they convert to one thing, their dollar equivalent. Things don't circulate; money circulates. Things in themselves are lost in the translation. All that is solid melts into air. To which structural problem Thoreau has two responses. The first is to confound the singularity of the measure. There is no gold standard in *Walden*. Things – the things of nature in particular – do not find their equivalent in a single other thing. This is why Thoreau is always measuring: because there is no single measure, because the project of finding a single measure can result only in a distortion and diminution of that for which a measure is being sought. I am talking in part here, obviously, about academic bureaucracy, about the insane project of trying to measure thought and books, of trying to reduce the possibilities of the humanities to a notation of stars. Which is one of the reasons it is good to hear from Thoreau, who had, as Emerson noted, though again dismissively, a highly developed talent for mensuration.

> He could pace sixteen rods more accurately than any other man could measure them with a rod and chain. He could find his path in the woods at night, he said, better by his feet than by his eyes. He could estimate the measure of a tree very well by his eyes; could estimate the weight of a calf or a pig, like a dealer. From a box containing a bushel or more of loose pencils, he could take up with his hands fast enough just a dozen pencils at every grasp. (Ex, 15)

There is a comedy in all this, as if Thoreau were an eccentric uncle performing his party tricks, and among other things *Walden* is a comedy of measurement, Thoreau parodying the accountancy that wants to price everything up. But by the same token, Thoreau's mensuration is deeply in earnest, because above all what Thoreau wants in *Walden* is to take the measure of things. There is a world of difference between these two operations, between the act of measuring and the process of taking the measure of, the latter project calling not for a single currency, but a constantly varying unit of measure; where the variation depends on familiarity with the thing in question, and where the ambition is always the same, somehow to measure things on their own terms, to measure things as they are and in themselves. Take, for instance, the pond.

Walden is measured throughout *Walden*, but nowhere more thoughtfully than in the chapter entitled 'The Ponds', where the neighbouring ponds

White Pond and Flints' Pond, are used to bring Walden into view. Combining his own research and historical findings, Thoreau judges Walden according to its differing height, or depth, and its varying temperatures, with both of these measures being viewed chronically and seasonally. But while, clearly, it can be measured in these terms, it is itself a measure, an infinitely subtle recording instrument: 'not a pickerel or shiner picks an insect from this smooth surface but it manifestly disturbs the equilibrium of the whole lake' (W, 169). In fact, 'Not a fish can leap or an insect fall on the pond but it is thus reported in circling dimples, in lines of beauty, as it were the constant welling up of its fountain' (W, 170). And then also, especially on the kind of September day he is commenting on here, the pond is a kind of mirror – 'a perfect forest mirror, set round with stones as precious to my eye as if fewer or rarer' – and as such, as a mirror, in revealing other things so it reveals itself (W, 170). The trajectory of 'The Ponds' is typical: from the externally imposed unit of measure (feet, and degrees Fahrenheit) to a fathoming determined by the pond's defining properties; from a measure conducted in alien terms to a measure in terms of the thing itself. Not, of course, that Thoreau has the thing's own terms available to him. Unlike Marx's commodity, the things in Walden are never invited actually to speak. Except that in *Walden*, and it is central to his experiment, Thoreau goes beyond both Marx and (as we shall see) Kant – the Enlightenment tradition's major commentators on the disappearance of things – in formulating a language that might act as the kind of measure that, for instance, money is not: responsive, equal, open to things.

One way Thoreau succeeds in this objective is to accentuate the analogical character of language. What this means is not that Thoreau is, as a writer, forever making analogies – though he is and the practice is important to *Walden*. What it means, rather, is what Stevens is driving at in his essay 'The Effects of Analogy', where language is understood not simply as a medium in which analogies are made, but as itself an analogy, careful sequences of words (in their varying weights and measures) achieving an analogy for, or a correspondence with, the world. Thus, perhaps,

> The shore is irregular enough not to be monotonous. I have in my mind's eye the western indented with deep bays, the bolder northern, and the beautifully scalloped southern shore, where successive capes overlap each other and suggest unexplored coves between. (W, 168)

Here the sentence – and this time the critical phraseology points towards the Pound of 'Vorticism' – is itself the measure, with the not-monotonous irregularity of the shoreline caught not so much in the relayed descriptive sense – in the references the words make to things – as in the varying and continuous play of sounds: in 'western indented' and 'beautifully scalloped', an effect which requires the words to be spoken, or at least heard out loud, for the writing to be sounded. Also, though, beyond analogy, is the thought that underpins all of Thoreau's writings, that if you dig deep enough what you find at the roots of words are things. *In pecunia*, for instance, cattle.

Thoreau's second response to the uniformity effected in the circulation of things by money is to detail endlessly, or as if endlessly, the other ways the world has of effecting circulation. Always there is a process of transmission to be observed, one thing passing through another thing to become a different version of itself, or just passing through, unaffected by the transition. Thoreau's beans, for instance, his cultivation of which is in all commercial respects a comical failure,

> have results which are not harvested by me. Do they not grow for woodchucks partly? The ear of wheat, (in Latin *spica*, obsoletely *speca*, from *spe*, hope,) should not be the only hope of the husbandman; its kernal or grain (*granum*, from *gerendo*, bearing,) is not all that it bears. How, then, can our harvest fail? Shall I not rejoice also at the abundance of the weeds whose seeds are the granary of the birds? (W, 150)

Distribution, the way things are kept or put into circulation, Thoreau wants us to understand, doesn't work like you think or are encouraged to think, one thing becoming another in many more ways than one. Look at my beans, he says, which didn't do so well as a cash crop, but did serve to keep the woodchucks going. Witness also 'The Succession of Forest Trees', the whole of which significant early essay – significant as a staging post in Thoreau's development, but also, as it has turned out, as a work of still usable scientific observation – is a detailing of the mechanisms and modes of circulation whereby the perpetuation of trees is ensured. These can be delicate, as with pines, in which case, 'a beautiful thin sack is woven around the seed, with a handle to it such as the wind can take hold of' (Ex, 138). Or they can be gloriously indelicate: 'Eating cherries is a bird-like employment, and unless we disperse the seeds occasionally, as they do, I shall think that the birds have the best right to them' (Ex, 140). We know what he's talking about here – he's talking about excretion.

There are many such descriptions of countermodes of circulation – Thoreau's writing precisely teems with them – accounts of how fish, or apples, or trees or beans go round, or keep themselves going, or are kept going round. Just as often, though, there are metaphorical or allegorical variations on these, where the operations by which nature circulates – operations through which things either remain themselves or, better still, fulfil their potential – are allowed to suggest, or are related to, the circulation of human society and culture, or even thought itself. For instance, from the concluding paragraph of 'The Pond in Winter':

Thus it appears that the sweltering inhabitants of Charleston and New Orleans, of Madras and Bombay and Calcutta, drink at my well. In the morning I bathe my intellect in the stupendous and cosmogonal philosophy of the Bhagvat Geeta, since whose composition years of the gods have elapsed, and in comparison with which our modern world and its literature seem puny and trivial; and I doubt if that philosophy is not to be referred to a previous state of existence, so remote is its sublimity from our conceptions. I lay down the book and go to my well for water, and lo! there I meet the servant of the Brahmin, priest of Brahma and Vishnu and Indra, who still sits in his temple on the Ganges reading the Vedas, or dwells at the root of the tree with his crust and water jug. I meet his servant come to draw water for his master, and our buckets as it were grate together in the same well. The pure Walden water is mingled with the sacred water of the Ganges. (W, 266)

The passage goes to the essence of Thoreau's enthusiasm, and of his sense, presented most fully in *Walden*, of enthusiasm as a mode of circulation counter to money. It follows a lengthy account of how, in the winter of 1846–7, a local farmer had men break up the ice on the pond for subsequent sale. By this transaction the ice will become dollars, given over to private use and so taken out of circulation. Thoreau's response, prompted by his environment, is to posit a different form of transaction. Thus, as the ice is removed, so the water of the pond again begins to evaporate, hence the thought that the inhabitants of Charleston and Calcutta might drink at his well; evaporation, one thing become another but preserving itself in the process, becoming in turn a model for the readerly thought. Except that, as so often with Thoreau, what he happens to be reading is scripture, and so the passage of thought or words from one speaker to another, from book to book, is associated with the divine. Enthusiasm, the breathing in of the God, is thus cast, via citation, as a mode of circulation.

We know how this works. Enthusiasm, even, or especially, in its most colloquial sense, is a means of circulating: if somebody enthuses about a book – *Walden*, for instance – they heighten the possibility of its being passed on. 'My heart is in my / pocket, it is Poems by Pierre Reverdy', as O'Hara has it at the end of 'A Step Away from Them', a statement of enthusiasm which, when it was published in *Lunch Poems*, caused an unlikely rush on the works of the semi-Surrealist French poet. By this kind of gesture are words and works kept in circulation. More than this, money-losing ventures of all kinds – poetry for instance – are fuelled and sustained by enthusiasm. In the most colloquial sense, then, where money is either not available or not desired, what stands in its stead is enthusiasm. Thoreau's contribution is to sound the deeper implications of this conventional procedure, presenting a sense of enthusiasm as circulation which takes us back to scripture, or to his reading of it, or to his presenting of it. To spell this out: we have already heard Thoreau define enthusiasm as an oracular gesture. In an enthusiastic state the individual self does not utter speech, but is spoken through. This is the substance of accounts of inspiration – the muse – and also of some forms of religious testimony, in Quakerism for instance. Enthusiasm, in other words, is a voicing of, at very least, words, and, ideally, entities and agencies, not oneself. And Thoreau is always doing this. Always he is arriving – his chapter endings provide notable instances – at the serenity whereby he might speak enthusiastically, as an enthusiast, and invariably when he does he quotes. Thus much more so than Emerson's essays, *Walden* is made up explicitly of other people's words: of the anonymous words of scripture, of Ovid's, of Virgil's, of Shakespeare's, of Bunyan's, of Addison's, of Confucius', of Menu's, of Lovelace's, of Chapman's, of Cato's, of Milton's, of Cowper's, of Thomas Gray's. Drop into the text at any moment and you will find the putative diaristic or autobiographical self clearing out, so that others' words might come through. Not that the autobiographical self is ever entirely dismissed – Thoreau's enthusiastic gesture is predicated on there being a discernible voice there in the first place. The work's enthusiastic self depends on the quotidian self; *Walden* is not *The Cantos*.

This shift, from the circulating quotidian self to the circulation of enthusiasm – from the self that does this and does that, to the self that breathes out the God – is most carefully presented in 'The Village'. What Thoreau purports to do in that chapter is to show himself re-entering circulation: 'Every day or two I strolled to the village to hear some of the gossip which is incessantly going on there, circulating either from mouth to mouth, or from newspaper to newspaper' (W, 151). Thoreau names circulation here, but only immediately to set about redefining it. Thus, the chatter of the citizens is made equivalent to the noise of leaves and frogs, while the chatter itself is shown not to be the self-motivated exchange of individuated citizens, but the hollowed-out transmission of barely conscious thoughts. Thoreau, in other words, goes back into society, re-enters circulation, to find that what is circulating there isn't worth a bean. The contrast is with the end of the chapter, the moment when he leaves the village, when as convention would have it he steps out of circulation, but when in fact as we should by now expect he instead steps into it. The issue at this point is property, Thoreau explaining how he never locked or bolted the desk which contained his papers, and never fastened his door behind him even if he was to be absent for a few days, and that in all his time at Walden he never had anything stolen, save, as he is delighted to point out, a volume of Homer. This probably apocryphal anecdote relayed, the chapter ends with two quotations, the first, from *The Elegies of Tibullus*, indented, the second, from the *Analects* of Confucius, absorbed into the body of the text. The point is made: Thoreau's language is a medium of circulation through which words and thoughts pass unaltered, or perhaps with an aspect of their potential fulfilled. Anticipating Pound – an association prompted by the reference to Confucius – Thoreau's version of *The Dial* would frequently give its pages over to extracts from major classical writers, ensuring their continued presence in New England in the 1840s. Quotation is circulation. Thoreau was never out of circulation, though nor, if we were reading him carefully, did he ever pretend to be. Right from the beginning he borrowed: the materials for his house came in part from other people. Then, of course, there were the tools without which he could never have got started:

> It is difficult to begin without borrowing, but perhaps it is the most generous course to thus permit your fellow-men to have an interest in your enterprise. The owner of the axe, as he released his hold on it, said that it was the apple of his eye; but I returned it sharper than I received it. (W, 38)

So there you go, he made it new.

Knowing

Shifting from circulating to knowing in Thoreau – from the question of how things are distributed and distribute themselves to the question of how one might know them – one runs up against a paradox. Always one is running up against paradoxes in *Walden*, much more so than in his other works, the end of the sentence invariably giving way to a *volte face*, a contradiction, a counterthesis, or a self-annihilating change of tone or persona. Such shifts define the book's style and are integral to its lesson, the unresolved break forcing decision (or at least the acknowledgement of indecision, or of the necessity and burden of decision implicit in existence) on the reader, while the book itself has to be understood as containing a multiplicity of elements, a manifold, to use a term from Kant, that steadfastly remains as such. We come to expect paradoxes, in other words, in Thoreau: paradox is part of how he writes. Still, though, some paradoxes are more pressing than others. Thus where, on the question of the circulation of thought and expression, and of economy generally, Thoreau has just been heard to announce himself not-self-reliant, a cheerful borrower of other people's words and tools, on the question of knowledge he refuses to accept the second-hand.

This is particularly evident in 'The Bean-Field':

> It was a singular experience that long acquaintance which I cultivated with beans, what with planting, and hoeing, and harvesting, and threshing, and

> picking over, and selling them, – the last was the hardest of all, – I might add eating, for I did taste. I was determined to know beans. (W, 145)

More even than to grow them, Thoreau is determined to know beans, the comical aspect of which, it should be noticed, he is happy to acknowledge by his 'long acquaintance'. Thoreau is deeply in earnest in *Walden*, but he knows also that, from time to time, he cuts a ludicrous figure; we would be less able to take him seriously were it not that sometimes he knows he looks odd. Still, what's at issue is knowing, and as he presents it knowledge is a practical affair: planting, hoeing, harvesting, threshing. It is also an affair of the present tense, the immediacy of the present participle being, apparently, a factor in how Thoreau knows. I am hoeing, therefore I am knowing. (In which, to say it again, there is something serious but also something unavoidably funny; 'I'm ploughing North America,' Stevens wrote, 'Blow your horn!') To know beans is also, as Thoreau points out, to know other things also, for instance the weeds it is necessary to clear to make way for the chosen crop. 'Consider,' he says, 'the intimate and curious acquaintance one makes with various kinds of weeds...That's Roman wormwood, – that's pigwee, – that's sorrel, – that's piper-grass.' And so Thoreau documents his intimate and curious acquaintance with beans, signing off, as when he built his house, with a balance sheet. 'This,' he says emphatically, 'is the result of my experience in raising beans.'

There is a radical independence of mind being asserted here – 'this', 'my' – one which Thoreau had previously generalized upon at the end of *A Week on the Concord and Merrimack Rivers*, when by way of conclusion he offers a justification for his excursion – a justification which he perhaps senses is due, the week in question having been, by any standards, a long one: 'for knowledge is to be acquired only by a corresponding experience. How can we *know* what we are *told* merely? Each man can interpret another's experience only by his own' (*Week*, 296). This would seem like the worst aspect of mid-century self-reliance, with Thoreau casting himself as a kind of anti-intellectual, an American know-nothing. Except that, as we have seen already, Thoreau is not afraid to show dependence, *Walden* precisely, and enthusiastically, opening itself up to its sources. The issue is not, then, as it can seem with Thoreau, whether or not one should make do with other people's knowledge. The question, rather, is what constitutes knowing. Or as he put it much more emphatically, towards the beginning of *A Week on the Concord*, recovering his environment as he goes:

> The white man comes, pale as the dawn, with a load of thought, with a slumbering intelligence as a fire raked up, knowing well what it knows, not guessing but calculating ... He comes with a list of ancient Saxon, Norman and Celtic names, and strews them up and down this river, – Framingham, Sudbury, Bedford, Carlisle. (Week, 44)

What's at issue, then, is not whether Thoreau is prepared to take another person's word for it. What's at issue, rather, as he wants to present it here, is a whole cultural and racial mentality, a whole disposition towards the world, a disposition caught in the phrase 'a load of thought'. It is a good phrase, communicating well the burden under which people go into the world, or fail to go into it; a phrase that implies, in Kantian terms, a critique of pure reason.

The importance of Kantian thought to American writing, its principles and the problems it brought forth, cannot be overstated. Which is neither to say that all significant American poets have been Kantians, nor even that Kant has been on most American poets' reading lists – though famously, of course, he was on Stevens'. Kant is central because he was foundational for the Transcendentalists, and because since the 1850s American writers, poets especially, have been working on the house that Emerson and Thoreau built, a structure designed to house or at least to accommodate Kant, hence Emerson's explanation of the otherwise unhelpfully numinous term by which he and his contemporaries made themselves known:

> It is well known to most of my audience that the idealism of the present day acquired the name of transcendental from the use of the term by Immanuel Kant of Konigsburg, who replied to the skeptical philosophy of Locke which insisted that there was nothing in the intellect which was not previously in the experience of the senses, by showing that there was a very important class of ideas, or imperative forms, which did not come by experience, but through which experience was acquired: that these were intuitions of the mind itself; and he denominated them Transcendental forms.[12]

Emerson presents quite clearly, and quite contentedly, here, the *a priori* nature of Kant's contribution to philosophy which was his seeming appeal to the Transcendentalists, and out of which Emerson developed his wrongly untroubled sense, most fully articulated in *Nature*, of the harmony between the intellect and the world.

Thoreau's habit on hearing a proposition was, as Emerson said, to controvert it. This is not to imply that as Kant circulated among his contemporaries Thoreau's response was straightforwardly negative. The suspicion of 'a load of thought' is not, then, in any simple-minded way, a 'no' to thought, but strikes instead the same relation to a *Critique of Pure Reason* as Thoreau strikes, in effect, to Marx's critiques of political economy. Caught in the elaborate apparatus of intellection, as *Capital* is caught in the elaborate processes of manufacture, Kant's *Critique*, unlike Emerson's version of it, is hardly happy with itself, finding in reason's operations the conditions of experience but also the severity of their limitations. Again the issue is alienation, the problem Kant passed on to nineteenth-century thought being how to get beyond understanding to the thing itself. From this point of view, when Thoreau went to live by Walden Pond he stepped away epistemologically as well as economically, out of the problem of pure reason into the world of things.

This, at any rate, is more or less how Stanley Cavell sees it. For Cavell, picking up some of *Walden*'s favoured terms, Thoreau achieves a nextness, nearness or neighborliness to the world that, as a lived relation, amounts to an acquaintance with things in themselves. 'I was determined to know beans,' Thoreau says, and Cavell asserts that he did.

> Epistemologically, [*Walden's*] motive is the recovery of the object, in the form in which Kant left that problem and the German idealists and the Romantic poets picked it up, viz., a recovery of the thing-in-itself; in particular, of the relation between the subject of knowledge and its object.

He pulls this off, Cavell argues (to paraphrase), by stepping away, where the gesture can be understood almost literally, Cavell's chief point of reference being the moment in the 'The Pond in Winter' when Thoreau witnesses a double shadow of himself: 'Being beside oneself is the dictionary definition of ecstasy. To suggest that one may stand there, stay there in a sane sense, is to suggest that the besideness of which ecstasy speaks is my experience of my existence.' Cavell's word is 'ecstasy', 'ecstasy' being not a million miles, or even a mile, from enthusiasm. Cavell, however, doesn't refer to enthusiasm in *The Senses of Walden*, except in the second edition, and then only in the expanded second edition, and then only in the expansion on Emerson, where again the central question is how, taking on board Kant, we can inhabit a world of things:

> I take Emerson's answer to be what he means by 'abandonment'. The idea of abandonment contains what the preacher in Emerson calls 'enthusiasm' or the New Englander in him calls 'forgetting ourselves', together with what he calls leaving or relief or quitting or release or shunning or allowing or deliverance, which is freedom ... together further with something he means by trusting or suffering.[13]

What the preacher in Emerson calls 'enthusiasm' is worth dwelling on here, because of its currency in New England in the middle of the nineteenth century, but also as it features in Kant, the significance of *Walden* to American literature being measurable in part in terms of the confluence that occurs there: Thoreau situating himself, for all his distance, in the mainstreams of Enlightenment and Romantic thought. Thus, if the problem that Kant calls forth is the unknowability of the thing-in-itself, and if that unknowability is a function of mind's conditioned relation to the world – if reason, like money, alienates things – it's as well, as Kant does, to take a look at what reason was brought forward to displace. To return, then, to the *Critique of Judgement*:

The idea of the good to which affection is superadded is enthusiasm. This state of mind appears to be sublime: so much so that there is a common saying that nothing great can be achieved without it. But now every affection is blind either as to the choice of its end, or, supposing this has been furnished by reason, in the way it is effected – for it is that mental movement whereby the exercise of free deliberation upon fundamental principles, with a view to determining oneself accordingly, is rendered impossible.[14]

The problem with enthusiasm – the value of which Kant wants to be seen not to underestimate – is that it renders 'determining oneself' impossible. But Thoreau doesn't want to determine himself, he is determined instead to know beans; and so he steps away; not, this time, from the prevailing networks of circulation, but from the networks that constitute the transcendental self. It is an enthusiastic gesture, except that where for Kant there is a more or less violent derangement in enthusiasm – 'every affection' being rendered blind, the imagination becoming 'unbridled' – for Thoreau, for whom Eastern religions were among the tributaries, enthusiasm (the state of being in which something other than the self is predominantly at work) is a moment of serenity. Again, 'You must be calm before you can utter oracles. What was the excitement of the Delphic priestess compared with the calm wisdom of Socrates? – or whoever it was that was wise. – Enthusiasm is a supernatural serenity.'

The argument emerging here – and which will be developed through the book, emerging, at is fullest, in the discussion of James Schuyler – is for something like an enthusiastic epistemology, or rather, that in the state of enthusiasm as Thoreau describes it here, things can be known; that in enthusiasm there is knowing. It is a claim Thoreau makes quite often, *Walden* frequently presenting as its object state a condition whereby unburdened of the load of thought, a person is not apart from things but among them. 'Every man,' he observes in 'The Village',

has to learn the points of the compass again as often as he awakes, whether from sleep or any abstraction. Not till we are lost, in other words, not till we have lost the world, do we begin to find ourselves, and realize where we are and the infinite extent of our relations. (W, 154)

As a claim this is interesting, but not, in itself, compelling. It is not sufficient, one might well think, to counter the elaborate workings of the transcendental deduction with a metaphor, or at best, perhaps, a pun. What we need to know is 'how'. How, we want to know of Thoreau, do we 'realize where we are', given that in realizing where we are, in making our environment real, the promise is made that we might become properly acquainted with things? Cavell points to the state of mind *Walden* repeatedly depicts, to the 'nearness' to things that comes of the 'besideness', the being beside oneself, the being outside of reason, that is a function of ecstasy or enthusiasm. Cavell's commentary characterizes this psychology brilliantly, getting as close as one can imagine to the state of mind Thoreau wants to present. What I want to suggest here, however, is that for Thoreau, the answer to the question 'How do we realize where we are?', or 'How might we become properly acquainted with things?', has to do with how he derives, with how he does things with words.

Deriving

Like the Emerson of, in particular, *Nature*, and like Pound after him, Thoreau has a faith in the origins of words, a faith that if you track words back to their origins you find in them a more exact rendering of things. Words themselves, in their tangle of roots and meanings, seem to promise this. Etymology derives from *etymon*, being 'the earliest recorded form of a word', which comes from the Greek *etumon* meaning 'basic meaning', which comes in turn from *etumos* meaning 'true or actual'. This is to derive the word: to derive from being 'to draw on (or in) the source or origin of a thing, to obtain by reasoning, in the sense of deduction or inference', and, as the verb applies to words, 'to trace the source or development', to derive coming from the Latin *derivare*, meaning 'to draw off', which derives in turn from *rivus*, meaning 'a stream'. Taken this way, what words promise is knowledge. It is this promise that the classicist in Thoreau finds attractive, his knowledge of the language apparently conducting him back to a knowledge of things. The supposition is that in the first act of naming there was an intimacy between words and things. It is a limited claim in that it is only ever made for specific examples, and also in that the claim is about words and not about language as a whole. It had a special appeal, though, to the Concord writers who thought themselves to be the beginning of American literature, the new first namers. Later it became an element in Heidegger's response to Kant.

Often, then, in Thoreau, we are taken back through etymologies to hear the meanings that will speak through words if they are allowed to. There is an analogy here with the act of quotation, the poet's task – Thoreau considers himself a poet when he is writing like this – being to so handle the language as to enable it to speak all that it knows, which is more than it knows in any contemporary usage, contemporary usage serving to restrict words. Deriving, then, is a further act of clearing, a tracking back which is a making way in order that words can perform their revelatory function. Old words speak through new words the way, in quotation, one voice speaks through another, the writer's task being to guide words back to their better originals. Sometimes this requires only a minimal realignment, as for instance at the end of the first day, the Saturday, of *A Week on the Concord and Merrimack Rivers*, when Thoreau and his brother are kept awake by the novelty of their situation, by the foxes and the owl and the house dogs and eventually the cock:

> All these sounds, the crowing of cocks, the baying of dogs, and the hum of insects at noon, are the evidence of nature's health or *sound* state. Such is the never-failing beauty and the accuracy of language, the most perfect art in the world; the chisel of a thousand years re-touches it. (Week, 35)

There is knowledge here, the sounds of the animals serving as 'evidence' of nature's health. Nature sounds and she is heard to be *sound*: she sounds and she is sounded, in her sounds she is revealed. These are seductive moves – revelation is a function of prophecy, prophecy, as was pointed out earlier, derives from the Greek for speech. What I want to draw attention to, though, is not just the moves (and their validity or otherwise) but also the mood in which they are made. Quite often such slight readjustments are made at the end of a chapter or a section, when what has been arrived at is a state of contemplation. It is at these moments and in this mood, often, that words are heard to speak more fully and, as it were, knowingly. 'Enthusiasm,' it will be recalled, 'is a supernatural serenity.' In the chapter in *Walden* devoted to 'Sounds', what eventually comes through the silence, after the noise of the train has died away, is not a repositioned word, but the sounds themselves of the neighbouring animals: '*bor-r-r-r-n*', '*tr-r-r-oonk, tr-r-r-oonk, tr-r-r-oonk!*'. The implication is that given a sufficiently serene state, a sufficiently careful listening, things will sound themselves, onomatopoeia pointing to the intimacy between words and things that Thoreau hopes for in language.

Walden is always leaning on words in this way – *grain*, *com-munity* – and invariably Thoreau will give the Latin names for animals and plants. Sentences frequently hinge on the different inflections afforded by current and earlier meanings. All the time in Thoreau's writing the impression is of something else coming through. The most spectacular example of this is to be found in 'Spring', when, as Thoreau observes the thawing of the sand, he discerns there the emergence of forms which resemble foliage, and which in their springing into being put him in mind of the primordial moment when the 'Artist who made the world' was first 'strewing his fresh designs about'. This is the end of *Walden*, and Thoreau's claim is that he is as close to things as he ever has been or, perhaps, ever will be: his proximity consisting in part in the fineness and accuracy of his observation. But it consists also in derivation, Thoreau tracking the words he is compelled to use right back through their etymologies to the constitutive phonemes or sounds. 'I feel,' he says, 'as if I were nearer to the vitals of the globe', and then proceeds to situate the reader there also, the sands anticipating the leaf in which form the earth 'expresses itself outwardly', but with which also 'it labors inwardly'.

> The overhanging leaf sees here its prototype. *Internally*, whether in the globe or animal body, it is a moist thick *lobe*, a word especially applicable to the liver and lungs and the *leaves* of fat, (λειβω, *labor*, *lapsus*, to flow or slip downward, a lapsing; λοβος, *globus*, lobe, globe; also lap, flap, and many other words,) *externally* a dry thin *leaf*, even as the *f* and *v* are a pressed and dried *b*. The radicals of lobe are *lb*, the soft mass of the *b* (single lobed, or B, double lobed,) with the liquid *l* behind it pressing it forward. In globe, *glb*, the guttural *g* adds to the meaning the capacity of the throat. The feathers and wings of birds are still drier and thinner leaves. Thus, also, you pass from the lumpish grub in the earth to the airy and fluttering butterfly. The very globe continually transcends and translates itself, and becomes winged in its orbit. (W, 273)

There are two things to say in response to this extraordinary passage of writing, presented here, at the end of *Walden*, not as a typical instance of Thoreau's practice but as an ultimate version of it. The first thing is that standing here, feeling nearer to the vitals of the globe, to the lumpish grub and the fluttering butterfly – nearer, note, and not, as Emerson blithely asserted, at one with; this is not antinomianism, but the meditative enthusiasm of Fox and Penn – Thoreau finds himself where Kant never stood: so close to things – expressed outwardly, labouring inwardly – that they are known as and in themselves. In one way, of course, one can always counter that this is illusory; in another way, equally, there is a generous sense in which Thoreau really could be thought here to find and take the measure of things. Either way, what we need to notice is that as he responds to the problem of the transcendental deduction, he does not simply revert to empiricism. To do so, by a Kantian way of thinking, would be to reduce experience to the manifold, a move Thoreau does sometimes make – '*bor-r-r-r-n*', '*tr-r-r-oonk*' – but which here he goes beyond. Thus here he gets beyond Kant without diminishing Kant's sense of experience, doing so by retaining in his picture of knowledge an equivalent to Kant's concepts and categories. The world presents itself as fully as it does here partly because there are, as Thoreau has observed, structural similarities to the elements of the world, but partly, also, because the basic structural principles have their counterpart in language. Words, carefully used, listened to carefully, so Thoreau would here assert, sound things and realize the world.

The second thing to say in response to this passage has to do with the state in which its realization can be thought to occur. The passage hovers between gibberish and sense. It *sounds* nonsensical. As the word is sounded out, as globe becomes leaf and as the transition is followed up through and out of the throat, the full extent of the words is sounded, their constituent elements loosened and unleashed. But the passage makes sense also, in that what it aims to do is to make sense of the world: the words, their etymologies, their derivations and ultimately their constitutive phonemes are understood here to sound the objects they refer to in the way that the onomatopoeically rendered birdsong *sounds* birds. This, I think, this passage in particular, is an example of Thoreau's enthusiastic use of words, where enthusiasm works both in Kant's sense of the unbridled self, and in William Penn's sense of the 'nearer' testament, and in Thoreau's own sense of supernatural serenity. Thus, that words are ungoverned here is plain, and also that as they are unbridled so they present a kind of frenzy: albeit a frenzy in which, if we find Thoreau persuasive, they speak more than in their governed, buttoned-down sense they are capable of. More than this, as the words are unbridled so something is conceived as speaking – or even passing – through them, the thing in question being the world, or the globe. And so there's one sense of verbal enthusiasm, the sense that seventeenth-century commentators were so worried about, and that twentieth-century writers, in their even more acute confrontation with the implications of bureaucracy and rationality – one might think, here, of William Burroughs – would find so appealing. But Thoreau's sense is here also, both because he could arrive at this level of insight only through the prolonged period of serenity that he enjoyed while living at Walden, but also because the passage itself is among the most carefully worked and heavily revised passages in the book, its knowledge made available only by the Delphic calm of writing.

Ungoverned and calm? Ungoverned because calm? Whatever – in this startling performance Thoreau echoes a claim he made at the start of his book. He is crowing, or at least his words are: sounding and resounding, bragging of that which is not them. *Walden* is an enthusiastic book.

Notes

1 Henry David Thoreau, *Walden*, ed. Stephen Fender, Oxford, Oxford University Press, 1997, p. 1; henceforth referred to in the text as W.

2 For a discussion of the choices Thoreau's writing presents, see Stanley Cavell, *The Senses of Walden*, Chicago and London, University of Chicago Press, p. 49.

3 See Cavell, *Senses*, pp. 17–29, and Lawrence Buell, *The Environmental Imagination: Thoreau, Nature Writing and the Formation of American Culture*, Cambridge, Mass., Belknap Press of Harvard University Press, pp. 339–69.

4 Henry David Thoreau, *Early Essays and Miscellanies*, ed. Joseph J. Modenhauer, Edwin Mower and Alexandra C. Kern, Princeton, NJ, Princeton University Press, 1975, p. 17; hereafter referred to in the text as EE.

5 Henry David Thoreau, *A Week on the Concord and Merrimack Rivers*, New York, Library of America, 1985, p. 103; hereafter referred to in the text as Week.

6 Germaine de Staël, *Major Writings of Germaine de Staël*, tr. and intro. by Vivian Folkenflik, New York, Columbia University Press, 1987, p. 321.

7 Robert D. Richardson, *Henry Thoreau: A Life of the Mind*, Berkeley, Los Angeles and London, University of California Press, 1986, p. 19.

8 Buell, *Environmental Imagination*, pp. 339–69.

9 Ralph Waldo Emerson, 'Biographical Sketch', in Henry David Thoreau, *Excursions*, New York, Corinth Books, 1962, p. 11; hereafter referred to in the text as Ex.

10 Karl Marx and Friedrich Engels, *Selected Works in one Volume*, London, Lawrence & Wishart, 1980, p. 38.

11 Ibid.

12 Ralph Waldo Emerson, *The Collected Works of Ralph Waldo Emerson*, Cambridge, Mass., Harvard University Press, 1971, pp. 206–7.

13 Cavell, *Senses*, pp. 95, 104, 136.

14 Immanuel Kant, *The Critique of Judgement*, tr. James Creed Meredith, Oxford, Clarendon Press, p. 124.

2

Ranting: Herman Melville

As he was writing *Moby-Dick*, from February 1850 to November 1851, as he composed the book he felt certain was his greatest work, Herman Melville understood himself to be inspired. This understanding – one might call it an insight – is evident wherever during that period Melville catches himself in the act of composition, whether in his barely containable excitement at the prospect of the novel's achievement, or as a metaphor articulating the writing state. Here, for instance, is a passage from a letter to Nathaniel Hawthorne, whom he had met for the first time in August 1850, and whose work and presence he experienced as a spur:

> My development has been all within a few years past. I am like one of those seeds taken out of the Egyptian Pyramids, which, after having been three thousand years a seed and nothing but a seed, being planted in English soil, it developed itself, grew to greenness, and then fell to mould. So I. Until I was twenty-five, I had no development at all. From my twenty-fifth year I date my life. Three weeks have scarcely passed, at any time between then and now, that I have not unfolded within myself. But I feel that I am now come to the inmost leaf of the bulb, and that shortly the flower must fall to the mould.[1]

The same note of inspiration is apparent in 'Hawthorne and his Mosses', the review of Hawthorne's *Mosses from an Old Manse* that Melville wrote shortly after their first meeting. Signing himself 'A Virginian Spending July in Vermont', which is as much as to say 'Call me Ishmael', Melville finds Hawthorne – and here we have to keep an eye on the anatomy – 'content with the still, rich utterances of a great intellect in repose … which sends few thoughts into circulation, except they be arterialized at his large warm lungs, and expanded in his honest heart.'[2] The lungs and the heart here are, as we shall see, borrowed from a whale. Elsewhere in the review Melville borrows from Plato, 'Ion' in particular, urging contemporary American readers to ensure Hawthorne's transmission, 'For genius, all over the world, stands hand in hand, and one shock of recognition runs the whole circle round'.[3] Hawthorne – as who wouldn't be? – was delighted by Melville's review, as was his wife, Sophia, who wrote about it to Evert Duyckinck: 'I keep constantly reading over & over the inspired utterances ... There is such a generous, noble enthusiasm as I have not found in any critic of my writer.'[4]

The phrase is right: 'inspired utterance'. Few writers ever, probably, have felt as capable of the inspired utterance as Herman Melville did when he was writing *Moby-Dick*. The evidence is all through the novel, but here's a passage that seems particularly to the point:

> My hypothesis is this: that the spout is nothing but mist. And besides other reasons, to this conclusion I am impelled, by considerations touching the great inherent dignity and sublimity of the Sperm Whale; I account him no common, shallow being, inasmuch as it is an undisputed fact that he is never found on soundings, or near shores: all other whales sometimes are. He is both ponderous and profound. And I am convinced that from the heads of all ponderous profound beings, such as Plato, Pyrrho, the Devil, Jupiter, Dante, and so on, there always goes up a certain semi-visible stream, while in the act of thinking deep thoughts. While composing a little treatise on Eternity, I had the curiosity to place a mirror before me: and ere long saw reflected there, a curious involved worming and undulation in the atmosphere over my head. The invariable moisture of my hair, while plunged in deep thought, after six cups of hot tea in my thin shingled attic, of an August afternoon; this seems an additional argument for the above supposition.[5]

The passage comes from the chapter called 'The Fountain'. The question on Melville's mind has to do with how the whale breathes, with what it takes in and what it pushes back out, except that as he composes the question gets caught up with the act of thinking, with the circulation of thought. Writing about the whale, Melville wants us to understand, has given him a way of thinking about thinking: or to put it another way, writing about the whale has led him to an understanding, or at least a way of articulating, the process by which composition occurs. And the spout is the key, the author, here, figuring himself precisely as spouting. *Moby-Dick*, as Melville understood it, was written in a fit of enthusiasm.

The enthusiasm of *Moby-Dick* is a complicated matter. There is, as we have already begun to see, a generalized Romantic sense of enthusiasm surrounding the composition of the novel, as that is discussed in contemporaneous reports and in the novel itself. It is part of Melville's understanding of himself as a writer during this period that he presents himself as inspired, and to that degree, at least, his thinking has an affinity with the Transcendentalists. Indeed a Transcendental enthusiasm (its headline, Emersonian sense at any rate) surfaces in all of Melville's intellectually ambitious novels. *Mardi*, his Rabelaisian tour of social and political possibilities, makes its penultimate island stop at Serenia, 'that land of enthusiasts ... where Mardians pretend to the unnatural conjunction of reason with things revealed; where Alma, they say, is restored to his divine original'. For the Serenians 'Love is a fervent fire', and they 'care not for men's words', but look instead

> for creeds in actions; which are the truthful symbols of the things within. He who hourly prays to Alma, but lives not up to world-wide love and charity – that man is more an unbeliever than he who verbally rejects the Master, but does his bidding.[6]

These are careful formulations, catching both the essentialism of Emersonian symbolism and the enthusiast's defining disregard for the sacraments. *Mardi*, however, is a series of enquiries, and so the novel's account of Emersonian enthusiasm cannot be thought its end point. *Pierre, or The Ambiguities*, on the other hand, written out of the acute disappointment Melville experienced at the immediate commercial and critical failure of *Moby-Dick*, is a self-portrait of the artist as an ardent young man whose coming of age consists precisely in his first-hand acquaintance with the ruinous implications of literary enthusiasm. Pierre is cast as an enthusiast from the beginning – 'To a less enthusiastic heart than Pierre's the foremost question in respect of Isabel ... would have been, *What* must I do?' – and chief among the ambiguities the novel's subtitle points towards is whether or not in light of Pierre's (which is to say Melville's) disappointments, enthusiasm is a sustainable mode of existence. Whether, that is, advanced minds should risk 'those hyperborean regions, to which enthusiastic Truth, and Earnestness, and Independence, will invariably lead a mind fitted by nature for profound and fearless thought.'[7]

The question posed throughout *Pierre*, and ultimately with appalling intensity, is whether, given the worldly devastation, born of intellectual marginalization, to which it can lead, an enthusiastic epistemology is advisable, or bearable, to the individual. The question by the time of *The Confidence-Man*, Melville's most exacting argument with Transcendentalism, is whether enthusiasm, and the confident ontology on which it is founded, the underlying belief in the possibility of a non-alienated relation with people and the world, isn't in fact flawed at its root. Enthusiasm is thus among the several concepts probed by the novel's unrelenting irony. It is first endorsed by the Confidence-Man himself:

> 'I fear you are too enthusiastic.'
> 'A philanthropist is necessarily an enthusiast; for without enthusiasm what was ever achieved but commonplace?'

This is a sort of joke: the sentiment itself is by now plainly commonplace, that which can or cannot be achieved by enthusiasm recalling Emerson, who recalled Kant. Later in the novel, however, enthusiasm is shown to be fragile, susceptible to mood and fortune: 'If a drunkard in a sober fit is the dullest of mortals, an enthusiast in a reason-fit is not the most lively ... for, if his elation was the height of his madness, his despondency is but the extreme of his sanity'. Finally, as with all concepts of human interaction, enthusiasm in *The Confidence-Man* is rendered fundamentally corruptible: '"You deceived me," smiled the cosmopolitan ... "you roguishly took advantage of my simplicity; you archly played upon my enthusiasm."'[8]

There are significant questions arising from these samplings of Melville, questions that will be addressed later: why, for instance, and with what degree of interest, does Melville press at enthusiasm's indifference to the sacraments in *Mardi*? What might it mean, in his case, to speak of an enthusiastic epistemology? The object for the moment, however, is to picture a body of work pivotal on and for the American mid-nineteenth century, as having, among its major themes, a fascination with enthusiasm: which returns to the theme and reconvenes there, which tests it from all the narrative angles its sets up for itself, and which figures enthusiasm throughout as a culturally defining force. And nowhere more so than in *Moby-Dick*, without which there would barely be a body of work to speak of, and in which Melville, as elsewhere, through Ishmael not least, shows himself to be wary of the headline sense of enthusiasm he found in Transcendentalism. As, for example, at the masthead, where, as Ishmael describes the sensation, 'lulled into such an opium-like listlessness of vacant unconscious reverie', in 'this enchanted mood' in which 'thy spirit ebbs away to whence it came',

> There is no life in thee, now, except that rocking life imparted by a gently rolling ship; by her, borrowed from the sea ... from the inscrutable tides of God. But while this sleep, this dream is on ye, move your foot or hand an inch; slip your hold at all; and your identity comes back in horror. (MD, 257)

What this famous burlesque on Emersonian abandonment should not be taken to mean is that in questioning enthusiasm – Melville questions everything – he rejects its potential as mode of being and writing. Rather, the novel transfigures the idea, the transfiguration taking two distinct and equally exacting forms. In the first place, then, Melville presses back through the idea of enthusiasm he picks up from American Romanticism, to the religious enthusiasm out of which it partly emerged, and which was foundational, at least in the ongoing controversies it provoked, for American culture right up to the middle of the nineteenth century. The best way to access this element in *Moby-Dick* is through the novel's Quakers, a glance back through the history of Quakerism exposing the cultural resources Melville had available to him as he pushed and probed at the implications of enthusiasm. One end of the argument through Quakerism, through the novel's shuddering sense of revelation, is Ahab, Ahab being an enthusiast whose conviction has become, to set the parlance running again, antinomian, and whose antinomianism is so driven that his actions have become those of a fanatic. But Ahab is not the end of the argument. The end of the argument – 'And I only am escaped alone to tell thee' – is Ishmael, and it is through Ishmael and his narrative that Melville's second transfiguration of enthusiasm occurs. Melville, Charles Olson said, 'went back, to discover us, to come forward' and this is true not least in his commentary on enthusiasm.[9] Ahab casts back, to the wilder fringes of early American religion. Ishmael cast forwards, his constant circulating of other voices, his sense of writing as citation, serving to draft a modern enthusiasm – a profoundly forward-looking sense of how an individual relates to language.

And also to literature – to books, to texts – because what *Moby-Dick* represents, above all things perhaps, is a radical and searching adventure in reading. This goes to the heart of the novel's enthusiasm. Thus when, in his letter to Hawthorne, he dated his life from his twenty-fifth year, he was referring to the beginning of his career as a serious and adventurous reader. An autodidact – 'a whale-ship was my Yale College and my Harvard' – he did not begin to acquaint with the world's great literature until after he had started to write, borrowing books, in the first instance, chiefly from his editor, the leader of the Young America Movement, Evert Duyckinck (MD, 208). From this point he read voraciously, finally getting round to Shakespeare at roughly the moment he began work on *Moby-Dick*. Which is to say that as he sat down to write the novel, he was swollen with other people's words, was full to the brim with the world's literature. He was also aware, however – Emerson's essays having been on his reading list – of an anxiety, one might call it a crisis, in American reading. 'Books,' as Emerson had told an audience of American academics, 'are for the scholar's idle times'.[10] It was a sentiment in Emerson that pointed back, again, to Quakerism, to the *Journal of George Fox*, which Emerson had read with 'a rising of joyful surprise at the correspondence of facts and expressions to states of thought and feeling, which are very familiar'. Thus 'The American Scholar', as critics have observed it, in the relation to textual authority it proposes, rehearses the experimentalism which characterized the Quaker relation to scripture; which found in scripture an incomplete statement of divine authority, which required the supplement of religious experience. To read *Moby-Dick* through its mid-century enthusiasm – and especially in the light of Quakerism, which was the background to that enthusiasm – is to bring to the fore the nature of its reading. Ahab and Ishmael are both demonstrably enthusiasts of sorts, but Ishmael, crucially, is also a reader.

And what *Moby-Dick* explores, among other things, is the possibility of an enthusiastic relation with books.

Quaking

Critics have long since understood *Moby-Dick* in terms of American religion. In *American Renaissance* Peter Matthiessen understood its presentation of the ongoing crisis in American religion to be central to the novel's achievement. 'The severe, bleak, and uninspired Presbyterian Church of Melville's experience had driven him inevitably,' Matthiessen reckoned, 'into questioning even the goodness of the Biblical God'.

> On the other hand, he could find no security in throwing over all the restraints of dogma, and exalting the God-like man. If the will was free, as the new faith insisted, Melville knew that it was free to do evil as well as to do good ... He had also seen in Ahab the destruction that must overtake the Man-God, the self-appointed Messiah ... Without deliberately intending it, but by virtue of his intense concern with the precariously maintained virtues of democratic Christianity, which he saw everywhere being threatened or broken down, Melville created in Ahab's tragedy a fearful symbol of the self-enclosed individualism that, carried to its furthest extreme, brings disaster both upon itself and upon the group of which it is part.[11]

The argument of Ahab, in other words, is rooted in contemporary (but also historic) crises of dogma in American Christianity, and out of which it comes to test Emersonian thinking to its implied Nietzschean limit. Laurence Buell has made a comparable observation, arguing that: 'One of the major intellectual forces behind the whole so-called literary renaissance to which Melville's work contributed was a religious ferment and anxiety resulting from the breakdown of consensual dogmatic structures and particularly the breakdown of biblical authority in Protestant America'. Emphasizing the relativist implications of this, Buell pushes the argument forward, finding in *Moby-Dick* both a 'document in the history of the clash in American and specifically northeastern post-Puritanism between Reformist Calvinist and Enlightenment Unitarian cross-currents', and a 'full literary efflorescence' of 'comparative religion as a discipline and as a literary force'.[12]

This is both affirmative of and true to the novel, but it shouldn't obscure the depth of the contemporary anxiety both Buell and Matthiessen point to, and which the book helped flush to the surface of American literary culture when it was first published. So here's Evert Duyckinck, Melville's editor and, if you like, friend – leader of the Young America movement and literary gate-keeper – reviewing *Moby-Dick* and finding it impossible not to voice the religious position with which, as he no doubt rightly understood it, the novel variously and fundamentally came into collision:

> This piratical running down of creeds and opinions, the conceited indifferentism of Emerson, or the run-a-muck style of Carlyle is, we will not say dangerous in such cases ... but it is out of place and uncomfortable. We do not like to see what, under any view, must be to the world the most sacred associations of life violated and defaced.

This is in substance the same point as Matthiessen and Buell make, though Duyckinck's tone shows a writer for whom something is really at stake, and except that for him the violating presence is not Ahab's, but Ishmael's. Thus,

> Here is Ishmael ... going down on his knees with a cannibal to a piece of wood ... Surely Ishmael, who is a scholar, might have spoken respectfully of the Archangel Gabriel, out of consideration, if not for the Bible (which might be asking too much of the school), at least for one John Milton.

Nor is the Bible the only authority at issue, because,

> Nor is it fair to inveigh against the terrors of priestcraft. ... It is a curious fact that there are no more bilious people in the world, more completely filled with megrims and head shakings, than some of those very people who are constantly inveighing against the religious melancholy.[13]

The issue raised by *Moby-Dick*, as Duyckinck saw it, was biblical authority, and with it priestcraft, and among the most significant and enduring challenges to such forces in American religious history, as his 'megrims and head shakings' acknowledge, was the never satisfactorily quelled phenomenon of enthusiasm.

Possibly Melville already had it in mind to write a novel which would disturb existing religious anxieties before he read and reviewed Hawthorne's *Mosses from an Old Manse*. Scholarly wisdom, however, is that Melville's conception of his novel, and of Ahab especially, altered radically upon reading Hawthorne, and in the appendix to his review of the book he documents the influence he already senses Hawthorne to have had on him. That influence has to do with the sense of what American writing should now aim for, and tangled up with that sense is the necessity to the American cultural imagination of religion:

> Whether Hawthorne has simply availed himself of this mystical blackness as a means to the wondrous effects he makes it to produce in his lights and shades; or whether there really lurks in him, perhaps unknown to himself, a touch of Puritanic gloom, – this, I cannot altogether tell. Certain it is, however, that this great power of blackness in him derives its force from its appeals to that Calvinistic sense of Innate Depravity and Original Sin, from

whose visitations, in some shape or another, no deeply thinking mind is always and wholly free.[14]

What Hawthorne showed Melville, in other words, or at least confirmed in him – the enthusiasm in the review of Hawthorne's work is at least in part enthusiasm for his own – is that if an American writer was to speak with real scope and force, he would do well to conduct the forces of the American religious personality into the fabric of his work. The prevailing religious temperament in *Moby-Dick* is not Puritan but Quaker, a fact which, in the main, criticism has tended to disregard. The intention here is to explore its meaning.

Nantucket was home to hundreds of 'Friends' in the first half of the nineteenth-century, and so it is simply a naturalistic detail perhaps – in the sense that you can't pin anything on it – that when Ishmael sets out to sign up for a whaling voyage, he should run into a couple of Quakers.

> Now, Bildad, like Peleg, and indeed many other Nantucketers, was a Quaker, the island having been originally settled by that sect; and to this day its inhabitants in general retain in an uncommon measure the peculiarities of the Quaker, only variously and anomalously modified by things altogether alien and heterogeneous. For some of these same Quakers are the most sanguinary of all sailors and whale-hunters. They are fighting Quakers; they are Quakers with a vengeance. (MD, 169)

Here, as elsewhere, Melville has done his research, their evolved 'peculiarities' being how Quakers, in the absence of a binding doctrine, characterized their way of life, religious and otherwise. Ishmael himself is not a Quaker, but, as he says, 'born and bred in the bosom of the infallible Presbyterian Church'. Except that as he has come to see it, and in the spirit of the relativism which matures through the novel into his defining intellectual quality, the Presbyterian Church is not infallible, or at least, so he concludes as he settles down to worship with Queequeg:

> How then could I unite with this wild idolater in worshipping his piece of wood? ... But what is worship? – to do the will of God – *that* is worship. And what is the will of God? – to do to my fellow man what I would have my fellow man to do to me – *that* is the will of God. (MD, 147)

This is one of the passages Duyckinck, an Episcopalian, objected to in particular. The objection was that here Melville showed a disregard for the forms of religion. Numerous American sects, emerging from the ferment of the English Civil War, demonstrated a disregard for the forms and procedures of religion. Unitarianism, the tradition out of which Transcendentalism developed – with its own insistence on the spirit over the text – is a good instance of such a practice. Denominationally, however, it wasn't Unitarianism but Quakerism that Emerson himself felt closest to, hence his 'frequent remark that he felt more kinship with the inner light of the Quakers than with any formal creed'.[15] Ishmael, this is likewise to suggest, as a sceptical Presbyterian, is a would-be religious relativist who in his disregard for the textual and sacramental trappings of religion approached the sometimes doctrinally neutral commitment of Quakerism. Much more significant in this respect, however, is Ahab, himself also a Nantucketer and also a Quaker, and whose relationship to his faith, his investment in it and his departure from it, is nothing less than the novel's dramatic premise:

> So that there are instances among them of men, who, named with Scripture names ... and in childhood naturally imbibing the stately dramatic *thee* and *thou* of the Quaker idiom; still, from the audacious, daring, and boundless adventure of their subsequent lives, strangely blend with those unoutgrown peculiarities, a thousand bold dashes of character, not unworthy a Scandinavian sea-king, or a poetical Pagan Roman. And when these things unite in a man of greatly superior natural force, with a globular brain and a ponderous heart; who has also by the stillness and seclusion of many long night-watches in the remotest waters, and beneath constellations never seen here at the north, been led to think untraditionally and independently; receiving all nature's sweet or savage impressions fresh from her own virgin voluntary and confiding breast, and thereby chiefly, but with some help from accidental advantages, to learn a bold and nervous lofty language – that man makes one in a whole nation's census – a mighty pageant creature, formed for noble tragedies. (MD, 169–70)

And so there's Ahab, the character whose presence the novel means us to be gripped by, 'the mighty pageant creature, formed for noble tragedies' Hawthorne had put Melville in mind of, whose 'bold and nervous lofty language' means to resemble and equal Shakespeare, and for whom, crucially, Quakerism is an essential part of the mix, the strange blend, its 'peculiarities' in him being – most emphatic word – 'unoutgrown'. Quakerism, in other words, was central to the formation of Ahab, in whose fate we are to understand a version of America's own, and so not only can you make something of Quakerism in *Moby-Dick* – not only are you entitled – but probably it is a mistake not to, Ahab emerging from that enthusiastic mould.

To build on the story sketched out in the introduction, Quakerism, from its inception, was understood as one form among many of religious enthusiasm, religious enthusiasts – whether Anabaptists, or Familists, or Ranters, or Quakers, or any of the many fervent sects that emerged in Britain and Europe in the period after the Reformation – showing a desire for a more direct acquaintance with God than conventional Protestantism, or even Puritanism, permitted. Such acquaintance was to be unmediated by either priests and priestcraft or even, in some cases, texts. Implicit in this anti-formalism was, in some cases anyway, and in Quakerism certainly, an extension of the franchise, all people being judged equally capable of receiving and acting upon the divine spirit. A further point of commonality was a strong attraction to the New World, where the religious constraints that contained and thwarted enthusiastic worship, so it was felt, need not apply. And so enthusiasts made the journey, from which adventure it followed that at moments of crisis in American religious history, enthusiasm, the belief in the possibility of a greater nearness to God, was invariably, in some sense or another, at issue. Whether in the antinomian crisis triggered by Anne Hutchinson's prophesying, in the Great Awakening, or in the Great Revival of the second half of the nineteenth century, the enthusiastic voice sounds loud through American history.

Quakerism was a pure strain. Perplexed and unconvinced by the many reformist Christian sects available to him in the 1640s, George Fox determined, or was led to the conviction, that God was available to him only through personal revelations, 'openings' as he termed the experience, which is to say by a process of spiritual intuition. It followed that all people, non-believers and believers alike – Pagans for instance, Queequeg for instance – were capable of divine revelation, from which it also followed that in the government of Quaker belief, religious experience, the individual's experience of the promptings of the divine spirit, took precedence over scripture. Thus, as the historian of American religious enthusiasm David Lovejoy puts it, for Fox, 'God's truths in the Scripture were universal, but they were not complete, and from them new truths were discoverable with God's help'. What was called for, theologically speaking, was an 'experimental spirit', and so as Lovejoy has suggested it, 'Fox read the Bible only to discover … truths he already knew "experimentally", a key word he frequently used and one which became central to enthusiasts' understanding of spiritual life'.[16] The Bible being judged incomplete, Quakerism was, by definition, unbound by a text-based doctrine, evolving instead, out of its forms of devotion and way of life, the 'peculiarities' Quakers in Britain and America became identifiable with: a repudiation of priestcraft and predetermined liturgy or ritual, in favour of a relatively free-form worship acknowledging the possibility that anybody present might be moved by the divine spirit to speak; a rejection of physical sacraments, communion being held to be a purely spiritual affair; and a commitment to social equality, flowing from spiritual equality, hence the 'stately dramatic', but also socially levelling, '*thee* and *thou* of the Quaker religion'.

Two aspects of Quakerism suggest themselves in this context in particular, seem 'unoutgrown', as it were, by *Moby-Dick*. The first is prophesying, the spiritual mechanism by which radical Protestants generally, but early Quakers in particular, sought to avail themselves of, and to communicate, the further light. To 'prophesy', in this sense, meant 'to interpret and expound upon Scripture, to discuss and explain to others the Word of God, the divine mysteries, from experience with divine prompting, even inspiration, and usually at public meetings and services'.[17] This makes it sound like a relatively measured procedure, though non-Quakers did not typically view it as such, Francis Higginson reporting of the phenomenon of prophesying that,

> many of them, sometimes men, but more frequently women and children, fall into quaking fits ... Those who are taken with these fits fall suddenly down, as it were into a swoon, as though they were surprised with an epilepsy or apoplexy, and lie groveling on the earth, and struggling as if it were for life ... While the agony of the fit is upon them their lips quiver, their flesh and joints tremble, their bellies swell as though blown up with wind, they foam at the mouth, and sometimes purge as they had taken physic. In this fit they continue sometimes an hour or two, sometimes longer, before they roar out horribly with a voice greater than the voice of a man ... greater sometimes than a bull can make.[18]

To prophesy was to speak with another voice, 'a voice greater than the voice of a man'; it was to avail oneself of, and to make oneself available to, words and agencies not one's own. Quaking and roaring was part of it, but so too, and especially as Quakerism developed, was silence or quietism, revelation of the divine will coming also 'through introspection, silence, emptying their minds of all distractions, and totally crucifying and eradicating any evidence of human will, or what Friends called "creaturely activity"'.[19] From this emptying a second significant element of Quakerism follows, that in its rejection of conventional modes of mediation, it became known, and sometimes seemed to assert itself, as an anti-intellectual faith. This is arguable, and has historically divided Quakers, was dividing them in fact as Melville was writing, in the guise of the Hicksite controversy: Elias Hicks casting back to the original freedom Fox's inner light had secured for Quakers from 'dependence upon Scripture, book learning, ordinances, church discipline and magistrates' and all practices deemed to get 'in the way of the Spirit'.[20] Whether properly understood as anti-intellectual or not, what is at very least the case is that Quakerism was a textually anti-bureaucratic movement, its enthusiasm, as with all forms of religious enthusiasm, having its original dispute with the alienating consequences of interpretive and organizational apparatus.

This is not the place for a history of Quakerism, for an account of its transition from the early enthusiasm of Fox, to the quietism – where silence and retreat became the emphasis rather than transmission – under the leadership in Philadelphia of William Penn, to Quaker involvement in political reformism, especially the anti-slavery movement, as led by John Woolman and as rooted in the Quaker sense of religious equality. What do need to be drawn out are the elements of what one might call Quaker sensibility: a commitment to revelation, a faith in the possibility of immediate contact with the divine, an experimental spirit, an opening of the self to other words and voices. As Quakerism – and then as Quakerism overlapped with other manifestations of religious enthusiasm, including, on occasion, the suicidalism of the martyr – this sensibility can be thought variously critical to the emergence of major American writing in the middle of the nineteenth century, and to avail oneself of it in relation to *Moby-Dick* is to release in the novel its wilder, more ruinous, but also more forward-looking forces.

Raving

It is a feature of *Moby-Dick* that just when everything seems like it might settle down, somebody, somewhere, starts to rant and rave. No sooner, then, have Ishmael and Queequeg successfully signed up for a voyage with the *Pequod* (chosen by Ishmael as dictated by Queequeg's idol Yojo) than they encounter Elijah, 'The Prophet' as the chapter heading names him. Ishmael's word for Elijah's talk is 'jabbering', or 'gibberish', and he advises Queequeg that 'this fellow has broken loose from somewhere' (MD, 189). Even so, he can't quite dispel Elijah's words as nonsense, reflecting subsequently that, 'This circumstance, coupled with his ambiguous, half-hinting, half-revealing, shrouded sort of talk, now begat in me all kinds of vague wonderments and half-apprehensions' (MD, 191). Nor can the reader dispel Elijah's words, both because as they are spoken they appear to have genuine prophetic force within the narrative, and also because the narrative generally takes prophecy seriously, a function in part of Ishmael's experimental religious sensibility. As with Queequeg's idol, so with Elijah's jabbering, his first thought is to pronounce the procedure as humbug. Ishmael, however, is on a spiritual journey all of his own in *Moby-Dick*, away from the infallible prescriptions of Presbyterianism, and so lacks the conviction whereby he might outright reject another's commitments or claims. Queequeg and Ishmael meet Elijah again, more ominously this time just before they go on board, at which point his ranting is more extreme:

> 'Morning to ye! morning to ye!' he rejoined, again moving off. 'Oh! I was going to warn ye against – but never mind, never mind – it's all one, all in the family too;–sharp frost this morning, ain't it? Good bye to ye. Shan't see ye again very soon, I guess; unless it's before the Grand Jury.' And with these cracked words

he finally departed, leaving me, for the moment, in no small wonderment at this frantic impudence. (MD, 195)

There are a lot of 'cracked words' in *Moby-Dick*, a lot of jabberings, a lot of gibberish, many occasions when a speaker is speaking words not entirely his own. Often the words are associated with prophecy, which is to say they are a speaking before, or are spoken before; and often with such utterances – 'inspirational utterance' Sophia Hawthorne called it – there is, or there is claimed to be, a movement of the spirit. From one point of view, in fact, *Moby-Dick* is an investigation of such states, a cataloguing and assessing of modes of delirium, of supernatural serenities and fits and flurries, of enthusiastic articulations of all sorts.

The *Jeroboam*'s story is a case in point. Gabriel, who first appears with 'a deep, settled, fanatic delirium' in his eyes, and who had been 'originally nurtured among the crazy society of the Neskyeuna Shakers, where he had been a great prophet', has had a career straight out of the annals of early American religious history (MD, 420). He left Neskyeuna for Nantucket on 'a strange, apostolic whim', the same kind of whim, say, that took Anne Hutchinson to Massachusetts or which drove the early Quaker Mary Dyer to her martyrdom at the hands of the Puritans. Thereafter, once having joined the *Jeroboam*, and once the ship's journey was under way, he announced himself as the archangel Gabriel, successfully recruiting disciples and generally investing himself with an air of sacredness through the 'dark, daring play of his sleepless, excited imagination, and all the preternatural terrors of real delirium' (420). Gabriel is a warning. 'Nor,' as the narrative points out, 'is the history of fanatics half so striking in respect to the measureless self-deception of the fanatic himself, as his measureless power of deceiving … others' (MD, 421). The phrase which draws one in here, which makes Gabriel's case-history exemplary rather than anomalous, is 'the history of fanatics'. The novel itself is a history of fanatics, the unravelling of Ahab's governing fanaticism occurring against a background of numerous walk-on and cameo fanaticisms, with the whole crew – even, ultimately, Starbuck – eventually getting caught up in the central fanatical quest. But the novel is also *predicated* on the history of fanatics, as Gabriel's carefully outlined background suggests, drawing on and drawing in the history of American enthusiastic religious traits and practices, showing and using the culture's capacity for extremism. Witness the novel's speech, its cracked words, which point, in the automatic speech of the carpenter, say, to twentieth-century developments in the presentation of language, but which are unimaginable in the context of the novel without the inspired utterances, the rantings and ravings, of religious enthusiasts. Melville mentions the Shakers as an instance of this, but perhaps a purer form is to be found among the Ranters, the Ranters being a relatively short-lived seventeenth-century sect best characterized here as extreme Quakers. Thus, while for Quakers the divine spirit 'justified and, according to some, perfected ... it did not deify; possessed with it Quakers did not equate themselves with God'. And so, 'While Quakers reduced the Scriptures and human reason to externals, they still believed them aids of a sort to religious life ... Ranters denied this, accepted the Spirit as all there was, and as perfectionists in spiritual things lived as they pleased.'[21]

In America the Ranters hovered at the fringes of Quakerism, doubtful Ranters sometimes being drawn back within the limits of Quakerism, extreme Quakers sometimes being attracted to the antinomian freedoms of the Ranters. Antinomianism is the extreme view that Christians are released by grace from observance of the moral law, and is as such a form of perfectionism; perfectionism holding that as it is possible for a human being to know the spirit of God on earth, therefore it is possible for a human being to be as God. The possibility of the Ranter was always implicit in the inward light of Quakerism, ranting being an extreme freedom of speech that flowed from an unquestioning investment in the motions of the Spirit. Once privilege the inner light, in other words, the extremes of the Ranter become possible. The person who rants, from the point of view of orthodoxy, is the Quaker overdeveloped, the Quaker gone wrong. *Moby-Dick* is a ranting novel, not in the sense that Melville identified the Ranters, of all sects in the history of fanaticism, as an explicit model for his more extreme characters, but in the sense that ranting is one of its modes, and because the novel's ranting is identified with and understood through the religious background out of which such forms of utterance most spectacularly entered American culture. To rant, as the dictionary has it: to speak or shout in a wild, impassioned way: from Du. *ranten* 'talk nonsense, rave'.

Ahab's 'transfiguration' (the word is Melville's) is explicitly the result of a psychological process made the more possible and imaginable because of the 'unoutgrown peculiarities' of his Quaker inheritance. Thus it is through and over the mechanisms of Quaker revelation and conversion – the glimpse of the inner light and the gradual unfolding thereafter – that Ahab's monomania is able to grip and take hold. The process, as Melville is careful to describe it, is not sudden, not the instantaneous consequence of his injury at the jaws of the whale, but the result, rather, of a protracted and painful spiritual rebirth. Thus, and necessarily to recall the transfiguration at length:

> When by this collision forced to turn towards home, and for long months of days and weeks, Ahab and anguish lay stretched together in one hammock, rounding in mid winter that dreary, howling Patagonian Cape; then it was, that his torn body and gashed soul bled into one another; and so interfusing,

made him mad. That it was only then, on the homeward voyage, after the encounter, that the final monomania seized him, seems all but certain from the fact that, at intervals during the passage, he was a raving lunatic; and, though unlimbed of a leg, yet such vital strength yet lurked in his Egyptian chest, and was moreover intensified by his delirium, that his mates were forced to lace him fast, even there, as he sailed, raving in his hammock. In a straitjacket, he swung to the mad rockings of the gales. And, when running into more sufferable latitudes, the ship, with mild stun'sails spread, floated across the tranquil tropics, and, to all appearances, the old man's delirium seemed left behind him with the Cape Horn swells, and he came forth from his dark den into the blessed light and air, even then, when he bore that firm, collected front, however pale, and issued his calm orders once again; and his mates thanked God the direful madness was now gone; even then, Ahab, in his hidden self, raved on. (MD, 283–4)

Beyond this, in one sense, beyond the ravings of the transfiguration, it isn't necessary to press, other commentators having observed perfectionism in Ahab; that, having shed all vestige of moral orthodoxy, he demonstrates a tendency to identify a divinity in man. What matters, rather, from the point of view of enthusiasm is the process whereby such an overestimation of his powers occurs. Quaker revelation, as Thomas D. Hamm reports it, did not come in 'a single, transforming experience'. Rather, 'the Inward light constituted a kind of seed' – the same kind of seed, perhaps, with which Melville understood his own transformation into a writer to have begun. A seed that would, if observed, gradually flourish, the process being 'strengthened by experiences that Friends called baptisms, seasons of divine visitation that often took the form of suffering or depression'.[22] And so there's Ahab, victim unquestionably of an 'opening', condemned by his isolation to look deeper and deeper inwards, raving so extremely his shipmates had to lace him down, his strength, apparently, intensified by his delirium. From which state he emerges, finally, converted to a new belief, baptized, as he says later, not in the name of the Father, but in the name of the Devil, apparently calm but inwardly 'raving on', always capable, as the novel shows us, of speaking with a voice greater than a man. This is the psychological process whereby 'torn body and gashed soul bled into one another', a process which, in its structural similarity to the enthusiast's conversion, would seem to confirm that Quaker 'peculiarities', if by no means observed to the letter, also remain 'unoutgrown'. And it is out of this process that, as he hoped in 'Hawthorne and his Mosses', 'a mighty pageant creature, formed for noble tragedies' emerges, with his 'nervous, lofty language', his ranting and raving.

Ahab emerges from his transfiguration an enthusiast in a strict sense of the term, in that, having breathed in the God he proceeds to breathe it out into others, a capacity which is crucial to the plot of the novel. Pip, likewise, becomes an enthusiast in the strictest, which is to say the etymologically informed, sense of the term, following the abandonment at sea from which he emerges raving. His transfiguration, more explicitly even than Ahab's, is presented in terms of an enthusiastic engagement with God:

> The sea had jeeringly kept his finite body up, but drowned the infinite of his soul. Not drowned entirely, though. Rather carried down alive to wondrous depths, where strange shapes of the unwarped primal world glided to and fro before his passive eyes ... He saw God's foot upon the treadle of the loom, and spoke it; and therefore his shipmates called him mad. So man's insanity is heaven's sense; and wandering from all mortal reason, man comes at last to that celestial thought, which, to reason, is absurd and frantic; and weal or woe, feels then uncompromised, indifferent as his God. (MD, 525–6)

And so Pip emerges, out of 'all mortal reason', a babbling idiot or a divine, depending on the point of view, jabbering ceaselessly, ranting and raving through the final quarter of the novel. The narrator's point of view, it should be noticed, is qualified or held back here, Pip's enthusiasm, his cracked speech, though unquestionably frantic and absurd, being held open for consideration as 'heaven's sense'. Ishmael's reluctance to judge is continuous with this toleration for the varieties of religious experience, but it is predicated also, as he promptly observes, on an affinity he necessarily feels with Pip's condition. 'The thing is common in that fishery; and in the sequel of the narrative, it will then be seen what like abandonment befell myself' (MD, 526). This is true, of course, Ishmael drifting for two days after the Pequod was destroyed by the whale before he was picked up. The question is, what is meant by 'like abandonment'? What does it mean in this context, for Ishmael to compare himself with Pip? One implication, perhaps, is that his own utterance – the book we are just now reading – was likewise the product of abandonment, that in some sense or other the narrative itself, Melville's own cracked speech, is the product of enthusiasm.

Writing

One way of thinking about enthusiasm against the religious background being sketched into this chapter is as a coming or speaking through. *Walden* was construed in these terms. Thoreau's language, it was argued, can be thought of as revelatory in manner, his recourse to etymologies, brought out by careful reinflection, designed to show old, unused and, in his view, valuable meanings, coming or speaking through familiar words. Melville's language, likewise, can be thought of in terms of a coming through, his writing itself as being, in some sense, enthusiastic; in two senses, actually, Romantic and proto-Modern, the divergence having to do with reading, and with the ways words can be thought of as originating somewhere else.

It is axiomatic to Quakerism that, in the act of worship at least, the individual's words come from elsewhere, Quakers historically desiring that, in the act of worship, they would never speak 'according to their own inclination, wisdom, or inspiration', but under 'a divine leading'.[23] At the time of writing *Moby-Dick*, Melville thought of the act of composition like this, or at least he figured it like this, his presentation of writing in review and in letters being according to the idea of something passing through the writer. The clearest statement of this is in 'Hawthorne and his Mosses', beginning, as it does, with a testimony to literary genius:

> I know not what would be the right name to put on the title-page of an excellent book, but this I feel, that the names of all fine authors are fictitious ones, far more so than that of Junius, – simply standing, as they do, for the mystical ever-eluding Spirit of all Beauty, which ubiquitously possesses men of genius.[24]

This is August 1850. The basic figuration had not changed much by the summer of 1851, Melville observing to Hawthorne:

> This most persuasive season has now for weeks recalled me from certain crotchety and over doleful chimearas the like of which men like you and me and some others, forming a chain of God's posts around the world, must be content to encounter now and then, and fight them the best way we can.[25]

The coming through thus pictured in the commentary surrounding the composition and completion of *Moby-Dick* – the image of enthusiasm or inspiration whereby the writing self opens up to the operations of another agency – is also, crucially in Melville, almost always a passing on, a circulation. The images presented are of transmission, continuity and fellowship, and as such, as a mode of circulation, the theme of inspiration spills into the texture of the novel itself, Melville in *Moby-Dick*, much more than in any other of his works, being obsessed, like Thoreau, by the processes whereby one thing passes through or turns into another.

Often these processes are physical, *Moby-Dick* being, among other things, a natural history of the whale, the novel repeatedly turning its attention to gases and fluids, to breath, to blood, to excreta of all kinds. Thus the preamble to the story, its various pre-texts and premonitions, brings to the fore all manner of modes of circulation. On the opening page, for instance, as Harold Beaver is delighted to observe, the first of the etymological entries comes from Hackluyt:

> While you take in hand to school others, and to teach them by what name a whale-fish is to be called in our tongue, leaving out, through ignorance, the

letter H, which almost alone maketh up the signification of the word, you deliver that which is not true. (MD, 75)

And so the fun begins. The letter H 'maketh up the whole signification of the word' because it is as the 'H' is aspirated that breath enters the word 'whale', which delivery of breath is an essential part of the truth of the whale; how the whale breathes, as Melville is careful (comically) to note in 'Cetology', being, after all, core to its being. The fictional usher who supplies the etymologies is likewise breathless, being consumptive and therefore tubercular, suffering from the growth of nodules on tissue – as the dictionary has it, most likely the lungs. The usher's entries contribute to the novel, but in themselves are dry as dust. What they want, in order to be animated, is the writer's breath. In 'Loomings' it is in the interest of 'circulation' that Ishmael decides to go to sea: 'It is a way I have of driving off the spleen, and regulating the circulation' (MD, 93). And then in 'The Sermon' – which takes as its text 'Jonah', the pre-text for the novel as a whole, and an allegory whose theme is, in multiple ways, the passage through – Jonah, when he is out of favour with God, is himself described, by Father Mapple, as breathless. Jonah throws himself into his berth to find 'the little state-room ceiling almost resting on his forehead'. 'The air is close, and Jonah gasps' (MD, 138). 'But God,' as Father Mapple notes, is everywhere, and so as Jonah, 'the prophet', repents:

God spake unto the fish; and from the shuddering cold and blackness of the sea, the whale came breeching up towards the warm and pleasant sun, and all the delights of air and earth; and 'vomited out Jonah upon the dry land' ... Jonah did the Almighty's bidding. And what was that, shipmates? To preach the Truth to the face of Falsehood! (MD, 142)

These are suggestive processes – Melville arriving at the idea of utterance he wants in *Moby-Dick* in part through the repeated attention the novel pays to forms of circulation – but none more so than the act of spouting.

Of all the unknowable aspects of the whale, the spout, Melville points out, has proved least available to analysis. It is a noteworthy thing, surely, that 'for six thousand years – and no one knows how many millions of ages before that – the great whales should have been spouting all over the sea', and yet,

down to this blessed minute (fifteen and a quarter minutes past one o'clock P.M. of this sixteenth day of December, A.D. 1850), it should still remain a problem, whether these spoutings are, after all, really water, or nothing but vapor. (MD, 477)

And the point is that in the spout, in the whale's characteristic 'spoutings', Melville finds an archetype for writerly enthusiasm:

> And so, through all the thick mists of the dim doubts in my mind, divine intuitions now and then shoot, enkindling my fog with a heavenly ray. And for this I thank God; for all have doubts; many deny; but doubts or denials, few along with them, have intuitions. (MD, 482)

With spoutings come intuitions, you could call them revelations, the revelation here being that as he contemplates the spout Melville finds an analogy for the processes of his own thought.

Nor is it only as it repeatedly details circulatory processes that the fabric of *Moby-Dick* is structured by the idea of one agency passing into and through another. In its devices also, in its characteristic rhetorical manoeuvres, the novel reads like an enthusiastic text. This claim made in relation to *Walden* emphasized Thoreau's investment in etymology, his inclination towards derivation releasing meanings such that otherwise unnoticed and neglected senses and inflections came through familiar words. Melville, for all his debt to the usher, is not an etymological writer. His defining devices, rather, are metaphor and simile, but used such that always the thing being described comes to bear the presence of some other, or previous formal incarnation. The whale often appears like this:

> mid most of them all, one grand hooded phantom, like a snow hill in the air (MD, 98)

But so too other phenomena, as when

> faith, like a jackal, feeds among the tombs, and even from these dead doubts she gathers her most vital hope. (MD, 131)

The point about simile and metaphor in *Moby-Dick* has to do with the relation between the subject of the comparison and the thing to which it is compared – between, as it were, the tenor and the vehicle. And the point about this is that, invariably in this relationship, the tenor is overwhelmed by the vehicle; that what comes through is not a sharper sense of the subject but a graphic and often quite overpowering image of what it is likened to, which is, by definition, something it is not. This epic tendency – because what this describes is epic simile – is underwritten by the novel's other most characteristic rhetorical move, its continuous reaching after genealogy as a mode of explanation, whether what's at issue is the genealogy of cetologists, or of monstrous pictures of whales, or, most famously, of the tradition of 'standing mastheads', to which Melville admits the builders of the pyramids, the tower of Babel, Simon Stylites, Napoleon 'upon the top of the tower of Vendome', George Washington and Admiral Nelson. The implication with each of Melville's genealogies is of an infinite series, the effect of the act of associating being to have one thing show through another, so that finally the form of each particular instance is lost, substituted by the likening feature, the continuous element.

There are various words one can bring to this process, to this sense, variously presented, of one thing coming through another. One of Melville's is metempsychosis, being the supposed transmigration after death of the soul into a new body:

> Oh! the metempsychosis! Oh! Pythagoras, that in bright Greece, two thousand years ago, did die, so good, so wise, so mild; I sailed with thee along the Peruvian coast last voyage – and, foolish as I am, taught thee, a green simple boy, how to splice a rope! (MD, 539)

This is thrillingly put, Melville using the idea of metempsychosis both to render the past immediate – the immediacy of things being a dominating concern in the last quarter of the novel – and to further explore the enthusiastic process whereby one agency passes into and through another. Another word for that process, however, is Ishmael. 'Call me Ishmael', Melville's narrator insists, in one of the most devastating openings in all literature, thereby investing in his own identity just precisely in so far as to ascribe to it a name. Implicit in that opening, however, is the fact that the narrator may or may not be Ishmael; that's just what we'll be calling him for the time being. Ishmael, as far as we can be certain, is just Melville's persona's persona, the form that the novel is speaking through. Which is to say that he is the form of writing, Melville's view being that 'the names of all fine authors are fictitious ones … standing, as they do, for the mystical ever-eluding Spirit of all Beauty, which ubiquitously possesses men of genius'. 'Call me Ishmael' in other words, in the manner of its address, introduces but also exemplifies an enthusiastic text.

To which point, as we consider the writing of *Moby-Dick*, the novel would seem to be pursuing a broadly Romantic sense of literary enthusiasm, pushing it, perhaps, to its ultimate statement, but even so, and in its excess, holding to an Emersonian sense of self-abandonment. It is a view of writing, however, significantly tempered and countered by Melville's reading, and by his sense of how reading relates to the process of composition; how to read, and more precisely, what to do with one's reading, being central questions in *Moby-Dick*. The question is implicit in the presence of the 'consumptive usher to a grammar school' on the opening page of the novel, 'threadbare in coat, heart, body, and brain', who 'loved to dust his old grammars' (MD, 75). It is posed also by (and to) the sub-sub-librarian, who belongs to the 'hopeless, sallow tribe which no wine of this world will ever warm'. The question is present, also, in the novel's satire on scholarship. This is ongoing, even as Melville openly borrows from the whaling manuals and histories, but is most apparent in his presentation of 'cetology', the chapter itself being a highly scholarly anatomy of whaling, the scholarship emphasized and satirized by the use of book-formats (folios, quartos, octavos and duodecimos) as categories for the cataloguing of whales according to size. There is an enthusiasm in this, an enthusiasm of the order implied by modern usage – a usage which, later in this book, Marianne Moore will be seen to bring into play – the enthusiasm of the antiquarian, or the collector, or the specialist, or, even, the statistician. It is not, however, an enthusiasm the novel looks to endorse, even as it indulges in it. The question being posed by the cetology, as elsewhere, is whether such bureaucracy of scholarship adds to knowledge and understanding, or whether the person who wants to know the whale shouldn't instead cut to the chase. Thus, 'Some pretend to see a difference between the Greenland whale of the English and the right whale of the Americans. ... It is by endless subdivisions based upon the most inconclusive differences, that some departments of natural history become so repellingly intricate' (MD, 233).

The repellingly intricate subdivisions of scholarship, the intrusive overlay of apparatus designed to categorize and measure, the procrustean formalization of knowledge and understanding go to the heart of this book. Which is also to say *this* book, this being a moment after all, 25 August 2005, as the whole machinery of British academia steams headlong into the maw of the RAE, when the forms and procedures of academic reading threaten constantly to overwhelm its content. But it goes to the heart of *this* book also because, as was observed earlier, enthusiasm, and especially religious enthusiasm, is born of a suspicion of the overweening form. Quakerism was precisely a departure from the prevailing apparatus of worship, risking, as a consequence, anti-intellectualism. Equally, and oppositely, however, and this is why *Moby-Dick* is so important in this respect, Melville was a voluminous and insatiable reader, and in particular a reader who considered his reading continuous with writing, with the process of composition. As Olson says, 'Melville's reading is a gauge of him, at all points of his life. He was a skald, and knew how to appropriate the work of others. He read to write.'[26] Nor, of course, is this process submerged. The extracts, the quotations, with which the novel opens are obviously sources, matter influential on the novel being directly passed on. Similarly there is little disguising the use of whaling histories and scholarship, Melville not so much passing words off as his own as, from time to time, simply giving his text over to others.

The matter of reading, as conducted through the tradition of enthusiasm, brings one to a central question posed in and by *Moby-Dick*; the question being – and I mean to present Melville as having been in the fullest sense conscious of this – how should a novel, in a cultural tradition founded, in part, on a suspicion of textual authority, handle and communicate reading? The answer, in various ways, and in a decisive development in the term's meaning, is that Melville communicates reading enthusiastically. There are three ways this might be thought true, three senses of enthusiasm at play here. In the first place, reading sometimes passes through writing in *Moby-Dick* in such a way that it is kept intact, word for word often, as when Melville is re-presenting his sources. A word for this is citation, but another word for it, as Thoreau might have thought, is prophecy: that which is said before, that which has before been said. Writing as agency, in other words, is like the enthusiastic self as agency; or, writing, as Melville shapes it, is an enthusiastic medium. A second sense in which Melville presents reading enthusiastically comes out of the readerly tradition of writing that Melville was keen to identify himself with, a tradition which might be thought to begin with Rabelais – whom Melville first read with an excitement critics usually associate with his reading of Shakespeare – and which continued through another work that featured prominently on his reading list, Robert Burton's *The Anatomy of Melancholy*. In both Rabelais and Burton, both of whom tease the scholar, the presentation of reading matter is charged with excitement, the purpose of the text being very much a means of accommodating other writing. Burton's metaphors for this are familiar [the passages in brackets being translations]:

> The matter is theirs most part, and yet mine, *apparet unde sumptum sit* [it is plain whence it was taken] (which Seneca approves), *aliud tamen quam unde sumptum sit apparet* [yet it becomes something different in its new setting]; which nature doth with the aliment of our bodies incorporate, digest, assimilate, I do *concoquere quod hausi* [assmiliate what I have swallowed], dispose of what I take. I make them pay tribute to set out this my *Macaronicon*, the method only is mine own ... Our poets steal from Homer; he spews, saith Aelian, they lick it up.[27]

Burton's method is the collage, the text as presentation of others' words, a mode of writing through reading implicit in Thoreau but made more apparent in Melville, and which Marianne Moore, a student of seventeenth-century prose stylists, would make unmistakably Modern.

There is, however, a third, no less important but more naive sense of enthusiastic reading at work in *Moby-Dick*; the simple sense that Melville is audibly excited about reading. He had had, as Hershel Parker points out, an irregular education, and so was not, as a consequence, a trained reader. Nor did he come to reading early, but when he did it was with all the enthusiasm of the autodidact, with the sense that his reading had inaugurated a new life. There are numerous revivals in *Moby-Dick*: Lazarus, Jonah, Queequeg, Tashtego, Pip and Ishmael, all presented as experiencing something akin to rebirth. Melville thought of the composition of the novel itself in comparable terms. 'From my twenty-fifth year,' he told Hawthorne, 'I date my life.' The writing of *Moby-Dick*, he thought, was the final unfolding of the process which that date had seemed to him to inaugurate; and what that date marks is Melville's life as a serious reader, a process through which he was, as he suggests, reborn. Or as he puts it in the novel, 'I have swam through libraries, and sailed through oceans,' both media altering him decisively as he passed through (MD, 230). And then, of course, the book itself nearly died. As the editors of the Newberry and Northwestern edition tell the story, it is possible *Moby-Dick* would have slipped completely from view, following bad reviews and poor sales, and Melville's own disillusioned disappearance from the literary scene, but for the fact that in the second half of the nineteenth century British working-class readers took it up, circulating it through their societies and institutions. The question arising is why the novel should have found such a committed readership in this social group, and one answer, no doubt, would have to with Melville's focus in the book on working life and practices. Another answer, however, has to do with the book's enthusiasm. Hayford, Parker and Tanselle identify among the novel's British readers a network of secret sharers, in which the novel served as 'a self-identifying and other-identifying token'. It is a historically grounded claim. 'We gather,' *The Nation and Atheneum* reported of such secretly sharing readers, '[that] they had been in the habit of hinting the book to friends they could trust, so that *Moby-Dick* became a sort of cunning test by which genuineness of another man's response to literature could be proved'.[28]

Moby-Dick, in its autodidactic enthusiasm for literature, contained its own means of circulation – and especially, perhaps, among a class of reader who appreciated in that enthusiasm a non-institutionalized means of transmission and address. *Moby-Dick*, this is to suggest, continued to circulate, in the face of such orthodox disapproval as Duyckinck articulated, in part because of the enthusiasm with which it circulated other people's books; because it understood the ceaseless passing on of words and values that is an essential function and feature of literature. What Melville teaches is that literary work is never complete, both in the sense that one work always leads back to, and on from, another, but also in that the work itself has its meaning in being passed on. Like *Walden*, like *The Cantos*, like O'Hara's *Collected Poems*, Melville's novel is an engine for the ceaseless circulation of culture; a circulation out of which, historically, communities of readers have formed. To read *Moby-Dick*, in other words, is to read an argument for the enthusiastic passing on of books, for the ceaseless and unlimited circulation that bureaucracy, with its whole lexicon of foreclosing, with its outcomes as endpoints, operates to prevent.

Knowing

Thoreau went to Walden Pond because, among other things, he was 'determined to know beans'. Asked by Captain Peleg why he wants to go 'a-whaling', Ishmael can offer no better reason than that, 'I want to see what whaling is'. *Walden* and *Moby-Dick* have a good deal structurally in common. In each book a narrative presence – Thoreau's 'I', Melville's 'Ishmael' – steps away from a circumstance with which they are familiar into a world they do not yet know. Each book, also, goes to unusual, sometimes self-parodying lengths, to document the experience in question, both writers being much more insistent on the value of fact, more dependent in their presentation of things on hard information, than had been any of their immediate predecessors, and perhaps more than any literary authors before them. Among the things that *Moby-Dick* and *Walden* have in common, in other words, is a dissatisfaction with how Romantic and before that Enlightenment writers had claimed to know the world.

This said, the dominant ways of knowing in *Moby-Dick* are, of course, Ahab's, the *Pequod*'s quest and the novel's plot being equally determined by the iron rails of Ahab's fixed purpose. Ahab's knowledge is complex. He knows what he claims to know about the whale, and the malign principle it reveals in nature, through a process of reflection. Left to dwell on the incident which has altered his life, and unable to accept its accidental quality, Ahab has attributed meaning to a meaningless event, has come to 'identify' with the whale 'all his intellectual and spiritual exasperations', 'all those malicious agencies which some deep men feel eating in them'. The process is not unreasonable, in that the process whereby meaning is attributed is not, internally, against reason. It is, however, a reasoning process unchecked, and ultimately in Ahab's case uncheckable, by externals. Depending on one's chosen lexicon, therefore, Ahab's conviction is the result of an intellectual process giving priority to inwardness, insight or the runaway capacity of pure reason; each or all of these, in his case, coupled with an indomitable will. Matthiessen was right to identify in Ahab an argument with Emersonianism, Emerson's Transcendentalism being quite precisely a Romanticization of the Kantian *a priori*. Which is not to say, however, at least as the novel shows it, that Ahab is without knowledge. He is knowledgeable from a narrative point of view in that the whale does, eventually, demonstrate something not unlike a malign intelligence. Less spectacularly, Ahab knows enough to locate the whale in the first place. This knowledge, the knowledge that drives the plot rather than the quest, is practical and technological, Ahab several times showing himself master of the ship's instruments, and willing always, where necessary, to make use of accumulated wisdom. Thus, as 'The Chart' has it, to any one not fully acquainted with the ways of the leviathans, it might seem an absurdly hopeless task thus to seek out one solitary creature in the unhooped oceans of this planet. But not so did it seem to Ahab, who knew the sets of all tides and currents; and thereby calculating the driftings of the sperm whale's food; and, also, calling to mind the regular, ascertained seasons for hunting him in particular latitudes: could arrive at reasonable surmises, almost approaching to certainties, concerning the timeliest day to be upon this or that ground in search of prey. (MD, 298)

It is not a digression to observe that in *Moby-Dick* – especially, perhaps, as viewed through the idea of enthusiasm – one finds exemplified the modes of knowledge that currently govern American's relations with the external world. Thus if, plainly – in a book which has as part of its intellectual apparatus 'the history of fanatics' – one has presented the mode of intuition and conviction that can drive a religious enthusiast to fly a plane into the side of a building; one has the counterknowledge presented also, the reasoned but unreasonable quest against an axis of evil facilitated by a technology capable of mapping the globe. There is a play of the sublime and the empirical here. You might no more think it possible to track down a given whale in all the waters of the globe than to track down a given, elusive Islamic fundamentalist – though actually, as it turns out, sometimes it is. But the point is, epistemologically speaking, that what Ahab knows is how to hunt down and catch whales. He doesn't, in the novel at least – perhaps he did before – know whales the way Thoreau knows beans.

Ishmael does; or at least, he means to. Like Thoreau, Ishmael is an empiricist of sorts, frequently reminding us that the only way to know the whale is to gain direct acquaintance with it. His authority rests, therefore, not only in the fact that he has swum through libraries, but also, as he immediately qualifies, in the fact that he has 'had to do with whales with these visible hands' (MD, 230). Similarly, he advises, if the reader wants to derive even a tolerable idea of what the whale looks like, the only way is to go 'a whaling yourself'. As with the determination to know beans, this can sound like an epistemologically simple-minded injunction, but as with Thoreau, what Melville offers is a thoughtful, subtle, rigorous and, I would suggest, enthusiastic epistemology. The enthusiasm rests in part in the image of the text Ishmael offers, and the relation he has to it as a person seeking knowledge. His cetology is 'a draught of a draught', his 'cetological System standing thus unfinished', which is just, he considers, as it should be, grand erections ever leaving 'their copestone to posterity' (MD, 241). 'God keep me,' Ishmael exhorts himself (and his God), from completing everything. Ishmael, in other words, is neither, religiously speaking, a literalist nor a perfectionist, believing in neither the completion of his system or himself. And his cetology, as a consequence, is in just the state an authoritative text ought to be, offering guidance to the experimental spirit – Ishmael is nothing if not an experimental spirit – but leaving room for and requiring further light.

What the cetology, the book within the book, requires by way of supplement, and which Ishmael's narrative sets out to supply, is immediate acquaintance. What the novel is moving towards, in other words, from Ishmael's point of view, is an ideal of acquaintance, a state in which things are present. He achieves this, or wants to be thought of as achieving this, in two ways or moods. Thus at times the novel achieves immediacy, or, at least, the impression of immediacy, in the midst of action – Melville, as Lawrence pointed out, being a great poet of action. Of all the pictures of whales he considers, monstrous and less erroneous, it is the action paintings Ishmael most admires, the paintings where the artist is most inside the event. This aspect of *Moby-Dick*, the sense of immediacy that comes through action, through the various deliriums of trashing and flailing, is among its most significant contributions to the American sensibility, which in the figure of, say, Jackson Pollock – as the chapter, here, on Frank O'Hara will observe – came greatly to prize the intimacy of the event. Serenity equally, however, is held by the novel to be conducive to immediacy, periods of imagined calm permitting in the writing a state of self seemingly conducive to the presentation of things. Thus, late in the novel, Ishmael restates his ambition to 'see what whaling is', only this time in the manner of the book's mature poetry. Speaking of the lamp, Ishmael notes, it is the whaleman's great privilege that,

> He burns, too, the purest of oil, in its unmanufactured, and therefore unvitiated state; a fluid unknown to solar, lunar, or astral contrivances ashore. It is sweet as early grass butter in April. He goes and hunts for his oil, so as to be sure of its freshness and genuineness, even as the traveller on the prairie hunts up his own supper of gain. (MD, 536)

There is a phase towards the end of *Moby-Dick* when the writing achieves something like 'freshness and genuiness'. The conclusion of the book, dominated by Ahab's sensibility, is a violent fit, the last thirty pages or so being consumed by the fatal chase. For a period prior to that, however – from, say, Chapter 93, 'The Castaway', to Chapter 114, 'The Gilder', as the *Pequod* drifts towards the South Pacific – the prevailing mood is one of supernatural calm. That something approaching an ideal state has been reached at this point is apparent from the higher lyrical charge in the writing. The burlesque is all but left behind, as are the more intrusive elements of scholarship, the novel approaching the immediate acquaint-ance with the world that has been one of its ambitions all through. And that there is a determination to know things immediately during this phase in the novel is apparent from chapters 103, 'The Measurement of the Whale's Skeleton', and 104, 'The Fossil Whale', which respectively address the whale in terms, as Kant had it, of the 'two pure forms of sensible intuition, serving as principles of *a priori* knowledge, namely, space and time'. But Ishmael has travelled a long way by this point, well beyond his ken, and so there is little or nothing, by now, he is confident of knowing *a priori*. So in both chapters the governing category is seen to collapse; the form giving shape to sensible intuition is held to be unsatisfactory. 'How vain and foolish, then, thought I', says Ishmael, contemplating the spatial representation of the whale,

> for timid, untravelled man to try to comprehend aright this wondrous whale, by merely poring over his dead attenuated skeleton, stretched in this peaceful wood. No. Only in the heart of quickest perils; only when within the eddyings of his angry flukes; only on the profound and unbounded sea, can the fully invested whale be truly and livingly found out. (MD, 565)

Likewise, as Ishmael contemplates the chronology of the whale, the time it has spent on earth, so that form of intuition also is understood as ceasing to mediate:

> I am, by a flood, borne back to that wondrous period, ere time itself can be said to have begun; for time began with man. Here Saturn's grey chaos rolls over me, and I obtain dim, shuddering glimpses into those Polar eternities ... I look round to shake hands with Shem. (MD, 569)

For a while, in other words, perhaps writing in the grass-growing mood, Melville can think of himself as stepping away from the apparatus of understanding and into a direct acquaintance with the world, with everything present, immediate and now. The mood in question is the supernatural serenity that Thoreau understood as enthusiasm. It was towards the present tense of this mood that Ezra Pound directed Modern poetry.

Notes

1 Herman Melville, *Moby-Dick*, ed. Hershel Parker and Harrison Hayford, New York, W.W. Norton & Company, 1967, pp. 540–1.
2 Herman Melville, 'Hawthorne and his Mosses', in *Moby-Dick*, ed. Parker and Hayford, p. 523.
3 Ibid., p. 528.
4 Hershel Parker, *Herman Melville: A Biography Volume 1, 1819–1851*, Baltimore and London, Johns Hopkins University Press, 1996, p. 769.
5 References to the novel are to the 1972 Penguin edition, edited by Harold Beaver, whose commentary threatens to equal the novel itself in bulk, but

which is, even so, an enthusiast's text. Herman Melville, *Moby-Dick*, Harold Beaver, Hamondsworth, Penguin, 1972, pp. 481–2; hereafter referred to in the text as MD.

6 Herman Melville, *Mardi*, Evanston and Chicago, Northwestern University Press and Newberry Library, 1970, pp. 622–3, 626.

7 Herman Melville, *Pierre*, Evanston and Chicago, Northwestern University Press and Newberry Library, 1971, pp. 87, 165.

8 Herman Melville, *The Confidence-Man*, Evanston and Chicago, Northwestern University Press and Newberry Library, 1984, pp. 41, 43, 167.

9 Charles Olson, *Call Me Ishmael*, Baltimore and London, Johns Hopkins University Press, 1997, p. 14.

10 Emerson, *Essays and Lectures*, p. 58.

11 Peter Matthiessen, *American Renaissance: Art and Expression in the Age of Emerson and Whitman*, London, Toronto, New York, Oxford University Press, 1941, pp. 458–9.

12 Lawrence Buell, 'Moby-Dick as Sacred Text', in Richard Brodhead, *New Essays on Moby-Dick*, Cambridge, Cambridge University Press, 1986, pp. 55, 69, 58.

13 Evert Duyckinck, 'A Friend Does his Christian Duty', in *Moby-Dick*, ed. Parker and Hayford, p. 612.

14 Ibid., p. 521.

15 Matthiessen, *American Renaissance*, p. 10.

16 David S. Lovejoy, *Religious Enthusiasm in the New World: Heresy to Revolution*, Cambridge, Mass., Harvard University Press, 1985, pp. 111, 112.

17 Ibid., p. 50.

18 Cited in Thomas D. Hamm, *The Quakers in America*, New York, Columbia University Press, 2003, p. 19.

19 Ibid., p. 30.

20 Lovejoy, *Enthusiasm*, p. 113.

21 Ibid., pp. 113, 114.

22 Hamm, *Quakers*, p. 30.

23 Ibid.

24 Melville, 'Hawthorne and his Mosses', p. 517.

25 Melville, *Moby-Dick*, ed. Parker and Hayford, pp. 541–2, 545.

26 Olson, *Call Me Ishmael*, p. 36.

27 Robert Burton, *The Anatomy of Melancholy*, New York, New York Review of Books, 2001, p. 25.

28 Herman Melville, *Moby-Dick, or, The Whale*, ed. Harrison Hayford, Hershel Parker and G. Thomas Tanselle, Evanston and Chicago, Northwestern University Press and Newberry Library, 1988, pp. 745, 746.

3

Distributing: Ezra Pound

Here is a portrait of an enthusiast:

> He has always been, first and foremost, a teacher and a campaigner. He has
> always been impelled, not merely to find out for himself how poetry should be
> written, but to pass on the benefit of his discoveries to others; not simply to
> make these benefits available; but to insist upon their being received. He
> would cajole, and almost coerce, other men into writing well: so that he often
> presents the appearance of a man trying to convey to a very deaf person the
> fact that the house is on fire. Every change he has advocated has always struck
> him as being of instant urgency. ... He has cared deeply that his
> contemporaries and juniors should write well; he has cared less for his
> personal achievement than for the life of letters and art. One of the lessons to
> be learnt from his critical prose and from his correspondence is the lesson to
> care unselfishly for the art one serves.[1]

This is T. S. Eliot on Ezra Pound, from the introduction to Eliot's selection
of Pound's *Literary Essays*. It is a good likeness: Eliot presenting his own
best sense of his poetic colleague while also drawing on Pound's idea of
himself; Eliot's terms being quite largely taken from the critical prose he is
introducing. The Pound on show is an enthusiast. He is a teacher, a
campaigner and an advocate; he is gripped by commitments that strike him
as instantly urgent; he has always wanted to make the benefits of his
discoveries available to others; he is one of the few writers for whom the
state of the art is more important than his own achievement. Which said,
his insisting and cajoling could border on coercion, though his was, as Eliot
presents it, a curiously passive coercion: he has 'always been impelled' to
make discoveries and to pass them on; everything was in the name of the
art he 'serves'. Poundian enthusiasm, in other words, as Eliot wants
apologetically to put it, can sometimes tip over into authoritarianism, and it
was founded – and here there is not an apology – on an act of servility.

Here's another portrait of the enthusiast:

> When I consider his work as a whole I find more style than form; at moments
> more style, more deliberate nobility and the means to convey it than in any

other contemporary poet known to me, but it is constantly interrupted, broken, twisted into nothing by its proper opposite, nervous obsession, nightmare, stammering confusion; he is an economist, poet, politician, raging at malignants with inexplicable characters and motives, grotesque figures out of a child's book of beasts. This loss of self-control, common among uneducated revolutionists, is rare – Shelley had it in some degree – among men of Ezra Pound's culture and erudition.[2]

As a description of Pound this is typical, W. B. Yeats, in the introduction to the *Oxford Book of Modern Verse*, piling up verbs and nouns to indicate the variousness of his subject. Primarily, though, there are two Pounds here, relating to Yeats' sense of early and late. It is the later that dominates – Yeats is writing in the mid-1930s amid a torrent of Poundian tracts and pamphlets – and what comes through is a picture of a writer who can neither stem nor order the flow, who presents the behaviour of the ill-educated, a writer who, above all, has lost self-control. Yeats' image thus supplements Eliot's, describing the Pound that Eliot – writing as he, Macleish and others were seeking to secure Pound's release from St. Elizabeth's – was keen to overlook: interrupted, stammering, raging at malignants.

And now here is Pound himself, presenting an image of enthusiasm in *Guide to Kulchur*, and smuggling through, in the process, a self-portrait or two:

There is no doubt whatsoever that human beings are subject to emotion and that they attain to very fine, enjoyable and dynamic emotional states, which cause them to emit what to careful chartered accountants may seem intemperate language ... which comes down into a man and produces superior ecstasies, feelings of regained youth, super-youth and so forth, not to be surpassed by the first glass of absinthe ...

Two mystic states can be dissociated; the ecstatic-beneficent-and-benevolent, contemplation of the divine love, the divine splendour with goodwill, toward others.

And the bestial, namely the fanatical, the man on fire with God and anxious to stick his snotty nose into other men's business or reprove his neighbour for having a set of tropisms different from that of the fanatic's, or for having the courage to live more greatly and openly.

The second set of mystic states is manifest in scarcity economists, in repressors, etc.

The first state is a dynamism. It has, time and again, driven men to great living, it has given them courage to go on for decades in the face of public stupidity.[3]

Establishing Pound's enthusiasm is a fraught and complicated business. Fraught because, in all his voluminous writings, 'enthusiasm' is a word

Pound rarely uses, and when he does it is without great charge, and typically to derogatory effect. Generally speaking, in fact, 'enthusiasm' features little in high Modernist writing, though Marianne Moore presents an exception. This is no surprise. Modernism, as directed by Pound, involved rebranding art as an anti-Romantic, aristocratic activity. Enthusiasm, from this point of view, was a Romantic idea, rehabilitated but also, as Jon Mee argues, regulated in the face of eighteenth-century political suspicions, suspicions recently rearticulated for Modernism by Nietzsche. 'In an even more decisive and profound sense,' Nietzsche asserts in *On the Genealogy of Morality*, 'the last political nobility in Europe, that of the *French* seventeenth and eighteenth centuries, collapsed under the *ressentiment*-instincts of the rabble, – the world had never heard greater rejoicing and more uproarious enthusiasm.'[4] Nietzsche's argument is with *ressentiment*, which he takes to be the principle of slave morality, a category, as he presents it and claims to historicize it, shot through with anti-Semitism. In this context enthusiasm features as a manifestation of the resentful rabble. This is not to imply a direct link between Nietzsche and Pound. It is, though, to make graphic the fact that given the aristocratic guise in which Pound was pleased to cast the artist, the term 'enthusiasm' was likely to have a limited or debased currency. All of which is frankly to acknowledge that to present Pound as an enthusiast is to argue against the grain.

Except that Pound was an enthusiast. He was an enthusiast in the Modern, less freighted sense that Eliot describes; in the sense that he campaigned for, advocated and promoted his contemporaries. Joyce, recognizing his own early debt to Pound, described him as 'a miracle worker'. He pressed and insisted and boosted and communicated. He put and kept Modernist art in circulation. But he was also an enthusiast in the stricter sense: the sense, as he presents it in *Guide to Kulchur*, of emotional states coming down into a person causing them to emit intemperate language. Or as he put it a few pages later in that work, and, as he notes for the benefit of Mr Eliot, who had asked him what he believes:

> our time has overshadowed the mysteries by an overemphasis on the individual. ... Eleusis did not distort truth by exaggerating the individual, neither could it have violated the individual spirit. Only in the high air and the great clarity can there be a just estimation of values. Romantic poetry, on the other hand, almost requires the concept of reincarnation as part of its mechanism. No apter metaphor having been found for certain emotional colours. I assert that the Gods exist. (GK, 299)

Pound, it will be argued, never did come up with an apter metaphor for the emotional colours he most wanted to claim for poetry. More than any Modern poet, including Eliot, Pound addressed himself to the question of the poet's vocation in the twentieth century, and central to that vocation – to the production and distribution of work – was the model of writer as enthusiast. It is possible to hear this in the first of the states he presents in *Guide to Kulchur*: the state characterized as 'ecstatic-beneficent-and-benevolent', and as supplying a person – Pound himself no doubt – with the courage to 'go on for decades in the face of public stupidity'. Pound's self-appointed function, according to this definition, as Modern poet, and in the face of public stupidity, is to circulate culture. But there is also the second state to reckon with: 'the man on fire with God and axioms to stick his snotty nose into other men's business'. Pound wants to associate this state with other people – 'scarcity economists, repressors etc.' – but clearly it describes him also. He was a fanatical anti-Semite, expressly reproving Jews for holding a 'set of tropisms' not his own.

This is why determining Pound's enthusiasm is complex. On the one hand, from a certain point of view, he invented the figure of the Modern poet, building into twentieth-century poetry a defining mobility of expression and action. On the other hand, in re-evaluating the poet's vocation, in his even contemplating 'vocation', he engaged in lines of thought which ran freely to fanaticism, and which produced a confidence that when turned to hatred resulted in unstoppable and unspeakable prejudice. And what has to be emphasized is that these two aspects of Pound's enthusiasm are, in him, deeply interlinked. So while in this book he is presented as a necessary development between the circulatory aesthetics of Thoreau and the cultural free-wheeling of O'Hara, another account – and not, it should be noted, necessarily a disapproving one – might show him leading poetry into isolation, exile and martyrdom. In Pound himself it is not possible to disentangle these two versions of enthusiasm. For readers what is presented, importantly, is a choice.

Calling

Pound's early poetry – the poems he published in the volumes *A Lume Spento* (1908), *A Quinzaine for this Yule* (1908), *Personae* (1909) *Exultations* (1909), and *Canzoni* (1911), from which he selected to form the first section of *The Shorter Poems of Ezra Pound* (1926) – can seem tentative, haphazard and quite un-Modern. Casting about for things to write, he translates, mostly from the Troubadours, writes versions of and poems after other poets' work, performs eccentric formal experiments, pastiches, lampoons, drifts in and out of mythology, addresses himself to historic figures, and every so often risks a manner of his own. In retrospect he made sense of these forays by gathering them up under the rubric of *Personae*, suggesting, as he had in his essay on Vorticism, a deliberate attempt to arrive at a sense of himself as poet through the adoption of others' style and modes. Or as he put it in his 1929 postscript to the preface on the republication of *The Spirit of Romance*:

> The detached critic may, I hope, find … some signs of coherence, some proof that I started with a definite intention, and that what has up to now appeared an aimless picking up of tidbits has been governed by a plan which became clearer and more definite as I proceeded.[5]

What this retrospective theorizing should not be taken to imply is that in his early poems Pound knew what he was doing. The lesser, truer, but aesthetically more far-reaching judgement is that in those early poems Pound was intelligently aware precisely that he didn't know what he was doing. There is not, therefore, an order to be found in early Pound. There is, however, a continuous impulse. What Pound somehow appreciated at a very early stage in his writing – and in a way not predicted by his early reading or education – was the foundationlessness of Modern art in general, but of contemporary poetry in particular. This insight was the germ of his decisive contribution to Modernism. It also remained a constant in his own work. So while there is a world of difference between the slim, sometimes exuberant, but more typically wan elegance of the early poems, and the scope, vigour and intermittent bad temper of *The Cantos*, what remains true is the sense of the poet always bringing himself, and his work – and its motivation, and its audience – into being. What Pound starts to investigate, in other words, in the work published between 1908 and 1911, and then never stops investigating, is what, if anything, constitutes the call for Modern poetry.

Call, 'the call', is, in this context, a loaded term, heavy as it with the idea of vocation – calling – without which religious enthusiasm, George Fox's say, would never get off the ground. It is loaded also in that, in a moment, I will be making reference to Heidegger, and in particular to his series of lectures *What Is Called Thinking?* But 'call' is also a Poundian term, and one that carries pressure and weight in his writing from the beginning. So amid all the various voices and voicings of the early poems, an idea of the call is relatively constant. Take 'La Fraisne', spoken by a once 'gaunt, grave councillor' – a bureaucrat, it is worth noting, for later reference – who is 'drawn' away from his old habits, but not just drawn, 'called':

> She hath called me from mine old ways
> She hath hushed my rancour of council,
> Bidding me praise.[6]

'She' is the muse. The poem's speaker reports that he responds to the call, and that 'now', as a consequence, 'men call me mad'. Another example –

there has necessarily to be some piling up of examples here – is in 'In Durance', a more Modern poem, in respect of situation and diction, predicated on the opening statement that 'I am homesick after mine own kind', where his own kind are not fellow nationals (this is a Crawfordsville poem) but kindred artistic spirits. The poem turns on a call:

> When come *they,* surging of power, 'DAEMON,'
> 'Quasi KALOUN.' S.T. says Beauty is most that, a
>   'calling to the soul.'
> Well then, so call they, the swirlers out of the mist of my soul,
> They that come mewards, bearing old magic.
>
>   (P, 20)

The call, and the need for a calling, is clear here, even though partly mystified, Pound's habit of reverting to semi-mythical formulations of the nature and source of art being a further constant in his career. One more example, from 'Guido Invites you Thus', with Cavalcanti, as in Dante's original sonnet, enunciating the call:

> Talk me no love talk, no bought-cheap fiddl'ry,
> Mine is the ship and thine the merchandise,
> All the blind earth knows not th'emprise
> Whereto thou calledst and whereto I call.
>
>   (P, 24)

The point here is not that Pound, speaking though these personae, considers himself called; rather, that he needs to be, that he needs the structure of demand, the impression of third-party requirement implicit in the idea of the call, in order to venture poetry. 'No apter metaphor having been found,' as he puts it in *Guide to Kulchur*, 'I assert that the gods exist.' There are two aspects to this statement, the assertion, which I'll come on to, and the metaphor. In one sense Pound never did come up with an apter metaphor for poetic production than the circuit implied in this assertion, no metaphor more equal to the experience of writing poetry than the taking in of the divinity registered by 'enthusiasm'. He resorts quite precisely to the metaphor at various moments through his career. His fixation on 'Eleusis' is an instance of this, but so is the formulation he presents in 'Axiomata' (1921), where he reproduces the metaphor albeit in semi-Modern, semi-technical terms:

1 The intimate essence of the universe is *not* of the same nature as our own consciousness.
2 Our own consciousness is incapable of having produced the universe.
3 God, therefore, exists. That is to say, there is no reason for not applying the term God, *Theos*, to the intimate essence.

4 The universe exists. By exists we mean normally: is perceptible to our
consciousness or deducible by human reason from data perceptible to our
consciousness.[7]

This sounds a bit Modern because of the bullet points, and the logical
positivist diction, but Pound is not asserting anything here that Emerson
could not have agreed with. Nor is there anything in the mode of
production described in the early poem 'De AEgypto' to which Whitman,
say, would have needed to object.

> To write the acceptable word ...
> My mouth to chant the pure singing!
>
> Who hath the mouth to receive it,
> The song of the Lotus of Kumi?
>
> I, even I, am he who knoweth the roads
> Through the sky, and the wind thereof is my body.
>
> (P, 18)

Whitman would not need have disagreed with this sentiment because in
one sense, in the manner of pastiche, it is him speaking it, and 'De
AEgypto' is unusual, even in early Pound, in formulating so conventional a
sense of the enthusiastic utterance. Such a resort to poetic convention is
more common in the prose. In the poetry the intention is almost always –
the assertion in *Guide to Kulchur* notwithstanding – precisely to formulate a
more Modern metaphor.

Early Pound, then, is not called but craves a call, and out of this craving
there evolves an ongoing investigation into what can be said to call poetry
and the poet into being. Often the call is implicit in a subject or an
addressee, as in 'Na Audiart', where 'Bertran of Born' has to compose a
woman equal to the 'Lady Maent of Montagnac', her rejection of him
imposing a demand on the poet which Pound revisited, and the sense of
which he made more complex, in '"Dompna Pois de me No'us Cal"' and
'Near Perigord'. The call on 'Marvoil' is simpler, his last will and testament
recording '"Vers and canzone to the Countess of Beziers / In return for the
first kiss she gave me"' (P, 22). 'Night Litany' calls directly to 'God',
'O Dieu, purifiez nos coeurs! / Purifiez nos coeurs!' (P, 24). 'Famam
Librosque Cano' calls to the future and to the audience it may or may
not hold for Pound. 'Cino' calls to those who have forgotten him, and to the
sun. Amid this welter of calls there is, in fact, no decisive call, Pound's
various voices in this period remaining resolutely hollow, sounding
utterances with no conviction of their necessity. And yet, or rather as a
consequence of this, he and his speakers are forever calling themselves

'poet', asserting themselves as such, as in the opening lines of 'And Thus in Nineveh':

> Aye! I am a poet and upon my tomb
> Shall maidens scatter rose leaves
> And men myrtles.
>
> (P, 23)

And again later, if a little less confidently: 'Yet I am a poet'. 'Cino' asserts that he has been and still is a poet – 'Bah! I have sung women in three cities'; likewise 'Piere Vidal Old' – 'And every jongleur knew me in his song'. And similarly, of course, Pound himself, who expended great energy once he got to London insisting to publishers and editors that he was, in fact, a poet. There's a photograph, for instance, reproduced in Humphrey Carpenter's *Life of Pound*, which records the so-called 'Poets' outing' to visit W.S. Blunt. Pound wrote subsequently that Blunt seemed uncertain whether 'we were a deputation of poets or horse-breeders'.[8] Of the six visiting, four – Victor Plarr, Sturge Moore, Richard Aldington and F.S. Flint – could, by the look of them at least, have been horse-breeders, or bank managers, or accountants, or pretty much anything else. The other two, by the look of them – Yeats with his round glasses and his bow-tie, and Pound with turned-out collar, goatee beard and swept-up hair – assert themselves as poets, as writers of calling.

It is a value of Pound's early poetry that it documents the difficulty of bringing Modern poetry into being, and one index of that difficulty is the complex sense of the call he quickly evolved. Thus the idea of the call, the idea that some external agency will be perceived to issue a call, is integral to the structure of much early Pound. Equally structural, however, is his continuing, almost systematic refusal to accept any of the metaphors articulating a requirement on the poet, and which he is himself enunciating, as apt. The strength of the early poems, and what carried Pound towards a Modernism, was this refusal. Later, his insistence on the idea of the vocation of the poet can be thought to be at the root of his authoritarianism and his martyrdom. At this very early stage, however, Pound's poetry should be understood as a quite coherent, increasingly definite enquiry into its own calling, as an ongoing, committed and defining consideration of what, if anything, calls for poetry. Which is where Heidegger can come in.

Heidegger's lectures, entitled *Was heisst Denken?* (equally well translated, so David Farrell Krell suggests, as 'What is called thinking?', and 'What calls for thinking?'), illuminate Pound's situation as a poet in his early work in various ways. Like Pound, Heidegger wants to preserve a trace of the enthusiastic circuit in his image of mental operations: 'What is thought is the gift given in thinking back, given because we incline toward it. Only when we are so inclined toward what in itself is to be thought about, only then are we capable of thinking.'[9] What Heidegger wants to preserve is the sense of external agency or presence, that in thought something is given. As with Pound, however, Heidegger can no longer presume in any simple way a relation between thinking and its object, or more specifically that such an object might be readily identifiable. Thinking, for Heidegger, must be, very largely, a self-sustaining activity, save for the sustenance that comes of the search for its proper object. As he says: 'Man learns when he disposes everything he does so that it answers to whatever addresses him as essential. We learn to think by giving heed to what there is to think about.'[10] There is a trace of Emerson here, in the fullness of the commitment called for, in the sense of the questions, 'What is a man good for without enthusiasm? and what is enthusiasm but this daring of ruin for its object?' Pound himself proceeded in something like the way Heidegger describes: becoming instrumental in and central to Modern poetry because he addressed himself to the question, constantly, of what might be essential. It is apt to think of him, in other words, as giving heed to what poetry might now properly be about.

There are cross-illuminations beyond the outlining of the basic predicament – the clarity in Heidegger's presentation of which owes in some part to the fact that he is writing some forty years after the predicament first began to make itself felt to the likes of Pound. Like Pound then (as we will see), Heidegger is suspicious of the university, having little confidence that it is an environment conducive to thinking, the problem being that universities have lost the relatedness to the media they work with, without which a craft of any kind – thinking is a craft by analogy for Heidegger, poetry being one in name – becomes determined exclusively by business concerns. The university, Heidegger wants to argue, cannot stomach the necessary risk and disjunction involved in thought, such that,

> In contrast to a steady progress, where we move unawares from one thing to the next and everything remains alike, the leap takes us abruptly to a place where everything is different, so different that it strikes us as strange ... Though we may not founder in such a leap, what the leap takes us to will confound us.[11]

This, though Pound spoke of jumping not leaping, is the thought of *The Cantos*. 'People think me crazy,' Pound observed, 'When I make a jump instead of a step, just as if all jumps were unsound and never carried one anywhere' (SP, 123). (Jumps do, of course, carry one somewhere, and *The Cantos* jump very productively at times. Equally, however, the step, as in

O'Hara, can sometimes prove just confounding enough.) Chiefly, though, it's through 'the call' that Heidegger can be thought to illuminate Pound, through his sense of the term's implications, remembering that as he formulates them he has a sense of enthusiasm in mind. Thus:

> We are playing with the verb 'to call'. ... But if we are to hear the question in a sense that asks for what it is that directs us to think, we find ourselves suddenly compelled to accept the verb 'to call' in a signification that is strange to us, or at least no longer familiar.
>
> We are now supposed to use the word 'to call' in a signification that one might paraphrase approximately with the verbs summon, demand, instruct, direct ... But the 'call' does not necessarily imply demand, still less command; it rather implies an anticipatory reaching out for something that is reached by our call, through our calling.[12]

Heidegger presents two operations here which, helpfully, carry us from an aspect of Thoreau's enthusiasm to an aspect of Pound's. Thus, in drawing out the meaning of calling, Heidegger pins his faith on what he terms the original signification. Old meanings, he, like Thoreau, wants always to argue, make a call to things that new names tend to obscure, and so for the call to be heard older significations have to be allowed through. What this implies is a power in the act of naming, as if naming a thing could bring it into being, as if 'By naming we call on what is present to arrive'. Pound believed this wholeheartedly: his entire early career was an act of naming as bringing into being. He named himself a poet to assert that he was one. He named a movement, Imagism, to bring it about. He named fellow writers major contemporaries – Eliot, Joyce, Lewis – to ensure that they became what he wanted them to be. And what this naming as calling into being points to again, and what Heidegger helps illuminate in Pound, is the nature of the pursuit of apter metaphors. The enthusiast's sense of the call is central to both writers' thought, without either being able in any simple way to envision the agency from which this might issue. Heidegger tries to get around this by paraphrasing, with the very verbs summon, demand, instruct, direct. Pound Modernised himself by taking a similar turn.

Demanding

With Ezra Pound it's good to think in terms of dates. Later, dates would feature in the fabric of his work, with the aim, in *The Cantos*, of rendering history present. Early in his career his thinking and, more precisely, his terminology, developed so fast – he modernized himself at such a rate – that dates are necessary as markers of transition. He introduced the idea of dating poetry and the development of the poet in his prose; his essay on

'Vorticism', for instance, followed by 'A Retrospect', clearly establishing the time frames first of Imagism then of Vorticism. The point, quite largely, was to make the shifts in the poet's thought a matter of moment – a practice O'Hara, immortally, carried on. To set the date, then, by 1911 Pound more or less knew what he was doing. It was in 1911 that he wrote the bulk of *Ripostes*, a more confident, well-directed book than any he'd published before, the title, this time, not waiting for a call but issuing a response. In 1911, also, he began to publish a series of articles in *The New Age*, under the un-Modern title 'I gather the Limbs of Osiris', in which he presented for the first time, to anybody who cared to listen, a 'New Method in Scholarship', being 'the method of Luminous Detail, a method most vigorously hostile to the prevailing mode of today' (SP, 21). That he had a sure sense of purpose by this stage is evident in the content here, the luminous detail subsequently becoming an enduring principle of his work. But it is evident, also, in the approach, the sales pitch, the 'I've-got-a-new-method-ism'. Pound's self-appointed purpose by 1911 was to establish a demand in England, and after that in America, for Modern art (writing in particular) where the word is properly 'establish' not 'create', though creating a demand was unquestionably part of it.

As Pound understood it, establishing a demand for modern writing was a complicated, risky, labour-intensive process. Thus on the one hand he set out, deliberately and concertedly, to establish what one can term an aesthetic demand for poetry. The question was, what, in the Modern period, could be thought to make a call on the poet such that his or her poetry might be deemed necessary? What might properly be called the source of Modern poetry? To what should the poet give heed? Simultaneous with this aesthetic sense of establishing a demand was the need, as Pound saw it, to create a readership or audience for the work which hadn't yet but probably would soon come into being. This was a practical measure in that writers need sustaining, but it was an aesthetic measure also in that partly what sustains a writer is the sense of readerly demand: the reader's demand acting as a call to the writer, confirming his or her sense of what is necessary work. Pound, in other words, was trying to replicate the enthusiastic circuit; he was trying to simulate the mechanisms and effects of the process whereby the writer's allure was secured by an appeal to an implied divinity. What this required was a complex relation to the market. Largely he worked in despite and in defiance of the market, circulating the work of his contemporaries in acts of peerless generosity. Lewis reported on this, noting that, 'Pound has been superlatively generous. ... He does not in the least mind being in service to somebody (as to other people it is usually found) if they have great talent'. Likewise Hemingway observed, 'Pound the major poet devoting, say, one fifth of his time to poetry. With the rest of his time he tried to advance the fortunes, both material and artistic, of his friends.' But what establishing a demand also required was, wherever possible, playing the market, or at least playing with the market's means, hence Lewis's double description of Pound as 'a poet and an impresario, at that time an unexpected combination'.[13] Hence the 'new-methodism', and also the hyperbole surrounding Imagism, both presenting that form of enthusiasm which critics, reading him through his nineteenth-century Idaho childhood, sometimes term boosterism; Pound catching on quick to the idea that if the Modern movement was to get off the ground, it had to be alluringly branded.

In his poems, the requirement to establish a demand for poetry involved Pound in a purposive if not systematic trying out of previous and new modes of poetic production or sources of poetry, *Lustra* being his single most dynamic book in this respect. The book opens with a definition, by way of an epigraph, which self-consciously determines a demand:

> Definition: *Lustrum*: an offering for the sins of
> the whole people, made by the censors at the expira-
> tion of their five years of office, etc. Elementary
> Latin Dictionary of Charlton T. Lewis.
>
> (P, 80)

This is the way of atonement, poetry by this definition finding its calling, in a secular age, in the sins of the people and the culture, where the sins are of the order of taste, discernment and language use. It is an odd note for the book to start on. There *are* poems in *Lustra* which seek a function in martyrdom: 'The Condolence' addresses itself to 'fellow suffers'; 'Ité' directs the poet's songs to 'Seek ever to stand in the hard Sophoclean light / And take your wounds from it gladly' (P, 83, 96). These, though, are strictly performances, melodramatisations of martyrdom. *Lustra*, on the whole, is a light-footed volume; the deeply unattractive image of modern poet as martyr being a production of late Pound, *The Cantos* in particular.

Another possible source of poetry in *Lustra* is the milieu, 'Causa', for instance, aiming to establish a cause in the form of a self-conscious elite. In full the poem reads:

> I join these words for four people,
> Some others may overhear them,
> O world, I am sorry for you,
> You do not know these four people.
>
> (P, 89)

The sense of demand built in here is that provided by the minority audience, the readership that will read exactingly enough to call for something from the poet. Actually, of course, the poem is both, also, a provocation to those who might overhear and a complaint against an existing milieu, Georgian literary London, which was not sufficiently exacting to call forth significant poetry. Pound had voiced this dissatisfaction before. In 'Au Salon' he had identified

> This our reward for our works,
>   sic crescit gloria mundi:
> Some circle of not more than three
>   that we prefer to play up to,
> Some few whom we'd rather please
>   than hear the whole aegrum vulgus
> Splitting its beery jowl
>   a-meaowling our praises.
>
> (P, 51)

The problem, however, was that if 'the whole aegrum vulgus' was inadequate to the task of making a demand for poetry, so were the salons. 'Portrait d'une Femme', in a characteristically misogynist positing of a modern woman as insufficient cause for writing, presents a society woman as degraded muse and so as an instance of poetry's absent demand:

> Your mind and you are our Sargasso Sea,
> London has swept about you this score years
> And bright ships left you this or that in fee:
> Ideas, old gossip, oddments of all things,
> Strange spars of knowledge and dimmed wares of price.
> Great minds have sought you – lacking someone else.
>
> (P, 57)

The misogyny here is especially gratuitous in that the woman barely exists. What she stands for is the absence in the environment Pound inherited in London of an urgent call on the poet's powers.

One response to the failings of the existing milieu to present an agency capable of demanding poetry was that the poet should act as source himself. A number of poems in *Lustra* thus practise a sort of summoning, the poet himself calling on and to himself, as in the opening to 'Further Instructions':

> Come, my songs, let us express our baser passions,
> Let us express our envy of the man with a steady job and no
>   worry about the future.
>
> (P, 95)

It is not needless to say that the man with a steady job had, no doubt, numerous worries about the future. His function in Pound's poem, as with the woman in 'Portrait d'une Femme' is simply to dramatize the poet's bohemian situation, to generate the impression of isolation that gives him a sense of himself. 'Salvationists', likewise, summons itself:

> Come, my songs, let us speak of perfection –
> We shall get ourselves rather disliked.
>
> (P, 100)

Such Poundian 'summoning' constitutes a significantly post-Romantic procedure. So while, by one definition, the term implies a third party, meaning authoritatively to call on somebody to be present, especially to appear in a court of law, a second definition means to cause to emerge from within oneself. These two meanings direct one to the predicament of the Modern poet as Pound experienced it. As he saw it there was no substantive third-party summons, there was no call, and at worst, therefore, the poet would have to summon himself. This, however, was not Pound's preferred option. For whatever reason, to do with the history of art or the history of self, what Pound appears to have wanted most of his life was that he should be summoned. What he craved was a call, a requirement made by somebody else – Mussolini, for instance – that he should act. Eventually, of course, he was summoned, to appear before a Washington court on the charge of treason, though characteristically the obligation was self-generated.

One further response in this period to the failure of the milieu to issue a demand was to seek out and present situations where the demand for poetry was clearly articulated. Medieval Provence had already provided one such situation, the troubadours' proximity to power, and the patronage of power, offering a model, or at least a historical consolation, to Pound. A better model, however, or at least an aesthetically more promising one, was the Chinese as mediated by Fenollosa and presented by Pound in 1915 as *Cathay*. The poems of *Cathay* are beautiful in many ways it would be a pleasure to expand on at length, but in ways also that probably do not need rehearsing here. Except to observe that more than any work in early Pound, with the exception of 'The Seafarer', 'Near Perigord' and 'Hugh Selwyn Mauberley', the poems that make up *Cathay* are driven and coloured by necessity. A number are enunciated in time of war, providing reports from the front or from the home front, presenting situations that would otherwise go unknown or forgotten. Thus from 'Song of the Bowmen of Shu':

> When we set out, the willows were drooping with spring,
> We come back in the snow,
> We go slowly, we are hungry and thirsty,
> Our mind is full of sorrow, who will know of our grief?
>
> (P, 131)

From 'Lament of the Frontier Guard':

> Ah, how shall you know the dreary sorrow at the North Gate,
> With Riboku's name forgotten,
> And we guardsmen fed to the tigers.
>
> (P, 137)

And from 'The River-Merchant's Wife: A Letter', communicating what otherwise she and her husband would experience together:

> The leaves fall early this autumn, in wind.
> The paired butterflies are already yellow with August
> Over the grass in the West garden;
> They hurt me. I grow older.
>
> (P, 134)

What Pound discovers, and passes on, in *Cathay* is a poetry that understands itself as necessary, providing reports on circumstances that would otherwise go unpresented. What he presents also, however, is a system of patronage summoning the poet to work, as in 'Exile's Letter', where Rihaku is explicitly called for:

> And one May he had you send for me,
>   despite the long distance.
> And what with the broken wheels and so on, I won't say it wasn't
>   hard going,
> Over roads twisted like sheep's guts.
>
> (P, 138)

But, or rather 'And', as the poem has it, 'what a reception'. In a Poundian sense the beauty of the surface of the *Cathay* poems should, very largely, be understood as an index of their demand.

What this account of how early Pound established demand has not yet mentioned is Imagism, Pound's contribution to which appeared chiefly in *Lustra*, but his fullest formation of which was published in 1914, as an essay on 'Vorticisim', in the *Fortnightly Review*, and then reprinted in *Gaudier-Brzeska: A Memoir*. 'Imagism' was first thrust onto the world in the form of a bogus pre-existing demand, Pound requiring F. S. Flint to put his name to an article to appear in *Poetry* in March 1913, in which he was to appear as investigative critic, writing, as the opening of the piece had it, 'In response to many requests for information regarding *Imagism* and the *Imagistes*'.[14] A retrospective – Pound had, by now, more than mastered the art of self-inflation – the essay on 'Vorticism' presents both movements as a complex of calls and urgencies, and is a high point in Pound's effort in this period to establish a need for Modern writing. Everything about the essay, in fact, serves the purpose of establishing a demand. As he re-presents the essay in

Gaudier-Brzeska, Pound opens by quoting his own fundamental tenet of Vorticism: 'Every concept, every emotion presents itself to the vivid consciousness in some primary form. It belongs to the art of this form. If sound, to music; if formed words, to literature'.[15] Whether this is true or not is not the issue; Pound, as Maud Ellmann points out, doesn't philosophize, he puts ideas into action. What matters here is the impression of 'necessity' created by the idea of 'belonging', and created also in the definitions of lyricism and Imagism:

> There is a sort of poetry where music, sheer melody, seems as if it were just bursting into speech.
> There is another sort of poetry where painting or sculpture seems as if it were 'just coming over into speech'. (GB, 82)

Poetry, according to these definitions, cannot be helped, is necessary; there is a call for it, it is a requirement of certain human situations. Art, Pound goes on, of the 'first intensity' – a phrase which both describes a demand (for enunciation) and creates a demand (by its allure) – is work which would 'need a hundred works of any other kind to explain it' (GB, 84). Imagism, as he records it, had this necessity about it – and here we have to notice that there is no change of rhetorical pitch as he moves from, for instance, *The Divine Comedy* to 'In a Station of the Metro'. That poem, he recalls, emerged out of the sense that 'I could not find any words that seemed to me worthy, or as lovely as that emotion'. What this means is that he was not equal to it yet; the emotional-intellectual complex (resulting in the image) had issued a demand to which he became equal, or which was, at any rate, equalled, not in the sense that he found words, but in the sense that 'there came an equation' (GB, 87). It is here, in this relation to his environment, that Pound considered he had established a demand for the Modern poet. The demand occasioning the poem was Modern in that the situation was urban and fleeting. The poem was necessary – was to be understood as necessary – in that as an 'equation' it had truth and inevitability about it. Nor did the necessity only consist in the relation of words to intellectual-emotional complex; it carried over also into the naming of the art that complex brought forth:

> The image is not an idea. It is a radiant node or cluster; it is what I can, and must perforce, call a VORTEX, from which, and through which, and into which, ideas are constantly rushing. In decency one can only call it a VORTEX. And from this necessity came the name 'Vorticism'. *Nomina sunt consequentia rerum* [names are the consequence of things], and never was that statement of Aquinas more true than in the case of the vorticist movement. (GB, 92)

What is apparent is how much Pound wanted to believe in the 'necessity' of the vortex. What he craved was to be able to call a thing by a given name on the grounds that no other name was permissible, that the unnamed thing called forth the name, and that the name called the waiting thing into being. He wanted, as a poet, to heed the call. What should be apparent also, however, is that in his seeking after an apter metaphor, he has, whether he would have liked it or not, fallen back on the trope of enthusiasm. Except that here it is not the artist that is enthusiastic but rather the word, 'from which, and through which, and into which ideas are constantly rushing'. One could, in all decency, name Pound an enthusiast at this point, or at least an enthusiastic writer, a writer for whom his medium existed to permit the rushing into and from of ideas, a rushing Maud Ellmann commented on under the rubric of impersonality when she noted the 'worded breezes of these early texts'.[16] Simply to name Pound an enthusiast, heedful as that term is of the conventional circuit Vorticism is here modelled upon, would, however, be largely to miss the point. What Pound did through the nineteen-teens was pursue and identify apter metaphors, not discarding the fundamental procedure of enthusiasm but making it new. The term 'Vortex' is part of this, but so too is the terminology with which, in his note, Pound ends his essay, and where, as he says, 'Certain things seem to demand metrical expression, or expression in a rhythm more agitated than the rhythms acceptable to prose' (GB, 94). The word here is 'demand'; the poetic word, as Pound had come to see it here, being 'demanded'.

The trouble was that, as Pound pressed on, no substantive demand emerged; in a supply and demand environment, or at any rate in England, there was little or no call for his work. Naturally enough, then, as he continued to investigate the requirement, or otherwise, for Modern poetry, what he wrote in the late nineteen-teens were a series of poems in which he rendered more complex the idea of writing and its demands. 'Near Perigord' is a strong instance of this, Pound massively complicating the relation between Bertran de Born and Maent that previously he had presented in 'Na Audiart' and '"Dompna Pois de me No'us Cal"', de Born being characterized in terms of his difficult and devious relation to political power. The culminating example, however, is 'Hugh Selwyn Mauberley', where the idea of the demand and the idea of the call are dissociated. 'What the age demands' in that poem, as articulated by the siren voices of its first part, is emphatically not what the age requires. And the trouble in part is with the rhetoric of 'demand' and the economy it implies, with the fact that in a literary marketplace poetry can barely survive. The preferred term is therefore once again the call, witness the poem's epigraph:

> 'Vocat oestus in umbram'
> – Nemesianus, Ec. IV.

'The heat calls us into the shade'. Wherever the heat emanates from – whether it is the heat of cultural hell or the warmth of the sun – the call is clear; the poet in the present age must retreat into the shade. It was a call that would eventually mean marginality, exile, martyrdom, arrest and incarceration.

Distributing

Pound reviewed C. H. Douglas's *Economic Democracy* in 1920. How he came to be reading economic theory at this time, he explained in another of his retrospectives, 'Murder by Capital', published in *The Criterion* in July 1933. Once again tracking the twists and turns of his own career, Pound puts the question: 'what can drive a man interested almost exclusively in the arts, into social theory or into a study of the "gross material aspects", videlicet economic aspects of the present?' (SP, 198). Writing in the midst of the depression, at a time of massive unemployment, Pound reflects that,

> The unemployment problem that I have been faced with, for a quarter of a century, is not or has not been the unemployment of nine or five million … it has been the problem of the unemployment of Gaudier-Brzeska, T. S. Eliot, Wyndham Lewis the painter, E. P. the present writer. (SP, 200)

Mass unemployment features in the Cantos. As Canto XLVI observes:

> FIVE million youths without jobs
> FOUR million adult illiterates
> 15 million 'vocational misfits', that is with small chance for jobs
> NINE million persons annual, injured in preventable industrial accidents
> One hundred thousand violent crimes. The Eunited States ov America
> 3rd year of the reign of F. Roosevelt, signed F. Delano, his uncle.[17]

Unemployment is waste of human potential, and as such, as waste, was for Pound unquestionably an aesthetic issue: the elimination of redundancy having been a central feature of his programme for the Modernization of poetry since at least 1913. More than mass unemployment, however, it is the unemployment of the artist that troubles him. Twenty years ago, he observes in 'Murder by Capital',

> before 'one', 'we', 'the present writer' or his acquaintances had begun to think about 'cold subjects like economics' one began to notice that the social order hated *any* art of maximum intensity and preferred dilutions. The best artists were unemployed … long before … the unemployment crises began to make the front page in the newspapers. (SP, 197)

Behind the word 'unemployment' one can hear the word 'demand', or lack of, and behind the word 'demand' one can hear the word 'call', or lack of.

There were, he notes in 1933, '15 million "vocational misfits"'. Pound, Eliot, Lewis and Gaudier-Brzeska experienced a crisis of unemployment *avant la lettre* because, as he saw it, in an economy organized according to the principle of the market, the works issuing from their vocation supplied no demand.

In *Economic Democracy* C. H. Douglas reads like Thoreau. 'Systems,' he says, 'were made for men, and not men for systems, and the interest of man which is self-development, is above all systems.' In part, as in Thoreau, the problem is one of time: the working day should be shortened, and by recourse, as Douglas sees it – this isn't Thoreauvian – to labour-saving devices. 'It is essential,' he says, 'that the individual *should be released*' for 'other pursuits than the maintenance of life'. In part also, however, and again as in Thoreau, the problem has to do with things. Thus in the first place, systems of production have resulted in a 'complete divorcement between the worker and the finished product'. And then, more acutely still, having been divorced sociologically and metaphysically from things in the production process, they are too often not reacquainted with the things they need at the point of consumption. Thoreau's response to these problems was to explore forms of circulation other than by money, money being that which effected the breach between people and things. Douglas, operating in a more advanced industrial environment, while clinging to the rhetoric of organic relations, requires a tougher mechanism than Thoreau provides, and so in his lexicon 'circulation' becomes 'distribution'. The objective of 'social credit' theory, he says, is 'a reasonably uniform and plentiful distribution of simple necessaries; food, clothes, housing'. His aim is to ensure that 'every individual can avail himself of the benefits of science and mechanism', to arrange, as he puts it, 'for the equitable distribution of the whole product'.[18]

Prior to reading Douglas, Pound's preferred term for the movement of things and artefacts through society and culture had been 'circulation'. In 'Cantico del Sole', published in 'Instigations' in 1920, he had ruminated that

> The thought of what America would be like
> If the Classics had a wide circulation
>   Troubles my sleep,
> The thought of what America,
> The thought of what America,
> The thought of what America would be like
> If the Classics had a wide circulation
>   Troubles my sleep.
>   (P, 182)

Is that good troubling or bad troubling? Does Pound lie awake worried or excited? The poem declines to be clear. What is clear is the terminology, and its place in Pound's thought at this time. Thus throughout the nineteen-teens, his enthusiastic mobilizing of Modernism had largely taken the form, straightforwardly, of getting, or trying to get, works into circulation. He had published writers in anthologies, presented them to editors, insisted on their value to publishers, and detailed their merits in review. And this activity could hardly be thought to have been to no avail, given the publication in 1922 of *Ulysses* and *The Waste Land*; but by then Pound had come to dwell on the lack of demand for the work he had championed, and distribution – with its promise of getting the things people needed to them – became central to his theorizing and practice. Like 'the call', and like 'demand', the idea of distribution in Pound is complex, demonstrating once again the fraught and dangerous nature of his enthusiasm. Thus as he came to put it in *ABC of Economics*, 'Probably the only economic problem needing emergency solution in our time is the problem of distribution. ... *There is Enough*. How are you going to get it from where it is, or can be, to where it is not and is needed?' (SP, 204–5). At its best, when it is not repeating itself or digressing beyond readability, *ABC of Economics* is a popularization, as Pound hoped, of Douglas and Silvio Gessell (author of *The National Economic Order*), the graphic, tub-thumping phrasing adding verbal force to the social credit message. And it is important not to underestimate the centrality of this to Pound; few things mattered more to him, as his thinking widened into political economy, than the movement of things from one place to another, the practicalities of which became integral to his thinking about culture. He was fond, for instance, of quoting Kipling's phrase, 'Transportation is civilization,' commenting that 'Whatever interferes with the "traffic and all that it implies" is evil. A tunnel is worth more than a dynasty'(SP, 169). From which it followed that Pound was an early advocate of a tunnel between England and France. What complicates this distributive thinking is that if *ABC of Economics* is a popularization of Douglas and Gessell, it is also a popularization of Mussolini, whose claim was precisely that he was able to get a thing from where it was to where it was needed. 'Distribution' in Pound thus came to be stained, like so much else, by his enthusiasm for Fascism, the stain running through this poetry, from *The Cantos* back.

Making things available had long since been axiomatic to Pound. When he argued, in *How to Read*, that when 'the application of word to thing goes rotten ... the whole machinery of social and of individual thought and order goes to pot,' he was amplifying the claim he had made in 'I gather the Limbs of Osiris' that 'it is not until poetry lives again "close to the thing" that it will be a vital part of contemporary life' (LE, 21; SE, 41). Pound was also recalling Imagism, of course, with its headline demand for a 'Direct treatment of the "thing"'. How to treat the thing directly, or what kind of thing he had in mind, is far from clear. More interesting, and more durable, is the subtler version of Imagism's first demand that emerged in the essay on 'Vorticism' as the idea of 'presenting'. 'Ibycus and Liu Ch'e,' he asserts by way of illustration, 'presented the "Image"', and likewise, 'when the poet speaks of "Dawn in russet mantle clad," he presents something which the painter cannot present' (GB, 83, 84). The subtlety here is that what Pound presents in such an image is not exactly the '"thing"'. What is presented, rather, so Pound would like to think, is the thing's precise equivalent. There is a proximity, a nearness, in such verbal formulations, in the arrangements of their sounds, to the situation at hand, such that the situation presented can be thought to have directed, or demanded, or required, or necessitated the expression. Thus if the thing – dawn – is not precisely made available in Shakespeare's formulation, language has been made available to the thing. As in Thoreau, then, the purpose of writing, if not quite to make things available – though neither writer ever relinquishes this yearning – is to be present at the scene of things, to be present at events, with such presence, as Pound argues, constituting the high points of a life and a culture.

Education, it followed for Pound, consisted in '"getting wise" in the rawest and hardest boiled sense of that … argot', the problem being that, 'This active, instant, and present awareness is NOT handed out in colleges and by the system of public and/or popular education' (GK, 52). Likewise religion: 'The essence of religion,' as Pound put it, echoing Thoreau's sense of oracular serenity, 'is the *present* tense' (SP, 72). And it is in the interest of such high points, such instances of being present, the 'top-flights of the mind' as Pound put it, that *The Cantos*, at their best, are directed. Thus if the least readable parts of *The Cantos* are among the history sections, the Adams Cantos for instance, so equally Pound's handling of history, in the first thirty Cantos, provides some of the work's most gripping moments. Clark Emery was right in suggesting that the intention in such Cantos is not to bring 'history to the reader' but to 'bring the reader into history', that the 'reader will not witness an event or an accomplished fact but will seem to be a participant in the event'.[19] The notion of presenting, of making present, thus never goes away in Pound, and there is a reading of *The Cantos* to be had from what they set out to make present. Even so, as regards poetry's relation to things and to their availability, 'distributing' becomes a more powerful term than 'presenting' in Pound's thinking, witness his remark, in *ABC of Economics*, that the problem of distribution is 'as much our question as Hamlet's melancholy was the problem of the renaissance dyspeptic' (SP, 205).

To complete Pound's analogy, if melancholy was integral to Shakespeare's major work, so distribution should be integral to major work of the Modern age, and *The Cantos* therefore can be properly understood as a distributive and distributing work. This is repeatedly evident in the poem's handling of economics, of course, Canto XII, like many other Cantos, asking what is 'likely to ease distribution'. It is evident, also, in the poem's politics, Canto XIII, for instance, the first of the Confucian Cantos, centring on a discussion of how the wise ruler might distribute order. But it is also in the poem's primary method, in its relation to and way of handling things, as is apparent, I would argue, in the justly famous Canto XLIX. A Confucian Canto, offering, as Pound saw it, a 'glimpse of paradise', Canto XLIX has as its familiar Poundian subject the relation between light and things:

> Comes then snow scur on the river
> And a world is covered with jade
> Small boat floats like a lanthorn,
> The flowing water clots as with cold. And at San Yin
> they are a people of leisure.
> Wild geese swoop to the sand-bar,
> Clouds gather about the hole of the window
> Broad water; geese line out with the autumn
> Rooks clatter over the fishermen's lanthorns,
> A light moves on the north sky line;
> where the young boys prod stones for shrimp.
> In seventeen hundred came Tsing to these hill lakes.
> A light moves on the south sky line.
>
> (C, 244–5)

This is exemplary Pound – Pound exemplifying and at his best – the passage pulling together many of the threads of his enthusiasm. Thus it matters, of course, that these 'are a people of leisure', that they are able to pursue things other than the maintenance of life. It matters also, as the Canto later implies, that they are outside, or above system. 'Imperial power is?', the people are heard quizzically to ask, 'and to us what is it?' It matters also, of course, that here, as so often, as Pound approaches a Thoreauvian oracular stillness, he is voicing another's words, the passage quoted having its source in a sixteenth-century manuscript of Chinese and Japanese poems which, as William Cookson points out, came into Pound's possession via his father. By this characteristic enunciatory gesture, one voice incorporated into another, *The Cantos* are always practising an enthusiastic mode.

What matters most, however, is this Canto's sense of things. As with the 'Image', the passage works by an equivalence. We are not in the presence of things, though we could perhaps be lulled into thinking so. Rather, Pound finds an equivalence in language for the way things are made available. What makes things available in the world, from a Poundian point of view, is light, a defining quality of which is precisely that it distributes itself equally. Things are shown. Light affords access. What the poetry does is to simulate that distribution, Pound's long process of Modernization – the ongoing elimination of unnecessary diction and emphasis – resulting here in lines whose poetic attention is distributed equally across all its elements; in which all the elements of the poem, all the nouns and all the actions, are rendered equally available, equally present.

Beyond a certain date, there is no escaping the stain of Fascism in Pound – stain in the sense that Philip Roth speaks of the human stain, as going all through, as affecting everything – and while there are great contradictions and inconsistencies in his writing, there are major continuities also, themes that find development in all aspects and corners of his work. So there is no difficulty in appreciating why Pound should have thought Canto XLIX a glimpse of paradise, suffused as it is with light, a light which makes all things available. But what's on show also is a Fascist aesthetic, the distributive poetic having made common cause with an authoritarian response to the problems of demand.

Preventing

The things Pound most wanted to move from where they were to where they needed to be were books. 'FOR A NATIONAL CULTURE,' he argued in 'NATIONAL CULTURE: A MANIFESTO 1938,' 'the first step is stocktaking: what is there of it *solid*. The second step is to make this available and to facilitate access to it' (SP, 136). Demanding as he was, and given that the demand on the poet and the reader was invariably difficulty – 'beauty is difficult' as he reiterates in the first of *The Pisan Cantos* – it is easy to overlook Pound's commitment (his terms) to access and availability. He is very clear about this: culture – he calls it 'heritage' in this manifesto, so that here again the stain of Fascism is apparent – should be made available; people should have access to it. He claims always to have thought this. 'For one thing,' he writes in 'Murder by Capital',

> I don't care about 'minority culture'. I have never cared a damn about snobbisms or for writing *ultimately* for the few. Perhaps that is an exaggeration. Perhaps I was a worse young man than I think I was.
> Serious art is unpopular at its birth. But it ultimately forms the mass culture. Not at full strength? Perhaps at full strength. (SP, 201)

Pound is coy here. Almost certainly in the nineteen-teens he wrote for a few, and not purely by accident but by design, as a way of generating a call for his work. What is undeniable is that in the 1930s Pound was actively committed to the task of popularizing literature, where popularizing meant getting books to people, making literature widely available. His term is access, and we should hear two implications in that. In the first place, there have been too few writers in the Modernist tradition since Pound who have felt the need to argue publicly for widespread access to literature, and writing in that tradition has almost certainly suffered for its failure to appreciate the non-compromising distinction between work which makes demands – 'beauty is difficult' – and the need for a cultural apparatus, and a demeanour toward the culture, that might ensure access (Pound's term) to such work. In the second place, however, there is absolutely no slither from access to what is now thought of as accessibility; no implication for the character of the work itself in the argument that it should be made available. Pound's strategy for holding this line was to construe himself as a distributor rather than a critic – in the terms of this book it seems fair to view him here as an enthusiast – so that significant work was to be presented, 'exhibited' to borrow the term he uses in *ABC of Reading*, with just sufficient (meaning minimal) critical apparatus.

To take Pound at his word here is to steer towards what Maud Ellmann termed his 'poetics of impersonality', and so towards the disingenuities that underpinned all aspects of his self-effacement. This is true on a simple level, in that, as *The Cantos* demonstrate consistently, an exhibition entails a selection, a mind mediating the spectator's relation with the apparently unmediated artefact. And it is true in the more complex sense that Pound, of all writers, requires commentary, and that where the critic is inclined simply to exhibit him, as in the case, for instance, of William Cookson's *A Guide to The Cantos of Ezra Pound*, what invariably follows is an apology for crimes of hate that criticism is prepared to expose. Thus, in Cookson's highly informative and in some senses invaluable guide, he observes how Pound quotes fondly from the Old Testament in *The Pisan Cantos* (the Bible being one of the few books he had available to him at the Disciplinary Training Centre), suggesting: 'It is to be doubted that anyone who was at heart an anti-Semite would have expressed these sentiments'. To confirm which he quotes Kenner (from a review of *Letters of Captivity*) remarking apropos the same debt to the Hebrew Bible in *The Pisan Cantos* that Pound's anti-Semitism 'may have begun to dissipate in the Pisan cage. I know that I once brought a Jewish friend to visit him at St. Elizabeth's, and they got on well, and the friend went back another time. And one moral is, beware of generalizations.'[20] So the defence is that 'in his heart' he was not an anti-Semite, or that he was friendly to friends of friends who were Jews. One moral, therefore, is beware the Poundian commentary whose primary method is presentation. At the same time, and without closing one's mind to the ways Pound's thought colluded with itself, there is something, especially now, to be learned from his impulse to exhibit, to ensure access. Take teaching, which as Pound argued meant allowing people to learn, where allowing people to learn meant, primarily, ensuring access. Which sounds uncontroversial, except when set against his claim, in 'Definitions', that 'The aim of state education has been (historically) to prevent people from discovering that the classics are worth reading. In this endeavour it has been almost wholly successful' (SP, 183). Central among the preventers were bureaucrats, educational bureaucrats in particular, and it is in this aspect of his thinking that Pound's popularizing speaks to the present moment.

Pound is good on bureaucrats. 'Bureaucrats are a pox,' he heckles at the beginning of his essay 'Bureaucracy the Fail of Jehovah' (SP, 187). 'They are supposed to be *necessary*,' but then, 'Certain chemicals in the body are supposed to be necessary to life, but cause death the moment they increase beyond a suitable limit.' (SP, 187). The abuse is gratifying, but the argument goes beyond abuse, chiming with his insistence on the need to make things present. Thus in its educational form, bureaucracy is quite rigorously addressed in an essay entitled 'Provincialism the Enemy'. The case is not difficult to understand (which is not, of course, to say that historically it has been understood); in its truthfulness, however, and its pertinence to the current British climate, it is worth hearing in some detail. Speaking as a former doctoral student, Pound observes: 'No one who has not been one of a gang of young men all heading for scholastic "honors" knows how easy it is to have the mind switched off ... all considerations of the values of life, and switched on to some minute, unvital detail.' (SP, 162)

This doesn't matter in the individual case, except that as individual cases are reproduced across the system the effect is of a general deadening and mechanization. He hears from the university only – note – 'boasts of efficiency and of "results produced"', and finds there the practice of 'hammering the student into a piece of mechanism for the accretion of details, and of habituating men to consider themselves as bits of mechanism for one use or another: in contrast to considering first what they are in being' (SP, 165). 'The bulk of scholarship,' he contends, 'has gone under completely: the fascination of technical and mechanical education has been extremely seductive.' Nor was the process of seduction difficult, the mechanization of the universities being entirely of a piece with critical and scholarly practice, with the development of 'apparatus criticus', and the insistence on '"original research"', the 'demand' for which results in a 'retabulation of data, and a retabulation of tables already retabulated' (SP, 167). Pound's career-long assault on the universities is sometimes put down to personal bitterness, his own academic career, following his failure to secure a PhD, having dwindled into nothing. But to dismiss it as such is to miss the force of his complaint. He was on to the modern university, and especially the English Department, early, and what he saw with great clarity was that,

> The moment you teach a man to study literature not for its own delight, but for some exterior reason … you begin his destruction, you begin to prepare his mind for all sorts of acts to be undertaken for exterior reasons "of State", etc., without regard to their merit. (SP, 167)

This might seem an easy charge to fling. What does it mean, a person might ask, 'to teach literature for its own delight'? What really is meant by destruction? What are 'exterior reasons "of state"'? What does it mean, as he claims elsewhere in the essay, that to take a person's 'mind off the human value of the poem he is reading will begin his dehumanization'?

Here, in answer to these questions, is a luminous detail:

MODULE PROPOSAL

1   **The title of the module:**

2   **The Department which will be responsible for management of the module:**

3   **The start date of the module:**

4   **The number of students expected to take the module:**

5   **Modules to be withdrawn on the introduction of this proposed module and consultation with other relevant Departments and Faculties regarding the withdrawal:**

6   **The level of the module:**

7   **The number of credits which the module represents:**

8   **Which term(s) the module is to be taught in (or other teaching pattern):**

9   **Pre-requisite and co-requisite modules:**

10   **The programmes of study to which the module contributes:**

11   **The intended subject specific learning outcomes and, as appropriate, their relationship to programme learning outcomes:**

12   **The intended generic learning outcomes and, as appropriate, their relationship to programme learning outcomes:**

13   **A synopsis of the curriculum:**

14   **Indicative reading list:**

15   **Learning and teaching methods, including the nature and number of contact hours and the total study hours which will be expected of students, and how these relate to achievement of the intended learning outcomes:**

16   **Assessment methods and how these relate to testing achievement of the intended learning outcomes:**

This is a form, generic enough no doubt, which a university teacher has to fill in when proposing to teach a course. The form can be completed with almost no reference to literary content: it has to be readable by bureaucrats, so the less subject-specificity the better. What are called for, almost exclusively, are external reasons for study: the form wants to know about outcomes, where outcomes will be externally determined measures. After completion, the form will begin an arduous journey, to a departmental Learning and Teaching meeting (and probably back), to a department meeting, and then on to faculty, where faculty Learning and Teaching will scrutinize it (for generic fit, for consistency with other such documents), and will probably send it back, via the departmental Learning and Teaching committee, to the teacher for a comment.

All of this is a problem. It is a problem because bureaucracy kills enthusiasm. Bureaucracy blocks – produces a series of structural interventions which amount to blockages – and so prevents the circulation of works and values that enthusiasm sets in motion. The terms of the form and the process infect and disrupt thinking. They become the medium through which teacher and student encounter each other, or rather the barrier erected between teacher, student and book. And yet bureaucracy, by default, also produces enthusiasm, in that historically enthusiasm has flared at moments of overbearing apparatus. Such structures produce an intense desire for immediacy, for a direct contact with things, and in his or her intensity the enthusiast is liable to become extreme.

Pound's thinking about bureaucracy was thoroughgoing, traced back through Church history. Thus 'Christ,' he contends, was not 'constructing a code for the administrating empire but a *modus vivendi* for the individual' (SP, 57). When this relation is lost, 'when this immediate sight is lacking the cult dilutes into verbal formulation ... a highly debatable intellectual paraphernalia usually without cultural force' (SP, 59). From which it follows that 'the Church, as bureaucracy and as vested interest was the worst enemy of "faith"' (SP, 121). Or as he puts it in *Guide to Kulchur*, 'A live religion can not be maintained by scripture. It has got to go into effect repeatedly in the persons of the participants' (GK, 191). This is Pound's enthusiasm. It goes to the heart of his thought. Or rather, it goes to the heart of his thinking about thinking. He draws a distinction in *Guide to Kulchur* between two kinds of 'ideas': 'Ideas which exist and/or are discussed in a species of vacuum ... and ideas which are intended to "go into action", or to guide action'; the history of a culture being, as he contends, 'the history of ideas going into action' (GK, 34, 44). What bureaucracy prevents – what, from this way of viewing things, it exists to prevent – is the kind of culture that can be produced by ideas going into action. *The Cantos*, at their best – chiefly in 'A Draft of XXX Cantos', 'The Fifth Decad of Cantos XLII–LI' and The Pisan Cantos LXXIV–LXXXIV – are a riposte to this. They incorporate into themselves the practices and languages which act as blockages and stops on the distribution of works and values. By contrast they advocate and embody movement. They jump in order to confound. They distribute by voicing words not their own. They testify to the difficulty of making things available to people, and to the necessity, always, of mobilizing thought.

'Ezra Pound speaking'

Just before Ezra Pound boarded the boat that would take him from America to Italy, after his release from St. Elizabeth's, following a twelve-and-a-half-year incarceration, he ended a conversation with attending journalists by giving a Fascist salute. It would be fortunate if one could disassociate such a gesture from Pound's enthusiastic mobilization of literature, but this can't be done. In the first place, his popularization of 'essential' literature was of a piece with his personal programme for Fascism, 'the publication of essential parts of our heritage' being central, as he saw it, to 'a national or racial culture' (SP, 131). More than this, his idea of mobility is deeply entangled with his anti-Semitism, as, for instance, Canto XXXV would appear to show. 'So this is (may we take it),' the Canto opens, 'Mitteleuropa'. Which is to say, we may take it, 'Mitteleuropa' as opposed to Confucian China or Malatesta's Tuscany. What we find there, as Pound has it, is a bourgeoisie, but more specifically, a community of Jewish people, and what the Canto presents are closed relations and closed circuits, 'the intramural, the almost intravaginal warmth of / hebrew affections, in the family, and nearly everything else ...' (C, 172–3). The Canto is expressly anti-Semitic, Pound going out of his way to mock the voice which speaks of 'a peautiful chewisch poy'. And what the Canto stands for, what it means to symbolize, is the absence of circulation, distribution and mobility; and the prevalence, by contrast, of overfamiliarity, networks and stasis. Prejudice is the opposite of presenting, the obtruding of pre-existing mental categories over detail, and in this sense only, a person might try to dis-integrate Pound's anti-Semitism from his enthusiastic commitment to good (which is to say, in his terms, direct as opposed to abstracted or generalized) writing. In another sense, however, his anti-Semitic rants – in *The Cantos*, but more so in the radio broadcasts – are consistent with his sense of calling. Through the late 1930s into the 1950s, as numerous friends, former friends and acquaintances avowed, and as the writings make all too clear, the role Pound cast himself in was that of prophet or martyr, calling on the culture to listen to what it ought, as he saw it, to hear; to what he, with the authority stemming from his sense of vocation, had to say. 'All he wants,' wrote Charles Olson, 'is the purring and tears of fellow fascists ... Poor, poor Pound, the great gift, the true intellectual, being confined and maltreated by the Administration. SHIT.'[21] And so, in the end, in his appearances in court and in his incarceration, Pound cut a historically familiar figure: the ranting, self-assured, self-elected individual versus the combined forces of the American state. Out of which standoff arises a choice. Pound presented Modern poetry with one of its favoured guises: poet as martyr, exiled, out in the cold. He also presented it with an image of mobility, with the task of keeping things moving. Marianne Moore, for one, as we shall see next, developed a language conducive to the latter.

Notes

1 T. S. Eliot, 'Introduction' to Ezra Pound, *Literary Essays of Ezra Pound*, London, Faber and Faber, 1954, pxii; hereafter referred to in the text as LE.

2 W.B. Yeats (ed.), *Oxford Book of Modern Verse, 1892–1935*, Oxford, Clarendon Press, 1936, p. xxv.

3 Ezra Pound, *Guide to Kulchur*, New York, New Directions, 1938, p. 223; hereafter referred to in the text as GK.

 4 Friedrich Nietzsche, *On the Genealogy of Morality*, Cambridge, Cambridge University Press, 2003, p. 36.
 5 Ezra Pound, *The Spirit of Romance*, Norfolk, Conn., New Directions Books, 1929, p. 10.
 6 Ezra Pound, *Personae: The Shorter Poems of Ezra Pound*, London, Faber and Faber, 1990, p. 5; hereafter referred to in the text as P.
 7 Ezra Pound, *Selected Prose 1909–1965*, ed. William Cookson, London, Faber and Faber, 1973, p. 49; hereafter referred to in the text as SP.
 8 Humphrey Carpenter, *A Serious Character: The Life of Ezra Pound*, London, Faber and Faber, 1988, plate 25.
 9 Martin Heidegger, *Basic Writings: Martin Heidegger*, tr. David Farrell Krell, London, Routledge, 2002, pp. 369–70.
10 Ibid., p. 370.
11 Ibid., p. 377.
12 Ibid., p. 386.
13 Carpenter, *Serious Character*, p. 188.
14 Cited in Carpenter, *Serious Character*, p. 196.
15 Ezra Pound, *Gaudier-Brzeska: A Memoir*, Hessle, Marvell Press, 1966, p. 81; hereafter referred to in the text as GB.
16 Maud Ellmann, *The Poetics of Impersonality: T.S. Eliot and Ezra Pound*, Brighton, Harvester Press, 1987, p. 149.
17 Ezra Pound, *The Cantos*, London, Faber and Faber, 1986, p. 235; hereafter referred to in the text as C.
18 C. H. Douglas, *Economic Democracy*, London, Cecil Palmer, 1920, pp. 6, 45, 34, 93, 5, 110.
19 Clark Emery, *Ideas into Action: A Study of Pound's Cantos*, Miami, Fla., University of Miami Press, 1958, p. 94.
20 William Cookson, *A Guide to The Cantos of Ezra Pound*, London, Anvil Press Poetry, 2001, p. 130.
21 Carpenter, *Serious Character*, p. 737.

4

Presenting: Marianne Moore

There was no frenzy about Marianne Moore. She composed not in fits and bursts, but patiently, sometimes over several years. She steadfastly refused to envisage herself as inspired. Her writing doesn't flirt with gibberish. Her principal mode of production was accumulation. In her various notebooks – of quotations and conversations – she amassed the materials that would sometimes, eventually, constitute the fabric of her poems. One readily available way to view her, therefore, is as a collector, an antiquarian, rooting among the archives for choice additions: as a sub-sub-librarian, extracting and compiling, as a consumptive usher dusting off texts. From which way of reading Moore's procedure – or rather, from which way of reading off her procedure on to her poems – one can quickly arrive at an image of an enthusiast of sorts: as the kind of enthusiast who, had she known other circumstances, might have founded a museum in an age when private collectors – Isabella Stewart Gardener or Henry Frick, for example – were accruing to American prestige the world's artistic riches. But such a way of presenting Moore, conflating as it does intellectual curiosity with acquisition, and privileging matters of procedure over questions of form and technique, significantly diminishes her sensibility, and in the process misses the point of her enthusiasm.

To get closer to the point, one might, perhaps, think in terms of the question with which George Oppen opens his sequence 'Five Poems about Poetry'. 'The question is,' Oppen writes, 'how does one hold an apple / Who likes apples?'[1] This is a difficult question; not a question it is hard to understand, maybe, but a question to which it is difficult to make an adequate response. Supposing one likes apples, and one has an apple, should one hold it in such a way as to keep it to oneself, or should one hold it in order that others might enjoy it? Should you hold it at all, in fact, or, as the verb allows one to think, ought you rather to behold it? Or should you just eat it? It all depends, of course, on what one means by 'likes'. This is to take the question literally. Taking the question analogously, understanding it to be in some sense 'about poetry', the same sort of options present themselves, though with further difficulties as regards medium and method. So if one likes apples, and wants to demonstrate that attitude in language, how does one do so? What operations in language are the equivalent to holding close and holding out, to beholding and consuming? And then what further questions arise if one is working in language because one enjoys words; so that not only does one like apples, but one likes 'apples' also – the 'p's' and the 'l', the way when you say the word you first have to open your mouth wide, before pursing your lips into a sort of pout, the way you breathe through the syllables as you activate your throat, the way the letters line up across the page. How, Oppen asks in his poems about poetry, should one handle language when one's object in using the language is to present some *thing* that one likes?

Marianne Moore is a poet of things. Isolated things – jewels, curios, familiar and exotic animals, common and rare species of plant – are often the ostensible subjects of her poems. She is also a poet for whom words have properties not unlike things, not in the sense that she thinks of words as a concrete poet might, but in the sense that when, for instance, she quotes, the value of the quotation is as likely – sometimes more likely – to lie in the discrete properties of the fragment as it is to lie in the text to which the fragment refers, or in its meaning as originally framed. She is fond of groups of words, this is to say, in a sense comparable to the way some people are fond of objects, and the attention she ostensibly gives to things in her poetry is, at one level, an analogy for the way she handles words. It is because of this analogy – this close relation in her poetry between the handling of words and the handling of things – that a reading of Moore as a hoarder can take hold, because when a *thing* is collected, however regularly it is exhibited, it stays collected, it remains in somebody's possession.[2] Even where, for instance, a painting is purchased by the state, it will be construed as public property, a vexed description which accords individual members of the public limited rights in relation to the object, but which serves primarily to indicate how difficult it is to construe a thing as standing outside the relationship of ownership, that 'property' is a deeply embedded cultural property of things. But this is not true of the published word, even if the procedure that arrived at that word resembles that of the collector, as Moore spelled out in her *Paris Review* interview with Donald Hall. Answering his question about her predilection for quotation (and in the process answering the question of value raised here through Oppen) Moore tells Hall, as she told numerous interviewers through her career:

> I was just trying to be honorable and not to steal things. I've always felt that if a thing had been said in the *best* way, how can you say it better? If I wanted to say something and somebody had said it ideally, then I'd take it but I'd give

the person the credit for it. That's all there is to it. If you are charmed by an author, I think it's a very strange and invalid imagination that doesn't long to share it. Somebody else should read it, don't you think?[3]

One task Moore set herself in her poetry, therefore, an obligation – 'should' – under which she wrote, was to present things, but more importantly words, she liked in such a way that she should be construed as sharing or passing on their value. In Oppen's terms, she wanted, in language, to hold an apple in such a way that its value for her is clear, but that built into that sense of value is the commitment that others should enjoy it also. And what this implies in Moore is a double operation, involving the demonstration of the value things and words have for oneself, cherishing them perhaps, while also presenting them clearly enough that they might have a similar value for other people.

This task has to do with enthusiasm. In *The Gift: Imagination and the Erotic Life of Property*, Lewis Hyde draws a partial analogy between religious enthusiasm and the gift, drawing the former into a picture of an economy which circulates without the aid, or intrusion, of money. The point of comparison is the direct communication upon which the idea of enthusiasm is founded. Hence,

> The deist's attachment to reasonable discourse and his caution before the trembling body placed the spirit of his religion closer to the spirit of trade than to the spirit of the gift. In gift exchange no symbol of worth need be detached from the body of the gift as it is given away. Cash exchange, on the other hand, *depends* upon the abstraction of symbols of value from the substances of value.[4]

'Cash exchange,' by this way of thinking, and as Hyde formulates it, 'is to gift exchange what reason is to enthusiasm.' Plunging us back into the post-Kantian landscape of Walden Pond, Hyde's analogy between gift economics and religious enthusiasm has the intention of showing how things can be made more available, how there are social practices which in their methods and modes desist from obscuring things behind symbols and mediations. There is in Hyde's thinking, it should be noticed, in Marianne Moore's terms, an 'element of unreason' – the phrase is from her poem 'Black Earth', subsequently retitled 'Melanchthon'. 'Will / depth be depth,' Moore asks, in relation to the elephant that is the poem's subject,

> thick skin be thick, to one who can see no
> beautiful element of unreason under it?[5]

In Moore, as in Hyde, as in Thoreau, there is a sense that things in themselves, in their depth and thickness, are made available by processes other than, or supplementary to, reason. The prime instance in Hyde of such a process is the relatively unmediated gift economy, though as he indicates here he thinks enthusiasm might also be so conceived. As far as he explores it, however, his analogy is only partial because his sense of enthusiasm deals not with things but exclusively with god. Marianne Moore, I want to argue, can be thought of as tightening Hyde's analogy. She does so by reorientating enthusiasm towards its Modern sense, so that in her habitual use of the term, enthusiasm shifts from a noun describing a state residing in a person, to a noun describing a relation between a person and a thing: 'she has enthusiasm for …', 'he is an enthusiast of …'. 'One applauds,' she says of Stevens, 'those analogies derived from an enthusiasm for the sea.'[6]

This shift in the history of the word – Thoreau spoke always only of enthusiasm, not enthusiasm for – is contributory to and an index of a significant shift in the history of writing. Thus when, in 1924, Moore published *Observations* – the collection on which this essay will largely concentrate, and in which she emerged quite as fully herself as Stevens did in *Harmonium* – she made fully manifest for the first time a process which had been developing in American writing since Thoreau. More even than *The Waste Land*, *Observations* was a book constituted by other people's words – words, as she told Hall, that she loved, words for which she had an enthusiasm. What Moore did in *Observations*, by the sheer density of her quotations, and in her demonstration (through her notes to the volume) of the integrity of quotation to her mode of composition, was to reconfigure the source of the poem. Thus, while Pound's poetry was, or was to become, quite as dependent on quotation as anybody else's, he held, in many of his prose statements at least, to a view of the poet as a divinely mandated figure. 'No apter metaphor having been found for certain emotional colours. I assert that the Gods exist.' For Moore, poetic assembler and arranger that she was, the sources of the poem lay very much less problematically in the world outside the poet: in the things she observed, and, crucially, in the statements people made about them, in the objects and words she found lying about her. Moore, in other words, was a Modern enthusiast, and in the forms of poetry that emerged from her enthusiasm she evolved a way of handling words which, while in its seeming connoisseurship can seem to invite it, in its instinct to pass on in fact denies the analogy of acquisition. One way to begin to understand this is through her prose.

Enthusing

Marianne Moore's prose was not a systematic, nor, in the senses such a body of work might be, a unified enterprise. It does not make the kind of claim on the reader that did the critical writing of some of her contemporaries. She did not set out, as Eliot did, to reorient the canon according to the virtues of a particular historical moment in an attempt to redirect modern taste; though like him she had arrived at an enduring commitment to the virtues of seventeenth-century prose stylists. She didn't campaign, as Pound did, on behalf of favoured contemporaries, nor did she exhort readers to particular modes of action. She tended to write reviews rather than essays, money being one of her motives, though she largely restricted herself to work she admired; she cited Leo Stein's resolve (as Patricia Willis, the editor of her *Complete Prose*, points out) 'never to review a book unless essentially in sympathy with it' (CPMM, 201). In this process she frequently returned to the work of major Modern writers, producing some of the most closely appreciative contemporary appraisals of, in particular, Stevens, Williams, Pound and HD. Pound she valued in part for a facet she termed his 'master-appreciation', and her collected prose has the miscellaneous quality it does in part because when reviewing her object was to show her subject not herself; her writing about others showed typical vigilance in the selection of quotation, and consisted in large part of intensely crafted, revelatory phrase-making. In part, also, the miscellaneousness comes from the subject matter: Moore was as happy writing about baseball, and movies, as poetry. There *is* an aesthetic at work throughout Moore's prose; her paratactical, digressive syntax is very much her own, if schooled in the sermonizing of Browne and Donne. For the most part, however, her determining ethos emerges only in the manner of her approach and in passing comments, not as statement; with the exception, that is, of the Comment pieces she wrote while editor of *The Dial* between 1925 and 1929.

Moore wrote no poetry while editor of *The Dial*. As Willis sees it, the Comment pieces were the poetry's substitute. There 'one finds the wit … the delight in quotation, and the unlikely juxtapositions that mark her poems' (CPMM, vi). For Margaret Holley, Moore's poetic silence through this period 'suggests the importance to her of *The Dial* undertaking as a public forum for the working out of … issues, trends, and practices' that had emerged in her poetry up to and until the publication of *Observations*.[7] These are true statements, and we are lucky to have Moore's Comment pieces. Intricately constructed, clearly benefiting from her otherwise dormant poetic attention, closely if illustratively argued and committed to a version of truth, this series of short pieces quite quickly developed into the working out of a highly significant twentieth-century aesthetic. Here, as in her poetry, Moore worked largely by observation and quotation rather than by pronouncement; there are no manifestos in Moore, no Poundian dos and don'ts. There is, however, in her Comments, an ongoing and deliberate amplification of the defining aspects of her poetic practice; a practice which, as her statement of it evolves, comes to turn increasingly on the question of enthusiasm. What I will show in a moment is how, taken as a whole, Moore's Comment series articulates a relation to things which takes the form of a circulatory aesthetic, which has a close bearing on her handling of language, and which she names enthusiastic. Her sense of enthusiasm, however, was finely calibrated, taking the outward, projective, transitive form that it did in proportion as her suspicion hardened towards conventional images of creativity. And to get the measure of this, to see how she came to formulate her defining attitude to words and things, it is necessary first to consider the prose she wrote prior to taking up the editorship of *The Dial*.

Determined though she was always to emphasize the laboriousness of her work – 'I never knew anyone who had a passion for words who had as much difficulty in saying things as I do' – Moore did not altogether expunge from her writing conventional images of creativity.[8] In her reviewing, in particular, certain divinities persisted, and she was happy, when convinced she had found evidence of it, to acknowledge the work of inspiration. Awe is one of her critical modes, albeit sparingly used, as in, for instance, her commentary on the work of the contemporary Italian artist Alfeo Faggi published in *The Dial* in December 1922. 'Remembering,' as she puts it, 'C.H. Herford's comment upon Sir Thomas Browne's contemporary Alexander Ross,' an introductory circumlocution which has a bearing on the issue, 'one hesitates,' Moore writes of Faggi's productions in general, 'to appraise work – even to praise it – the inspiration of which is spiritual.' Moore's hesitation in the face of Faggi's work has to do intimately with its manifestation of enthusiasm. Thus she notes in his *Ka*,

> as in all his work, the controlled emotion, the mental poise which suggests the Absolute – a superiority to fetishism and triviality, a transcendence, an inscrutable dignity – a swordlike mastery in the lips, which suggests the martyr secure in having found the key to mystery. (CPMM, 74)

One can't read this as anything other than admiration. Moore is unquestionably impressed. But she is also suspicious of the 'martyr secure in having found the key to mystery'. The suspicion is broadly Kantian; the state of enthusiasm in which Faggi creates diminishes Moore's capacity for 'appraisal'. This is significant, 'appraisal' being a key intellectual function in Moore, her poetry like her prose being centrally concerned with assessments of value. But it is key also in that in Moore's scheme 'appraisal' is a way of knowing: in 'Critics and Connoisseurs' the swan, initially unsure whether to trust the speaker's offering, cannot resist its 'proclivity to more fully appraise such bits / of food as the stream // bore counter to it' (BMM, 77).

The value of Moore's review of Faggi here is the productive uncertainty in which it finds her. 'To grasp the nature of the phenomenon which *Dante* represents,' she observes – *Dante* being a work by Faggi recently reproduced in an issue of *The Dial* – 'is perhaps impossible to many of us since one cannot discern forces by which one is not oneself unconsciously animated.' Moore, this is to say, does not think of herself as inspired, either religiously or aesthetically. Equally, Faggi's work and all that it represents has an allure for her, causes in her a sort of yearning, hence her concluding observation that, 'In the animating force of this bronze in its setting of physical power, is embodied the spiritual axiom that *Dante* has come to be' (CPMM, 74–5). What this comes down to, as the history of enthusiasm tells us it should, is differing ways of knowing. Moore admires Faggi's work not least for its certainty, for its direct acquaintance (martyr-like) with its source, with its 'animating force', a phrase which resonates with many a Moore animal poem. But she is also wary of the work, because of the way it disables her own way of knowing, appraisal being central among the ways she gets to know things. Arguably there is a lag here, arguably her poetry of this early period is more articulate on this tension than is her prose. The swan appraises because it cannot resist its proclivity to do so. Its knowledge is the result both of an unconscious animating force and an assessment of value. In her review of Faggi, however, there is a tension in Moore's structure of judgement, between the inspiration she finds, and admires, in his work, and her inclination to appraise.

Such a sense of 'animation', of the 'animating force', recurs on occasion in Moore's prose. With reference to Pound she later remarked, 'Most of us have not the tongues of the spirit, but those who have, tell us that, by comparison, knowledge of the spirit of tongues is as insignificant as are the clothes worn by one in infancy' (CPMM, 272). She is pleased, also, to quote George Saintsbury: ' "The religion of literature is a sort of Pantheism. You never know when the presence of the Divine may show itself, though you should know where it has shown. And you must never forbid it to show itself, anyhow or anywhere" ' (CPMM, 189). And then, of course, such a sense of 'animating forces' as she finds in Faggi is frequently present, as is discussed later, in her poetry. In 'When I Buy Pictures', she requires of any picture she might buy, that

> it must be "lit with piercing glances into the life of things";
> it must acknowledge the spiritual forces which have made it.
>
> (BMM, 101)

One has to register Moore's acknowledgement of such 'spiritual forces' to appreciate that, as she reconfigured the idea of the poem – as she reorientated her own and her reader's sense of poetry's sources – there lingered in her thinking another idea of art's animating impulse; that even as she displaced it she understood the sway of old-time enthusiasm, that its trace retained a grip on her imagination.

Still, for the most part, when Moore toyed with the idea of inspiration it was with a qualification firmly in mind, as in, for instance, her reviews of her friend and fellow member of the Others group, HD. In these pieces, conspicuously, she was both drawn to and drew back from the old enthusiasm. She wrote beautifully about HD, emulating Pound's 'master-appreciation', and nowhere more so than when considering *Hymen*:

> One recognizes here, the artist – the mind which creates what it needs for its own subsistence and propitiates nothing, willing – indeed wishing to seem to find its only counterpart in the elements; yet in this case as in the case of any true artist, reserve is a concomitant of intense feeling, not the cause of it. (CPMM, 80)

Again, as in the discussion of Faggi, there is a deep concern here for creativity and its impulses, for what drives, and compels, and sustains the artist. But here again, only this time more centrally to the image, there is reserve, the idea of which Moore amplifies when she notices also in HD's work, as 'suggested by the absence of subterfuge, cowardice and the ambition to dominate by brute force', a 'heroics which do not confuse transcendence with domination and which in their indestructibleness, are the core of tranquility and of intellectual equilibrium' (CPMM, 82). That description, of 'heroics which do not confuse transcendence with domination', is important for Moore, articulating as it does an aesthetic and political position which ran through the heart of her writing. So just as in 'When I Buy Pictures', she requires that art 'must acknowledge the spiritual forces which have made it', so she also demands that 'it must not wish to disarm anything: nor may the approved triumph easily be honored – / that which is great because something else is small' (BMM, 101). Transcendence must not be confused with domination. In a very early Comment piece, Moore takes as her subject for discussion a list of the world's greatest educators as issued by Charles W. Eliot, President Emeritus of Harvard. She is at pains to point out that the 'domination of these … sages [has] been implicit' in the work of 'lesser sages', and also to advocate those lesser sages on the grounds that, 'unmenaced as is the greatness of Dr. Eliot's decemvirs, the unbookish are intimidated by greatness so inclusive' (CPMM, 155). What this amounts to is a defence of miscellaneous reading. One of the 'Labors of Hercules', as her poem of that title puts it, is to persuade artists

> that one must not borrow a long white beard and tie it on
> and threaten with the scythe of time, the casually curious
> (BMM, 105)

Transcendence, this is to say, must not be confused with domination in any area of life, and the terms of her politics are apparent in her criticism of Dr Eliot, her politically motivated poems responding precisely to situations of domination by inclusion. 'Sojourn in the Whale', 'He Digesteth Harde Iron' and 'Spenser's Ireland' each coordinates its response to imperialism through a play of incorporation, the poetry absorbing the words of the dominant regime in the name of resistance, and incorporating alongside them hermeneutically stubborn elements. And then it was in the spirit, surely, of 'heroics which do not confuse transcendence with domination' that Moore arrived at her best-known self-presentation as an artist, repudiating poetry, and all that it might stand for in the public mind, and substituting for that image a sort of poetic administrator. 'I have,' she was pleased to recall from her early career, in answer to a question from Donald Hall, 'a little wee book about two inches by three inches, or two and half by three inches, in which I systematically entered everything sent out, when I got it back, if they took it, and how much I got for it'.[9] Here, as Moore recalls herself at the beginning of her career, filling in and ticking off, recording and amassing, is the poet as bureaucrat. It was a pose, but by no means entirely a disingenuous one. She was quite ready to admire the 'animating force' as and where she found it in another artist. Like HD, however, or at least as she presented her, it was Moore's practice, in the content and the processes of writing, to resist domination. Enthusiasm, as she scratched around it in the reviews she wrote alongside her early poems, was a vexed and largely unresolved subject.

In her earliest prose, then, in the reviews she wrote while composing *Observations*, there are, if you ask questions of them, significant uncertainties, albeit around issues Moore was fixing on as her own. In the later prose (and at times in the poetry) there is a tendency, as she began to formulate questions of poetics in essays and lectures for particular occasions, towards an over-awareness of the audience – an awareness which became a sort of defensiveness, a tendency to hide her practice behind a too readily formulated paradox. In the series of Comment pieces, however, undistracted by the pressure to produce poetry, she was able to draw out the principles and elaborate on the innovations which had informed and defined her work to date. As she did so she set out to establish a place for her sensibility within the mainstream of American literature. She coordinated herself with the major themes and figures of American writing, and what that coordination turns on, centrally, is 'things'.

Emerson is an early point of departure. Taking as her pretext, in March 1926, a study entitled *The Religion of Undergraduates*, and having prefaced her Comment with an epigraph from Sir Thomas Browne – 'I am sure there is a common spirit that plays within us, yet makes no part of us' – Moore quotes from 'The American Scholar': '"We, it seems, are critical ... We cannot enjoy anything for hankering to know whereof the pleasure consists; we are lined with eyes; we see with our feet; the time is infected with Hamlet's unhappiness"' (CPMM, 160–1). This is familiar territory. Emerson's argument is for a different relation with things, a less critical, less alienated, more direct relation. It was such a relation Thoreau settled at Walden to establish. It was towards such directness that Pound invented Imagism. Where Moore wants to be seen to differ from her fellow Americans is in her particular sense of how writing might acquaint itself with things. Thus, picking up what was clearly a salient feature of her own poetry in a Comment of three months later, she observed that 'Perfect diction is not particularly an attribute of America'. She finds it in Henry James, in his 'geometrically snow-flake forms', but identifies it more readily in European prose:

> We attribute to let us say Machiavelli, Sir Francis Bacon, John Donne, Sir Thomas Browne, Doctor Samuel Johnson, a particular kind of verbal effectiveness – a nicety and point, a pride and pith of utterance, which is in a special way different from the admirableness of Wordsworth or Hawthorne. Suggesting conversation and strengthened by etymology there is a kind of effortless compactness which precludes ornateness. (CPMM, 165)

The aim of 'perfect diction' is not, as one might half-suspect given the examples she presents, 'ornateness', but 'effectiveness', where the desired effect is a clearer relation with things. 'Perfect diction', in other words, is elemental to Moore's handling of that which she values, as for instance in her account of an exhibition of typography at the Grolier Club, where the excitement is held to lie chiefly in the way, for instance,

> The intensively stiff Lorenzo de Medici-like augustness of the Breydenbach fifteenth-century *Perigrinatio* detains one as does the perpendicular *esprit* and fencing-foil erectness of the lines on the page at which the 1491 *Schatzbehalta* is open, and there is a 1499 Aldus edition – open at pairs of elephants, flutes, harps, banners and other constituents of a triumph. (CPMM, 173–4)

By picking out the 'intensively stiff Lorenzo de Medici-like augustness of the Breydenbach fifteenth-century *Perigrinatio*' Moore situates herself in the mainstream of American literature, where that mainstream, starting with *Walden*, is post-Kantian in its resolve to renew people's acquaintance with things. Where Moore differs is in her sense of how this might be achieved. Exactness of diction is not as foreign to America as Moore would have us think – Thoreau's project, in all its erudition, was towards a perfected lexicon of the lake, and the scholarship of *Moby-Dick* was an essential, albeit not exhaustive component of Melville's presentation of the whale. But in both of these writers as in Pound there lurked the enthusiast's suspicion of the text, as if finally the purpose of writing was somehow to open itself up, so that the world and its items might rush directly through. Moore, by contrast, though quite as committed to things – as committed to ostriches and pelicans as Melville was to the whale – presents an epistemology which esteems, above all attributes, fineness of diction, hence her keenness for the nomenclature of the connoisseur. This, it would seem, is her response to the inspiration of the likes of Alfeo Faggi, her fastidious appraisal substituting for his direct acquaintance with his source. And so again, what would seem to emerge is a picture of Moore as poetic collector, acquainting with things through the fineness of her discriminations. What disrupts this image, however, or should disrupt it, is the fact that at every level of her expression Moore is concerned to circulate stuff. It might be as a connoisseur that she would seem to approach the world; her object, however, is not to amass things, but to pass them on.

Thus it is crucial to Moore, as she articulates her aesthetic in her Comments, that she should develop a language for transmission. Excitement is one means, as in the account of literary inheritance she gives in her Comment of April 1926:

> we may admire, and the shock of admiration may serve as an incentive to writing, quite as may that which has been experienced by us; but like the impelling emotion of actual experience, literary excitement must be assimilated before it can be reproduced ... Apperception is, however, quite different from a speedy exchange of one's individuality for that of another. (CPMM, 162)

This is a standard enough account, though it is worth noting in passing how Moore qualifies her remarks, and how her qualifications here – the assimilation preceding reproduction – check the easy flow of inspiration from one author to another that Melville wanted to assert by his allusion to *Ion*. A less standard, more far-reaching sense of transmission and its possibilities is offered in her Comment of June 1926, where the issue is not literary indebtedness, but charity. Addressing the present age's tendency towards conspicuous consumption – 'our present economically irresponsible detailed ornateness' – Moore considers the argument whether charity is selflessness or show. Focusing attention on cultural and artistic charitable gestures, she considers a litany of recent donations and endowments – for instance Mr. Rockefeller's funding of a museum of antiquities in Egypt – and wonders also 'what species of self-exultation is evinced by the recent anonymous gift to one of our universities of a million dollars for the establishing of an art school?' Moore's gently polemical, and by no means water-tight conclusion, is that, 'It does seem to us that there is active today, an altruism which is disinterested' (CPMM, 169). This is a hunch, and tells us little about what might actually be at work, psychologically and economically, in the donations and endowments of American capitalists. What the piece does clearly point to, however, is Moore's highly self-conscious pursuit of a sustainable, non-profit-accruing mode of transmission. The desire for such a way of passing things on goes deep with her, running, I will argue, freely from her prose into her poetry. 'To part with a valuable thing without losing it,' she asserts in her Comment, 'bespeaks for this thing, a very special kind of value.' It is in that statement, one could argue, that Moore speaks to George Oppen's question; that what one does with an apple who likes apples is somehow to part with it without losing it. One has a sense, perhaps, of what she means to say, though that does not remove the difficulty of the operation. But then, as elsewhere she quotes Chesterfield as saying, '"The manner of giving shows the genius of the giver more than the gift itself"' (CPMM, 194).

So here's the argument: in the Comment pieces she wrote while editor of *The Dial* Marianne Moore strives to articulate a principle which goes to the core of her poetry. The principle has to do with the way writing handles that which it most values, where the objects of value are both things and words, and where the aim is somehow to be able to part with a thing without losing it. It is a thing of special value, she suggests, that permits such an operation, but the operation itself would also be special. It would be a special kind of giving, and Moore's genius, one might argue, following Chesterfield, is precisely to be found in the manner of her giving. But giving is only one language of transmission Moore turns to as she tries to articulate the principle at stake in her writing. Literary inspiration is another nomenclature, and charity is another. And another, as she gets into her stride as editor and as Comment writer, and as her conceptualising of her own aesthetic impulses develops, is what she wants to call enthusiasm.

Moore admires enthusiasm. Writing in the Comment of November 1926, she was pleased to welcome Children's Book Week, which 'bespeaks as annually, the irrelevantly necessary enthusiasm of grown people. ... If it is possible to be both hidebound and hospitable, children's books presented collectively can perhaps more than others, make one so' (CPMM, 175). The approval is qualified. The enthusiasm grown people show for children's books is irrelevant, but it is also necessary – it demonstrates something vital in them. A similar claim is made in her Comment of March 1927, where in this case the argument centres on happiness, and on how modern existence seems to militate against it. The pre-texts for the discussion are books presenting old New York: Mark Sullivan's *In Our Times* and Henry Collins Brown's *The Elegant Eighties*. It is with obvious relish – she sounds like the Whitman of *Specimen Days* – that Moore catalogues the things and places, the 'prides, misfortunes, and whims of one-time New York'. And 'as Greek architecture rendered domestic by Thomas Jefferson, seems colonial, New York seems as one reads of it ... national; and although an occasional rococo facetiousness scarcely augments vividness, one's rhetorical ear pardons to enthusiasm, incidental offenses' (CPMM, 180). The argument in this piece is more looping, digressive and artful than ever, but what it comes down to is a thesis about loss, about the way Modernity homogenizes culture. This is the argument, in part, of 'To a Steamroller' also, where the forces in question 'crush all the particles down / into close conformity'. In her Comment piece what Moore considers has been lost, for all its rococo facetiousness, is 'enthusiasm'.

This is not Thoreau's enthusiasm, and it is not Melville's: the term doesn't have here its mid-nineteenth-century charge. But it does have a charge, a charge which, as she developed her argument, was all Moore's own. Witness her discussion of a recent book about Caxton featuring his prologues and epilogues, where, as she sees it, 'The antique strengths and refinements of speech and thought in these originals kindle by their substance and manner, enthusiasm for exactness of production and depth of learning' (CPMM, 181). Enthusiasm here is, as it were, transitive rather than revelatory. It is for, and fixes on, things and artefacts, rather than being of the spirit. But precisely as she resists an aesthetic which, as she sees it, implies domination – precisely as, apparently, she prefers not to construe her work as an opening up to other forces – so she recognizes enthusiasm to constitute a different kind of circulation. In her clearest statement of the importance of art's circulatory role, the Comment she wrote for *The Dial* in February 1929 (shortly before the closure of the magazine), she opens with a statement of the privileges and values of the marginalized artist: 'When an artist is willing that the expressiveness of his work be overlooked by any but those who are interested enough to find it, he has the freedom in which to realize without interference, conceptions which he personally values' (CPMM, 214). Such private valuing, connoisseurship if you like, is not to be discounted; but nor, she wants to argue, is its apparent opposite, advertising. Here again she qualifies: it is not that she wants to put her name to such advertising as places a 'strain upon credulity', but

> The semi-confidential impartial enthusiasm of the pre-auction descriptive catalogue suggests a desirable mechanics of eulogy and the same kind of honor without exaggeration is seen occasionally in guide-books and travel bureau advertisements. (CPMM, 215)

Here, surely, is a portrait of Moore: 'semi-confidential', 'impartial', 'descriptive', hunting among the catalogues, the travel bureau publications and the guide books. These are the media she likes, those by which she holds out against art which 'confuses transcendence with domination', against art which construes enthusiasm as an act of self-surrender. And here it is that she articulates another version of enthusiasm, 'enthusiasm' as 'a desirable mechanics of eulogy'. The question here, as in Thoreau, Melville and Pound, is how to pass things on. The secret, as she observes, is to do so in such a way that one parts with a thing without losing it. Enthusiasm, as she construes it, is a way of conceiving of this. To enthuse about a thing is to enjoy it and to make it available to another person. Enthusiasm is a 'desirable mechanics of eulogy'. It is a way of liking one's apple and passing it on.

This double operation – valuing and transmitting – is central to Moore's poetry, to its key devices and techniques. It is as an enthusiast, I want to argue, that Moore gives such thought to the way she displays her materials; and it is as a Modern enthusiast, I would suggest, that she gives her poetry over so frequently to other people's words. To put this another way, Moore's defining innovations as a poet flow from the new construction she came to place on enthusiasm in her series of Comments, the accumulated arguments of which amplify, and so better enable one to appreciate, the principles she had been bumping up against in her poetry.

Displaying

So as to resist the analogy of collection, the image of Moore as poetic hoarder, the question was asked, following Oppen, 'How does one hold an apple / Who likes apples?' Moore's response to this question, the question of how one handles what one values, was to try, as she put it in her prose, to determine a way of parting with a thing without losing it, a way, in language, of holding (where holding means, in part, cherishing) and at the same passing on. This is a matter, in the fullest sense of the term, of presentation, of how one presents a thing, or, as it surfaced in Moore's poetry, a question of display. How, she wanted always to establish, should she best display the elements of her writing such that the poem might be understood not to be possessing them but to be passing them on. Or to put this another way, what operations in language best accommodated and articulated her kind of enthusiasm?

The question of how the elements of her writing might best be displayed informed all aspects of Moore's thinking about her work from the beginning. She deliberated much longer than most poets, for instance, on the question of publication, telling Pound, in the first letter she wrote to him, 'I do not appear', 'I grow less and less desirous of being published, produce less and have a strong feeling for letting alone what little I do produce. My work jerks and rears and I cannot get up my enthusiasm for embalming what I myself, accept conditionally.'[10] The far-reaching thought here is that poetry does not display itself well, that publication is not, as Emily Dickinson thought, an auction, but an embalming. The more pressing question was when, or whether, to publish a book. Robin Schulze tells this story best. In the course of charting the 'Becoming' of Marianne Moore, she documents how to Moore's great dismay HD and Bryher took the matter into their own hands and produced a pamphlet of poems under the imprint of The Egoist Press. Moore's response to Bryher was categorical: 'I had considered the matter from every point of view and was sure of my decision – that to publish anything now would not be to my literary advantage' (BMM, 24). Only, in fact, when the call had become irresistible, when Eliot and Pound had both written urging her to publish, and when *The Dial* had offered its annual award (worth $2000) should she take her book to them, did Moore consent to 'appear'. And when she did appear she was more than particular about how: *Observations* came, complete with an index and a set of supporting annotations, and the poems themselves came carefully revised, differing in numerous cases from their appearance in magazines.[11]

One further index of its importance in her earliest work is the fact of display as content, the fact of the number of earlier poems which have as their central purpose an exhibition. Take for instance 'To a Chameleon', the third poem in *Observations*:

> HID by the august foliage and fruit of the grape vine,
> Twine
>   Your anatomy
>   Round the pruned and polished stem,
>   Chameleon.
>   Fire laid upon
>   An emerald as long as
>   The Dark King's massy
> One,
> Could not snap the spectrum up for food as you have done.
>   (BMM, 53)

This is a poem all about display. The chameleon is a display animal, deploying display to accommodate the elements of its environment, showing those elements to its own best advantage. Then there is the matter of the poem's entwining form; few poets, probably, since George Herbert have given as much care as Moore evidently wanted her reader to know she had, to the question of how to present a poem. It is the formal aspect of Moore's sense of display that I want to concentrate on here, though not chiefly as that implies Herbert-like mimesis. 'To a Chameleon' is in every sense, as commentators have pointed out, an emblematic poem, where part of its value is to give emblematic expression to Moore's concern for presentation. It is not, however, typical; Moore was rarely aiming for that kind of copy. What she sought, rather, were formal principles which might best accommodate her desire to part with a thing without losing it; formal principles of interest here not least as they point towards the enthusiasms of the New York School. Take the miscellany, which perhaps Moore developed a fondness for through her reading in the seventeenth century, and the case for which she made in her *Dial* Comment of May 1927. 'Academic feeling,' she notes,

> or prejudice possibly, in favor of continuity and completeness is opposed to miscellany – to music programs, composite picture exhibitions, newspapers, magazines, and anthologies. Any zoo, aquarium, library, garden, or volume of letters, however, is an anthology. ... The science of assorting and the art of investing an assortment with dignity are obviously not being neglected. (CPMM, 182)

The question the miscellany goes to answer is how best to present things; how to present things in such a way that they are most clearly themselves. Its response is difference. An apple, say, is perhaps best presented in its appleness by placing it alongside an orange, or for that matter a sardine; or a newspaper cutting, or a flag. Perhaps the best setting for an apple, in fact, would be a painting by Robert Rauschenberg. The miscellanist judges that the art of presenting lies in large part in juxtaposition. Moore understood editing like this. When asked about the value of *The Dial*, she told Donald Hall:

> It was a matter of taking a liking to things. Things that weren't in accordance with your taste ... And we didn't care how unhomogenous they might seem. Didn't Aristotle say that it is the mark of a poet to see resemblances between apparently incongruous things.[12]

Moore is right about *The Dial*, and she is right in general about the literary magazine, that it serves its elements best by not caring for homogeneity; though this, of course, is to make a demand on the reader, to require the same discernment of him and her as Aristotle called for in the poet. But Moore's discussion of miscellany points towards her own writing also. Thus, 'However expressive the content of an anthology, one notes that a yet more distinct unity is afforded in the unintentional portrait given, of the mind which brought the assembled integers together' (CPMM, 183). 'Integer' is 'perfect diction': a thing whole in itself, it is the root of integral and integrity, where the element is considered in relation to the whole. Moore thus asks us, here, to imagine a mode of presentation in which each item is whole in and unto itself, but also of the whole, and where both, unintentionally perhaps, present a portrait of the assembling mind. Assembling integers, by this way of thinking, is an act of enthusiasm, a way of displaying things in order that their singular value might best be appreciated.

The principles of the miscellany flow freely into other of Moore's characteristic formal and procedural choices. As, for instance, in her fondness for the catalogue, indicated early by 'A Fool, a Foul Thing, a Distressful Lunatic', with its amplified list of conventionally mis-apprehended birds: the gander, the Egyptian vulture and the loon, between them gesturing towards 'folly's catalogue'. Barely distinguishable from the act of cataloguing is the act, characteristic of early Moore in particular, of amassing, as in the amassed countries (and conventional prejudices) in 'England', and the amassed animals of 'My Apish Cousins', and the amassed illustrations of 'When I Buy Pictures'. Here again, of course, in the mention of amassing, one would seem to be recasting Moore as a poetic collector, as if, to repeat, her intention was an imaginary private hoard. And it is precisely from such easy readings of her procedural innovations that the image of Moore as an acquirer emerges. The problem is to do with the reading – no poet's procedure is their whole story; but the problem is also to do partly with the language available to poets, critics, readers and citizens alike, for the description of people's relations to things. Amassing and accumulating are among the best words we have for describing how Moore proceeds in her poems, and neither, given their financial connotations, is an instance of perfect diction. Actually, probably, the word Moore wants for the way she handles things doesn't quite exist; I hope, of course, I am getting close to it by speaking of her enthusiasm. In practice, though, it is a motivating fact in Moore's career that there is no simple way of describing the relation – somehow parting with but not losing – she wants to have with words and things. It is out of this linguistic deficit, in other words, that the poems are written.

Take 'When I Buy Pictures', which is at every stage an argument with the implications of amassing, but which is also its freely acknowledged procedure. An argument is stated clearly at the beginning. She doesn't buy pictures; she imagines herself their possessor. But this isn't the whole argument because she hasn't sufficiently rewritten the relation – the image is still of possession. Closer to the nub of the argument is the suggestion, patiently articulated, that

> Too stern an intellectual emphasis upon this quality or that,
>   detracts form one's enjoyment;
> it must not wish to disarm anything; nor may the approved
>   triumph easily be honored –

that which is great because something else is small.
It comes to this: of whatever sort it is,
it must be "lit with piercing glances into the light of things";
it must acknowledge the spiritual forces which have made it.

I want to say two things in response to this. The first has to do with emphasis. What is being called – what Moore herself called – the practice of amassing has an implication for emphasis. The implication, as the assorted things are placed beside one another, is that none carries too stern an emphasis, that none is emphasized more than any other, that the poem is free, in its even-handedness and evenness of tone, from domination. 'When I Buy Pictures' is thus a poem about not dominating, a poem about having relations with things which do not depend – as buying does – on domination. The second thing I want to say, or at least hazard, is that right at the end there, with the requirement that any picture in question 'acknowledge the spiritual forces which have made it', Moore, in her poem about possession, falls back on enthusiasm. Enthusiasm, I want to say, can be about possession – the religious enthusiast can very well be thought of as possessed – but it can also be about transmission, about the desire to pass things on, freely to acknowledge that which has 'made' it. There isn't a single word, perhaps, for the way Moore handles things in her poems, but one of her words was enthusiasm, that good mechanics of eulogy, and not without reason.

In shifting, here, to the question of emphasis, as qualification of the implications of amassing, the discussion moves from questions of procedure to questions of form, a poem's formal properties being the province of its emphasis, or refusal to emphasize – the chief means it has of displaying and presenting. Beneath the mechanics of her procedure, then, are the articulations of Moore's formal innovations, all of which are dedicated to an equality of display. Take light rhyme, her keenness for which Moore described clearly to Donald Hall, and which Margaret Holley writes about expertly in *Marianne Moore: Voice and Value*.[13] 'I like light rhymes,' Moore told Hall, 'inconspicuous rhymes and unpompous conspicuous rhymes.' A shimmering instance of this is her poem 'The Fish', which one has to read more than once to appreciate that the machinery holding the poem together consists in part of a rhyme featuring the first word of each stanza. This word – the only word of the line – rhymes with the third and final word of the second line. Another isolated word, the fourth line, rhymes with the last word of the fifth. Sometimes the words are feature words, 'wade' and 'jade'; sometimes they are incidental, 'an' and 'fan'. They are conspicuous only as far as everything in the poem is conspicuous, the point of this poem about water being that nothing can 'hide / there for the submerged shafts of the // sun' (BMM, 85). That such a contrived rhyme scheme can manage not to insist upon itself has to do with emphasis, is a consequence of Moore's predilection for prose rhythms rather than metre. Nothing is emphasized, and so everything is emphasized; parts come variously into view. Or to put it another way, the poem doesn't dominate its integers: rather they are assembled, and held out, for the reader's pleasure.

One might, with justice, say a similar thing of Moore's collage poems, 'An Octopus' being her most striking instance of this, where the achievement of the work is precisely in the assembling of the integers. One might cite, for instance, the line

> comprising twenty-eight ice fields from fifty to five hundred feet thick
> of unimagined delicacy
>
> (BMM, 125)

where a part of speech taken, very likely, from a 'government pamphlet', or a natural history, sits uncompromisingly, and uncompromised, next to a seemingly lyric utterance. Or one might observe such listed elements as:

> the birch trees, ferns, and lily pads,
> avalanche lilies, Indian paint-brushes
> bears' ears and kittentails.
>
> (BMM, 128–9)

Here we are somewhere between *Walden* and James Schuyler's *Freely Espousing*, where what is being placed before us are instances in the natural word, but more so the words that are picking them out. Moore relishes the words, that's why she uses them, and so she hands them on as unmediated (by cadence, emphasis or formal intervention) as she is able. She takes the words into her poem – where she holds them out.

One might say a similar thing again for the shift, in Moore, from the mainly free verse of *Observations* to the syllabics of her poems of the 1930s, where artfully designed stanzaic forms advertise the poet's desire to display, and where the forms are derived from rigorous syllable counts; so rigorous that one can become obsessed by them, and can start thinking again of Moore as no more than a proceduralist, as a bureaucrat of poetry, dogging content with questions of inappropriate form. Except that so supple are Moore's unmetred rhythms, and so light her rhymed emphasis, that the effect of the forms is not to dominate language but to show it anew. Charles Tomlinson picks out an early example in 'Melanchthon' (titled 'Black Earth' in *Observations*), observing that, 'We are, among other details, made by her syllabic lay-out to take cognisance of the humbler components of language, the "to it" and the "with it"'.[14] To put this another way, in her miscellaneousness, her assorting, her amassing, her cataloguing and her beautiful handling of emphasis; in her syllabics and her stanza formation, her unmetred rhythms and her light rhymes, Moore composed poems thoroughly dedicated to the act of presentation, intricate machines, one might think, purpose built for the display of their own bits and pieces. In her determination not to dominate the assembled integers of her poems, to hold them forth for the reader's equal and maximum enjoyment, she arrived at a medium capable of parting with but not losing that which she valued. In other words, she perfected an expression of her enthusiasm.

Quoting

In the event, Moore was right to have worried about the question of publication. When her *Poems* as presented by HD and Bryher appeared, it was to largely unsympathetic, not to say hostile reviews. Writing in the *TLS*, Harold Child went to the heart of the issue, accusing her, as Schulze reports, of 'writing pointless, contrived poems' in order to conceal her lack of inspiration. Harriet Monroe compiled a 'symposium' of responses to her work, affording most space to commentators who concurred with Child's line. Marion Strobel complained: 'she makes us so conscious of her knowledge! And because we are conscious that she has brains, that she is exceedingly well-informed, we are the more irritated that she has not learned to write with simplicity' (BMM, 26). While Bryher, 'the woman who,' as Schulze observes, 'had funded her volume', wrote that 'The temperament behind the words is not a passive one. ... The spirit is robust, that of a man with facts and countries to discover and not that of a woman sewing at tapestries. But something has come between the free spirit and its desire' (BBM, 26). Moore was dismayed, but, to her credit, not discouraged by this reception, such that when she published *Observations*, she accentuated the aspects of her writing to which reviewers had taken exception. The book appeared with a more elaborate apparatus than even sophisticated readers of Modern poetry might have expected, extensive notes on the poems' sources being supplemented by a comprehensive index (to the poems and the notes) of titles, phrases, key words and names. Not that Moore's early reviewers should be dismissed. In their antagonism to her work, in their complaints about its lack of inspiration and its mediating knowledge, and in Moore's subsequent response to these complaints, a significant question was being raised: where, Moore and her critics were asking, should Modern poetry come from?

Moore's notes on her sources can seem a sufficient response to this question. The poems, Moore wants us to understand, have their origin very largely in her reading, whether as tributes to other writers, or more straightforwardly, in that her writing is made up of other people's words. The notes underline what the quotation marks in the poems already indicate. They also add to the whole enterprise a scholarly or antiquarian air, as if, again, Moore was principally a collector of texts. Her early reflections on the act of composition would seem to confirm the point. Thus, in 'The Accented Syllable', a short essay she wrote for *The Egoist*, which opens, delightedly, with a series of quotations – presenting the pleasures of other people's words – she quotes Butler on quotation: '"As I have said over and over again, if I think something that I know and greatly like (in music) no matter whose it is, is appropriate, I appropriate it."' (CPMM, 31). Poets often speak boldly of theft. Just as in 'When I Buy Pictures', however, where the issue was precisely that the speaker didn't buy pictures – that there was a linguistic deficit when accounting for the relation between people and things – so 'appropriation' is not a satisfactory metaphor for Moore's art of quotation, and not least as it underestimates the force the practice has in her work.

In part the underestimation has to do with the sheer density of quotation in Moore. Thus, as we have considered the enthusiasms of Thoreau, Melville and Pound, citation has naturally surfaced as a significant element in their practice. Each writer opened writing to others' words, with, in the order given, growing self-consciousness. In none of these cases, however, was quotation quite as integral to their compositional practice as it was to Moore. Moore's notebooks of quotation run to thirteen volumes, this in addition to the numerous conversation notebooks (a variation on the theme). What the metaphor of appropriation doesn't answer to in this practice, what her own remark about ideal phrasing doesn't reveal, is its programmatic quality. It wasn't only, in other words, that she would defer or resort to a preferable way of saying a thing when that saying occurred to her; it was that absorbing other people's words was a foundational element of the compositional process. Moore, this is to say, didn't simply clutch at previous ways of saying as they happened to suit, but, as will be observed, in her systematic use of quotation she reconfigured the source of the poem.

There is a further sense, however, in which appropriation is not an adequate metaphor for Moore's citational practice, taking us back to the notes which, as Margaret Holley has observed, are neither complete – Moore mentions some sources but not others – nor provide a full account of all the phrases they reference, for the reason that often Moore will have altered for the purposes of the poem the words that appear in the note. Sometimes, also, the note will contain other words, which promise and sometimes deliver context – the notes on the fur trade in relation to 'New York', for instance, carry the poem beyond itself and towards the 'experience' it means to catch – though not infrequently the additional annotation will serve only as a digression. As Holley puts it, therefore, what looks like 'transcription' in Moore is quite often 'transformation'. The idea of appropriation, with all the connotations and analogies attendant on it, is deficient as an account of the value of quotation to Moore, of the way it figures in the origins of the poem, of the way it alters her writing. Rather, as it stirs the compositional process it functions as the poetry's enthusiasm.

One way to think of this would be as citation standing in for inspiration, for the force and impulse Moore's early critics found her poetry to lack. And *Observations* does act out this substitution. Thus, a number of poems comment on their own emptiness or hollowness. In 'Pedantic Literalist', for instance, it is charged – Moore anticipating her reviewers – that

> What stood
> Erect in you has withered. A
> Little "palm tree of turned wood"
>> Informs your once spontaneous core in its
>> Immutable production.
>
> (BMM, 75)

Ironically, teasingly, the 'excerpt' is from Richard Baxter's 'The Saint's Everlasting Rest'. Thus, a text which deals with the presence of the divine is made to make up for the lack of that presence in Moore's poem. What stands in for inspiration, in other words, is quotation, and quite often what seems to be at issue in *Observations* is this kind of incorporation, others' words being used in proportion as the poems want (or repudiate) inspiration. This is one version of Moore's practice. 'An Octopus' and 'Marriage' are the prime instances of it, where in both cases the real subject matter – the sublime and love respectively – would conventionally, in poetry, imply an animating spirit. In both collage pieces, however, the sources of the poem are, to all intents and purpose, other agencies' remarks, citation thus standing in for inspiration.

But true as this sometimes seems, it is not the whole truth, the metaphor of substitution, like the metaphor of appropriation, underestimating the degree to which citation informs the making of the poem, the degree to which, in her reconfiguring of the act of composition, Moore allowed the practice of citation to operate on her imagination. To state this as a claim: a Moore poem, I would suggest, is often – much of her most substantial work is like this – a seeking after another voice, where the mind (and language) in which that voice might be articulated is achieved through the act of quotation, through opening the poem up to the words of other agencies; where agency might mean poets, or friends, or passers-by, or (more literally) government departments, or park authorities. To trace this from the point of inception, when asked how a poem starts for her, she said: 'A felicitous phrase springs to mind – a word or two'. From the beginning, the poem is understood as being open to other sources, 'words' as 'springs', 'springs' as 'words'. And frequently, and throughout, as the poem develops, those sources are in the manner of quotations. There is, she observed, in an essay on 'Sir Francis Bacon' and by way of a commentary on sources – on what sustains a poem – 'a renovating quality in the work of early writers, as also in so-called "broken" speech in which we have the idiom of one language in the words of another' (CPMM, 98). This is integral to the process of a Moore poem: invariably others' words renew her work; invariably her work consists, one way or another, in broken speech. Often, however, the object of a poem seems to be to avail itself of some other source still, which is not the poet, and which is not simply a borrowed phrase.

'My Apish Cousins' is a good example of this, as of various aspects of Moore's procedure. The poem consists of more or less uniform stanzas – subject to the limitation of page size in *Observations* – with the stanzas having as a key formal principle the unemphasized rhyme. The poem sustains itself by the procedure called here, for want of a better word, 'amassing' (in this case various animals and their characteristics), breaking part way through into a transformed quotation, the note to the poem recalling that, 'An old gentleman during a game of chess' remarked: '"It is difficult to recall the appearance of what one might call the minor acquaintances twenty years back"' (BMM, 139). The poem only makes part use of this remark, and it fragments what it uses, interspersing the old chess players' words with words we take to be the poem's own. All of this is by way of preparation for – as setting or prelude to – a speech which comes as if from nowhere:

> "They have imposed on us with
> their pale
> half fledged protestations, trembling about
> in inarticulate frenzy, saying
> it is not for us to understand art; finding it
> all so difficult, examining the thing
>
> as if it were inconceivably arcanic, as symmet-
> rically frigid as if it had been carved out of chrysoprase
> or marble – strict with tension, malignant
> in its power over us and deeper
> than the sea when it proffers flattery in exchange
> for hemp,
> rye, flax, horses, platinum, timber, and fur."
>
> (BMM, 82)

Even within the grammar of the poem it is not clear who or what this speech is spoken by – by the cat likened to Gilgamesh, or by its resolute tail. Actually, of course, it is spoken by neither, and in being spoken by neither is, in effect, spoken by nothing, or by something else altogether. What we approach here, in fact, is oracular speech. A speech, that is, which does not properly belong to any of the poem's available speakers, but which nonetheless speaks through the poem. It is a speech, as we are to understand, of 'inarticulate frenzy', a speech, as the poem implies, spoken from a point of view of seeming intellectual disadvantage; a speech which ends, Thoreau-like, by giving voice to things.

Numerous Moore poems arrive at this kind of outcome, seem to have it as their intention. Invariably, in other words, what the poem is aiming to do is give articulate form to an otherwise voiceless, or unconscious, agency or force, to give voice to a force informing the subject of the poem, or the poem itself – which prior to writing the poem wasn't available. 'Black Earth' is like this, with its beautiful expression of the 'element of unreason'. 'Critics and Connoisseurs', likewise, identifies forms of, and gives voice to, 'unconscious / fastidiousness'. 'Virginia Britannia' documents and quotes, and in its supreme moment, 'unable to suppress' the brown hedge-sparrow's 'reckless / ardor', 'flutes his ecstatic burst of joy' (PMM, 215). A Moore poem, in other words, characteristically sets out to voice something which would otherwise, but for the writing of the poem, be unavailable, opening itself to quotation in a compositional process which has as its object, as Henry James' phrase in 'New York' has it, '"accessibility to experience"'; to, as Moore's own magnificent phrase puts it, 'articulate unconscious force'.

This is not to mystify Moore. Rather it is to suggest how deep her practice of quotation goes. Quotation, to recapitulate, the availability of the poem to others' words, was an integral part of Moore's compositional process. It is the poem's source, stirring and making it possible. The poem is available to other voices. Such voices open it up. They are its openings, to use George Fox's suggestive phrase, and once open, the poem can construe itself as voicing that which otherwise it doesn't know. There is an analogy here with Thoreau, where the uttering of others' words, and of the language as others' words, permitted – as Thoreau hoped – the voicing of that which was prior to language. The difference is that, more even than in Thoreau, the focus of activity in Moore is not the writer but the writing, not the poet but the poem. It is the poem which is quite deliberately opened up to other voices, and the poem which through that process hopes for an '"accessibility to experience"'. Because, this is to say, not in spite of, its practice of citation, a Moore poem is understandable as an enthusiastic text.

Knowing

Marianne Moore was famously suspicious of poetry. Writing for the *Christian Science Monitor* under the heading 'Subject, Predicate, Object', she invoked her most memorable riposte against the medium – 'Of poetry, I once said, "I, too, dislike it"' – in order to set up the version of the poet she could not subscribe to: 'Dazzled, speechless – an alchemist, without implements – one thinks of poetry as a divine fire, a perquisite of the gods. … As said previously, if what I write is called poetry it is because there is no other category in which to put it' (CPMM, 504). Against this picture of the poet as enthusiast, 'dazzled, speechless … under the spell of admiration or gratitude', she took every opportunity to document her fastidiousness, remarking frequently on the labour and perseverance necessary for her to produce a poem. The work itself makes this labour manifest, her poems being among the most carefully achieved, closely wrought of the twentieth century. Following her prose commentaries, however, the argument has been that in her fastidiousness Moore reconfigured, or redirected, rather than eliminated the enthusiasm of the poem. Her abiding formal innovations – her remodelling of the poem as miscellany, and her calculation of the line in terms of syllables rather than feet – were designed, as was observed, to perfect a medium (in the sense, perhaps, of 'perfect diction') in which the elements of her writing might be presented as immediately as possible, that she might pass on that which she valued with minimum interference. When she suspected interference in her work, she eliminated it: 'Considering the stanza the unit, I came to hazard hyphens at the end of the line, but found that readers are distracted from the content, so I try not to use them.'[15] Ornate as they are, Moore's poems have as their utmost object direct communication. Her intricate mechanics are in the service of her enthusiasm, have as their ambition a medium capable of parting with a thing without losing it. Likewise, in the same breath as Moore extinguished the divine fire as a source of poetry, she incorporated quotation more wholeheartedly than any other poet, thus continuing to open her expression to other voices and so preserving (in her miscellanies, collages and assemblies) the image of an utterance shaped and sounded by another's words. More than this, though, quotation in Moore has been presented as kind of conduit, not back, retrogressively, to an inspirational voice, but to a voice, or voicing, which cannot properly belong either to the poet, or to her subjects: voices which are sometimes allocated to animals but which are in fact the poem's best expression of what she terms, in various ways, an unconscious force.

This brings us to an important disjunction in Moore, which can be figured in terms of consciousness and unconsciousness: a disjunction whereby the unconscious force is figured as speaking through highly conscious poetic form. There is a sense, in other words, in which Moore's poetry endeavours to speak what it doesn't know, to give expression to the 'element of unreason'. And it is here, importantly, that for all her erudition, Moore will often identify the basis of knowledge. Thus as with 'When I Buy Pictures', the point of her great poem 'Critics and Connoisseurs' seems to be to depart from, or to advance on, the language advertised by the poem's title. What the title describes are epistemologies to which the poem does not fully subscribe. It does not endorse either the critic's or the connoisseur's way of handling things. Instead it likes the childish attempt to make an 'imperfectly / ballasted animal stand up', and the swan's 'proclivity to more fully appraise such bits / of food as the stream // bore counter to it', and the 'ant carrying a stick, north, / south, east, west', only to go through 'the same course of pro- / cedure' with a 'particle of white-wash'. There is fastidiousness here, but an 'unconscious / fastidiousness', in which, as she states in the poem's beautifully ungainly opening, 'There is a great amount of poetry'. The poetry is in the 'ambition without / understanding', in the direct acquaintance each agent gains with their object, in an unalienated relation with, or handling of, things held to be of value.

Or to hear this from the horse's, which is to say the poet's, mouth: reviewing Mabel Loomis Todd's edition of the *Letters of Emily Dickinson* for *Poetry* in January 1933, Moore suggested that,

> The chief importance of the letters for us, however, is in their establishing the wholesomeness of the life. They are full of enthusiasm. (CPMM, 290)

Dickinson's abiding enthusiasm is, Moore concedes, a cause of dissatisfaction in some readers: 'To some, her Japanesely fantastic reverence for tree, insect, and toadstool is not interesting; many who are "helped" by a brave note, do not admire the plucked string' (CPMM, 292). For Moore, however, such reverence for things is integral to Dickinson's work:

> A certain buoyancy that creates an effect of inconsequent bravado – a sense of drama with which we may not be quite at home – was for her a part of that expansion of breath necessary to existence. (CPMM, 292)

What Moore wanted of her own writing, and what she admires in Dickinson, in the sense of the 'expansion of breath necessary to existence', is a poet's enthusiastic relation with things. With trees and insects, with imperfectly ballasted animals: with yellow helmets and papaya juice, as Frank O'Hara might have thought.

Notes

1 George Oppen, *New Collected Poems*, Manchester, Carcanet, 2003, p. 101.

2 See, for instance, Cynthia Stammy, 'Quotation, Curio-collecting, and the Privileging of Detail', in her *Marianne Moore and China: Orientalism and a Writing of America*, Oxford, Oxford University Press, 1999, pp. 164–95.

3 Marianne Moore, 'The Art of Poetry: Marianne Moore', in George Plimpton (ed.), *Poets at Work: The Paris Review Interviews*, Harmondsworth, Penguin, 1989, p. 86.

4 Lewis Hyde, *The Gift: Imagination and the Erotic Life of Property*, London, Vintage, 1999, p. 168.

5 Marianne Moore, *Becoming Marianne Moore: The Early Poems, 1907–1924*, Berkeley and Los Angeles University of California Press, 2002, p. 89; hereafter referred to in the text as BMM.

6 Marianne Moore, *The Complete Prose of Marianne Moore*, London, Faber and Faber, 1987, p. 95; hereafter referred to in the text as CPMM.

7 Margaret Holley, *The Poetry of Marianne Moore: A Study in Voice and Value*, Cambridge, Cambridge University Press, 1987, p. 73.

8 Moore, 'The Art of Poetry', pp. 84–5.

9 Ibid., p. 84.

10 Marianne Moore, 'A Letter to Ezra Pound', in Charles Tomlinson (ed.), *Marianne Moore: A Collection of Critical Essays*, Englewood Cliffs, NJ, Prentice Hall, p. 17.

11 An essay on Moore's enthusiasm might be the place for a discussion of what Schulman calls Moore's 'passion for revision', were the revisions not so numerous as to warrant separate rather than passing comment. Suffice to say here that what clearly mattered deeply to Moore was how, at any given moment, a poem should be displayed. To revise published poems was to keep them alive, to prevent 'embalming'.

12 Moore, 'The Art of Poetry', p. 92.

13 Holley, *Poetry*, pp. 21–2, 149–52, 160–2.

14 Tomlinson, *Marianne Moore*, p. 8.

15 Moore, 'The Art of Poetry', p. 85.

5

Circulating: Frank O'Hara

The day Frank O'Hara died, following an accident on Fire Island – he was struck by a beach buggy early in the morning of 24 July, 1966 – 'the New York art world was,' as Peter Schjeldahl has said, 'collectively thunder-struck. In 15 years as a poet, playwright, critic, curator, and universal energy source in the lives of the few hundred most creative people in America, Frank O'Hara had rendered that whole world unprepared to tolerate his passing.'[1] 'A center,' as the painter John Button put it, registering the magnitude of the shock, 'had gone out of our lives' (H, 43). At O'Hara's funeral Larry Rivers told the congregation, 'Frank O'Hara was my best friend. There are at least sixty people in New York who thought Frank O'Hara was their best friend' (H, 138). To gauge the significance of this, in *In Memory of my Feelings: Frank O'Hara and American Art*, Russell Ferguson passes on the received wisdom that the New York avant-garde of the 1950s and early 1960s consisted of no more than 300 people. The premature death of any significant artist is always mythologized, as the composer Morton Feldman eloquently observes in relation to Jackson Pollock: 'To die early was to make the biggest coup of all, for in such a case the work perpetuated not only itself, but also the pain of everybody's loss'. Even after making full allowance for this, for the desire of all those who knew the artist in question to ensure his or her continued status, there is no question that in New York between 1951 and 1966, Frank O'Hara fuelled an extraordinary creativity.

There are numerous testimonies to this. Feldman, like many creative friends, described O'Hara's impact in terms of his energy: 'It is only now that one sees the truth about this intellectual's intellectual ... only now one realizes it was his capacity for work, his stamina ... that was the energy running through his life' (H, 13). For Alex Katz, O'Hara seemed, at times, like

> a priest who got into a different business. Even on his 6th martini-second pack of cigarettes and while calling a friend, 'a bag of shit,' and roaring off into the

night. Frank's business was being an active intellectual. He was out to improve our world whether we liked it or not ... The frightening amount of energy he invested in our art and our lives made me feel like a miser. (H, 99)

One expression of that energy was, as Rivers indicated, O'Hara's capacity for intimacy, where intimacy meant not just friendship but a detailed understanding of the artist friend's work. Philip Guston recalls a conversation with O'Hara:

Frank was in his most non-stop way of talking; saying that the pictures put him in mind of Tiepolo ... Suddenly I was working in an ancient building now a warehouse facing the Giudecca. The loft over the Firehouse was transformed. It was filled with light reflected from the canal. I was a painter in Venice. (H, 101)

The point here is the transformation, just as when Feldman, speaking of the conditions necessary to creativity, observes that 'what really matters is to have someone like Frank standing behind you. That's what keeps you going' (H, 13). What both painter and composer are alluding to is what Renée Neu, Kenneth Koch and Donald Allen refer to as O'Hara's enthusiasm. 'Perhaps,' O'Hara wrote of a posthumous Yves Klein show, in his third Art Chronicle, 'not for a non-enthusiast.' 'But,' as he went on to remark, 'I don't care about them.'[2]

There is no apology to make for the attention given here to O'Hara's life, or for the recourse to the anecdotes in which it is recorded; much more than most artists', O'Hara's actions, especially in relation to others, were a continuation of his aesthetic. This must, in part, have been why Bill Berkson and Joe LeSueur considered *Homage to Frank O'Hara* a necessary book, because the sum of his aesthetic was to be found not just in his writing, but also in his actions to which only friends and contemporaries could testify. It is an aesthetic they identify as Pasternakian, the book opening with an epigraph from *Doctor Zhivago* in which Zhivago (as O'Hara had quoted in his review 'Zhivago and his Poems') speculates that 'You in others – this is your soul'. Which said, however, and keeping his vital effect on others firmly in mind as an intentional consequence of his aesthetic, O'Hara's enthusiasm found its fullest expression in the writing itself. Koch wrote that 'His presence and his poetry made things go on around him, which could not have happened in the same way if he hadn't been there.' The early poem 'Easter,' he recalls, in his 'Note on Frank O'Hara in the Early Fifties', 'burst on us all like a bomb' (H, 27). Which is not to suggest, again, that the enthusiasm of O'Hara's writing is only to be identified in the responses it produced, and produces, in readers. What I want to argue, rather, is that the dynamic, sustaining and circulatory effect O'Hara had on the New York art world of the 1950s and 1960s flowed from the fact that, as he remodelled poetry to make it viable in the middle of the twentieth century, it was explicitly in terms of the modes and conventions of enthusiasm that he did so. This is apparent in the poems themselves, where the themes of immediacy, intimacy, directness and acquaintance that have constituted this book's reading of American literary enthusiasm find clear, deliberate and beautiful expression. It is apparent also, however, in the criticism, and in particular in a number of prose works he wrote between 1958 and 1962 – his book on Jackson Pollock, his review of Pasternak, reviews of Guston and Helen Frankenthaler, 'Personism: A Manifesto' – in which he quite self-consciously articulated and rearticulated a contemporary version of enthusiasm. These prose pieces are culminations, expressions of long-standing artistic interests, written at a moment when O'Hara was more than ever sure of how he had reconfigured the poetic act. O'Hara was able to have the effect on others that he did because more than any writer since Thoreau he explored the meanings of enthusiasm.

Painting

A significant difference between Frank O'Hara and Ezra Pound, who in their roles as artistic galvanizers had much in common, is that whereas when Pound arrived in London he had to create the movement which would generate the new demands to which, as he understood it, poetry should now look to respond, when O'Hara arrived in New York the movement had already begun – not in poetry, but in painting. As he told Edward Lucie-Smith:

> When we all arrived in New York or emerged as poets in the mid 50s or late 50s, painters were the only ones who were interested in any kind of experimental poetry and the general literary scene was not. Oh, we were published in certain magazines and so on, but nobody was really very enthusiastic except the painters. (SS, 3)

The painters, O'Hara specifies, 'the Abstract Expressionists in particular', acted as an '*example*', giving him the feeling that 'one should work harder and should really try to do something other than just polish whatever talent one had been recognised for, that one should go further' (SS, 3). The evidence of their example is *The Collected Poems*, testifying as the book does not only to O'Hara's willingness to work, his sheer productivity, but also to the relentless pursuit of the new and the better; early technical exercises giving way to the surrealist slabs of such poems as 'Second Avenue', giving way in turn to the 'I do this, I do that' poems, and then to the *Odes*, and then to the *Love Poems*. O'Hara worked harder, and went further, and what resulted was not just a style, but a series of radically different practices. In gratitude for their example, O'Hara took every opportunity, in his art criticism, to document the painters' value. Thus, for example, 'Despite the high level of ambition and execution witnessed in almost every country since the war,' O'Hara wrote with reference to Norman Bluhm, 'few artists can give to us that immensity and density which allows our spirits to elaborate and to founder, to leap and to fall back, with hope' (SS, 94). Likewise of Franz Kline, whose

> work embodies those qualities of individuality, daring and grandeur which have made the movement a powerful influence. The painters of this movement ... have given us as Americans an art which for the first time in our history, we can love and emulate, aspire to and understand. (SS, 89)

The poem of this relationship is 'Radio', in which, 'mortally tired', O'Hara calls on the radio for 'a little reminder of immortal energy'. All week long, he writes,

> while I trudge fatiguingly
> from desk to desk in the museum
> you spill your miracles of Grieg
> and Honegger on shut-ins.[3]

The poem turns on the verb, there in the third line, as if at its best the radio cannot help but issue marvels, as if, in its uncensored state, like a painter perhaps, it will spill miracles into the world. Except that at weekends, for whatever meanness of programming, it doesn't, and so it is to painting O'Hara has to turn:

> Well, I have my beautiful de Kooning
> to aspire to. I think it has an orange
> bed in it, more than the ear can hold.

The painting's value lies in the aspiration it produces, just as Kline produces aspiration, and where the source of the aspiration lies in the works' 'daring and grandeur', the permission it gives for 'our spirits to elaborate and to founder, to leap up and to fall back, with hope,' occasionally, perhaps, to spill miracles. Which steers us, unmistakably, into the territory of enthusiasm. Just as he enthused Guston, so O'Hara is enthused by the example of the painters; and it is, we should notice, enthusiasm in its most empowering form, that state of mind which prompted Emerson to ask, 'What is a man good for without enthusiasm? and what is enthusiasm but this daring of ruin for its object?', and which obliged Kant to observe: 'This state of mind appears to be sublime: so much so that there is a common saying that nothing great can be achieved without it'.[4] It was out of precisely this state of mind that, as O'Hara presented it repeatedly in his art criticism, the Abstract Expressionists issued their example.

O'Hara was a singular and deliberate art critic, asking questions that criticism, in its continuing preoccupation with hermeneutics, can too often neglect. Chief among these was how to present that which one values, his response to which, and his preferred critical practice, was to acquaint and reacquaint the reader with the work's own terms. This was his habit also when, rarely, he discussed his own work. As, for instance, in his 'Notes on Second Avenue', where in response to an editor's request for clarification of the poem, O'Hara attaches 'notes' to some 'excerpts': 'the remarks are explanatory of what I now feel my *attitude* was toward the material, not explanatory of the meaning which I don't think can be paraphrased' (SS, 37). In fact, very little sense is given of O'Hara's 'attitude' towards the material. Rather, extracts from the material are given minimal re-presentation, episodes being identified formally as 'a little Western story', 'a talk with a sculptor (Larry Rivers)', 'a description of a Grace Hartigan painting' (SS, 37–9). Coming as a critic to his own creation, O'Hara's question is not how can the work be explained, but how can it be positioned, or repositioned, such that its audience is most likely to gain acquaintance with it?

One might think of this as a curator's question, and it is as a responsible curator that O'Hara sometimes wrote, asking questions of galleries, museums and more generally of public arts policy, which were designed to ensure the best possible dissemination of works of value. As when he addresses the Lincoln Center on the question of sculpture. 'Modern American sculpture,' he urges the City Fathers responsible for the Lincoln Center,

> is presently at a very great height of development: what other country today can offer us such a splendid and brilliant array of masters . ... Most of these men, as in the case of Smith and Nakian, either have executed, or have projected, work of a scale and grandeur which cannot at present be accommodated in either our public or private situations. ... Lincoln Center is one of the few foreseeable possibilities to rectify this situation and, in so doing, allow our sculptors to make real their dreams, dreams which follow so closely Keats' great aspiration: 'I am ambitious of doing the world some good' (SS, 135)

As with Pound, it is a great virtue of O'Hara's criticism that he should sometimes address himself to policy makers on the question of presentation, and for O'Hara, as for Pound, this practical question of how best to acquaint the public with new work is also a matter of aesthetics. Hence his much quoted remark:

> In a capitalist country fun is everything. Fun is the only justification for the acquisitive impulse ... Abstract expressionism is not [fun], and its

justifications must be found elsewhere. Not to say it as justification, but simply as fact, abstract expressionism is the art of serious men. They are serious because they are *not* isolated. So out of this populated cavern of self come brilliant, uncomfortable works, works that don't reflect you or your life, though you can know them. Art is not your life, it is someone else's. Something very difficult for the acquisitive spirit to understand. (SS, 129)

There is an enthusiast's question in all of this, the question of what do with what one values, how to part with something, as Marianne Moore puts it, without losing it. It is a question here for museums, where the issue is how a public institution enables the requisite intimacy between work and audience. It was a question, also, for writing and publishing, for the choices O'Hara made about when and where to show his work, how to mediate it in such a way that an intimacy might be preserved between work and reader. Chiefly, though, it was a question for criticism, O'Hara aiming always to present the object in its own terms.

In particular, what O'Hara sought to familiarize his readers with was the creative or compositional process, a critical practice with him which amounted to a method. Thus if, as often as not, the question Pound was asking in his prose was 'What calls for poetry?', O'Hara's question, dispensing with the trace of passivity implicit in Pound's stance towards subject matter, was invariably 'What makes art happen, what fuels the creative process?' This is a question central to his poetry also, the point of an O'Hara poem being, as often as not, that it has found, in some unlikely situation, material on which poetry can feed. In the best of his criticism what the question leads to is a discussion conducted at the level of the creative process itself, showing the numerous applications and technical decisions that go into the making of a work of art. Which might seem to cast O'Hara as a Sontag-like critic before the fact, Sontag, in 'Against Interpretation', dismissing hermeneutic criticism in favour of accounts of the work's surface.[5] What O'Hara effects, however, is not an account of materials as opposed to meanings, but an account of *creation* as opposed to meanings, his model of criticism acquainting the reader with the work by showing how it happens.

His painstaking account of Fairfield Porter painting his daughter's portrait is a prime instance of this. The discussion is concerned with the numerous decisons that contribute to the making of the painting, as when, to sample the method, he notes how:

For the first oil sketch he used sized canvas but did not spread it with medium first, as is often done, because it makes colors blend more than he wanted them to. ... Instead, he merely mixed his tube colors with medium and applied them direct, drawing with the brush, a No.16 sable (he also uses oxhair and bristle brushes, finding oxhair a nice mean between bristle stiffness and sable softness). (SS, 54)

The issue here is the detail, the fundamental point about Porter's *Portrait of Katherine* being not what it signifies but that it exists, which means that the critic has to allow the reader to appreciate how it came into being. Likewise, and in case this seems just to be a point about the conventions of art criticism, in his sleeve notes to recordings of works by Morton Feldman, O'Hara inducts the reader into the process and markings that make the sounds (Sontag's surface) happen. Thus 'Intersection 3 for Piano' is

> A graph piece, it is totally abstract in its every dimension. Feldman here successfully avoids the symbolic aspect of sound which has so plagued the abstract works of his contemporaries by employing unpredictability reinforced by spontaneity – the score indicates 'indeterminacy of pitch' as a direction for the performer. (SS, 116)

Following which, for the direction of the reader, O'Hara presents the graph which is the music's pictorial life.

What these discussions underscore is O'Hara's commitment to technique, where technique means not the application of given rules, but the evolution of a method of composition which one might call a style, but which is really the process by which the artist's creativity is made possible. Which is to say that whereas O'Hara is implacably opposed to art understood as the performance of conventions, his enthusiasm is absolutely not opposed to technical proficiency. Rather, and quite the opposite, technical decision making is necessary for the operation of the artistic impulse. This is nowhere clearer than in his account of Feldman, where discussion of the graphic inner life of the music guides O'Hara to the creative wellspring itself, O'Hara taking great care to demonstrate how creativity is possible. Thus,

> I interpret this 'metaphysical place', this land where Feldman's pieces live, as the area where spiritual growth can occur, where the form of a work may develop its inherent originality and the personal meaning of the composer may become explicit. In a more literal way it is the space which must be cleared if the sensibility is to be free to express its individual preference for sound and to explore the meaning of this preference. That the process of finding this metaphysical place of unpredictability and possibility can be a drastic one is witnessed by the necessity Feldman felt a few years ago to avoid the academic ramifications of serial technique. Like the artists involved in the New American painting, he was pursuing a personal search for expression which could not be limited by any system. (SS, 115–16)

O'Hara could hardly be more deliberate in picturing creative work as a technical procedure, the object of which is a casting off of system in favour of an intimate acquaintance with the unpredictable promptings which constitute the force of the work. And in Feldman, crucially, the aim is to pass on this intimacy; hence his presentation of the music in terms of graphs not notes. Feldman's 'courageous assumption', as O'Hara sees it, is that 'the performer is a sensitive and inspired musician', and so his 'music sets in motion a spiritual life which is rare in any period and especially so in ours' (SS, 119, 120).

The tenor of this is clear, but it is clearer still in O'Hara's book on Jackson Pollock, where again O'Hara is keen to emphasize technique. Thus Pollock's glorious lines demonstrate his skill as a draughtsman, 'his amazing ability to quicken a line by thinning it, to slow it by flooding it', where again the object of the technique is the capacity to articulate that which in his creative state Pollock is capable of conveying. Thus,

> In the state of spiritual clarity there are no secrets. The effort to achieve such a state is monumental and agonizing, and once achieved it is a harrowing state to maintain. In this state all becomes clear, and Pollock declared the meanings he had found with astonishing fluency, generosity and expansiveness. This is not a mystical state, but the accumulation of decisions along the way and the eradication of conflicting beliefs toward the total engagement of the spirit in the expression of meaning. ... [T]he artist has reached a limitless space of air and light in which the spirit can act freely and with unpremeditated knowledge.[6]

Or as he puts it later:

> the action of inspiration traces its marks of Apelles with no reference to exterior image or environment ... It is the physical reality of the artist and his activity of expressing it, united to the spiritual reality of the artist in a oneness which has no need for the mediation of a metaphor or symbol. It is Action Painting. (AC, 35)

There are two things to observe about these remarks. The first is that, in the fullness of his admiration for Pollock, O'Hara puts behind him, artistically speaking, the Catholicism of his youth. Pollock articulates his inspiration without the mediation of metaphor or symbol, action painting being, in this respect, the art equivalent of religious enthusiasm. What is at issue here is proximity to the creative impulse. The object of action painting was to arrive at a technique – by way, largely, of rejections of technique – which permits as direct an expression as possible of that impulse. Pollock's paintings work because he was prepared to risk ruin in pursuit of this object, and because, therefore, there is nothing bogus in the claim of intimacy with the impulse to act. Or as O'Hara quotes Pollock as saying:

> When I am *in* my painting, I am not aware of what I'm doing. It is only after a sort of 'get acquainted' period that I see what I have been about. I have no fears about making changes, destroying the image, etc., because the painting has a life of its own. I try to let it come through. (AC, 39)

Finally, in this vein, consider O'Hara on Helen Frankenthaler, whose delicate and troubling work he reviewed in 1959: 'This sensibility is inclusive and generous, free-ranging and enthusiastic. One of her strengths is this very ability to risk everything on inspiration, but one feels that the work is judged afterward by a very keen and erudite intelligence' (AC, 121). Faced with the crucial decision for the contemporary artist, as O'Hara sees it, of 'whether to "make the picture" or "let it happen"', Frankenthaler's preference is to let it happen, where again technique is what allows the happening, and as a consequence of which she is able to be 'a daring painter … willing to risk the big gesture, to employ huge formats so that her essentially intimate revelations may be more fully explored and delineated' (AC, 125). It is this, perhaps, that carries over most directly from O'Hara's account of painters to the execution of his own work, his poetry aiming invariably at an intimate communication issued against the background of huge, abstract social and historical forces. More generally, as O'Hara presents it, Frankenthaler, Pollock and Feldman – and for that matter Kline, Motherwell and David Smith – are, artistically speaking, enthusiasts. Or to put it another way, O'Hara is immaculate in his reconstruction of the enthusiastic position, detailing precisely the intimacy, immediacy, directness, aversion to system and acquaintance with the creative impulse that constitutes enthusiasm in all its historical occurrences. So much so that, whereas with Pound one had to read his enthusiasm against his terminology, with O'Hara it is possible, through the deliberateness of his formulations, to name him an enthusiast.

Writing

In what has gone already, I have talked about the enthusiasm with which O'Hara embraced and motivated the New York art world of the 1950s and 1960s, and have shown enthusiasm to be a principle of his criticism – as the way he chose to articulate the creativity of a number of artists he intensely admired. The point now is to establish enthusiasm as a principle of O'Hara's own creative work, how it featured in and guided the composition of his poetry, and again it is helpful to draw a distinction between him and Pound. Thus, where Pound's innovations in writing were principally formal, the object being to arrive at a form that would accommodate the material which called for poetic attention, it was not his object, on the whole, to remodel the act of writing itself (save perhaps by default in *The Pisan Cantos*, composed as they partially were at the DTC). O'Hara remodelled the act. Inspired, perhaps, by the example of Pollock, who didn't so much change the content of painting as rethink the whole way painting was done, O'Hara sought new ways of doing writing, the intention of which was a reconfiguration of the relation between writer, poem and world. It is this reconfiguration of writing itself that I want to dwell on now, fundamental as O'Hara's changing sense of the act of composition is to questions of audience, content and theme in his work. And the claim I want to make is that as he sought ceaselessly to reconfigure the act of writing, his question was how, after the example of Pollock, one might arrive at a properly poetic, which is to say linguistically honest, articulation of enthusiasm.

It is arguable that early in O'Hara's career, Pollock served not just as an example, but as a model. Thus, among the aspects of Pollock O'Hara admires, as with other Abstract Expressionists, is the scale of the work, and in his book on Pollock he recalls that many painters of the New York School 'worked on the mural projects' of the Federal Arts Project, suggesting that 'this experience had an effect on [their] pictorial ambitions' (AC, 34). 'Scale,' as O'Hara notes, 'has a particular significance in Pollock's work,' having principally to do with 'the emotional effect of the painter upon the spectator'. This is the sublime, of course, and as such steers us towards the aspect of Pollock's enthusiasm which is most dubious: his propensity to be dominated by the work, and so in turn to dominate the viewer, to effect an overpowering intimacy, a tyranny as Locke would have called it. There are O'Hara poems which appear to have this ambition, works such as 'Easter', 'Hatred' and 'Second Avenue', where the intention is precisely to change the scale of the poem, as if the poem, in its proportions, could emulate 'that immensity and density which allows our spirits to elaborate and founder'. 'Second Avenue' is an immense work: it calls for a large and airy space; it requires ramps and walkways so that readers might become familiar with it as an edifice, so that they might become acquainted with its constitutive parts. This is what the notes were for, a way of coming at the work from a different angle. Even so, 'Second Avenue' doesn't have the impact of a Bluhm or a Pollock, poetry having as its principal mode of existence time. O'Hara later came to a profound understanding of this fact, as Geoff Ward has argued so insightfully in relation to his lyrics.[7] In the case of 'Second Avenue', however, the time it takes to read the poem militates against a Pollock-like immediacy of effect.

One might argue that in its mode of expression also 'Second Avenue' resembles Pollock, that in the extended syntax and the onrush of diction there is an analogy with Pollock's line. But the analogy founders as soon as it is made because the brush-stroke, or wrist action, carries over into the spectator's consciousness with a directness that the key-stroke on the typewriter can't very well emulate, the connotativeness of language making it pale, as a medium, by comparison with paint. A closer, more viable model for the outpouring of 'Second Avenue' is Surrealism, early O'Hara unquestionably demonstrating, even as it looks to go beyond, verbal qualities characteristic of Surrealism: syntax-busting sentences, irrational semantics, a willed variousness of diction and a high regard for the workings of the imagination as opposed to experience. And Surrealism can look very much like a mode of enthusiasm, like the verbal enthusiasm that results from the enthusiast's departure from, or abandonment of, the mechanisms of reason. Thus Breton can sound very much like an enthusiast when, in his first *Manifesto of Surrealism*, he recalls:

> Completely occupied as I still was with Freud at that time, and familiar as I was with his methods of examination which I had had some slight occasion to use on some patients during the war, I resolved to obtain from myself what we were trying to obtain from them, namely, a monologue spoken as rapidly as possible without any intervention on the part of the critical faculties, a monologue consequently unencumbered by the slightest inhibition and which was, as closely as possible, akin to *spoken thought*.[8]

Such a monologue, were you to hear it, might well sound like an enthusiastic utterance, like sceptical witnesses of early Quakers reported them as sounding, like Pip sounds – jabbering – after he has been abandoned by Stubb. And there *are* similarities: Surrealism conceived itself as a response to the Kantian view of the mind, endeavouring to bypass the critical faculties in its aim of establishing an intimacy with a creative impulse. But there are crucial differences also, implicit in Breton's statement early in the *Manifesto* that 'The mere word "freedom" is the only one that still excites me. I deem it capable of indefinitely sustaining the old human fanaticism'.[9] The divergence lies in the different problems in Kant to which Breton as opposed, say, to Thoreau, looks to respond. The problem Thoreau identifies is alienation, as proposed by the *Critique of Pure Reason*, from the thing itself – from which point of view, the point of view of Thoreauvian enthusiasm, Surrealism compounds the problem. Thus, the claim enthusiasm makes is to know better something that is external to the self, God originally, but, following Romanticism's repositioning of the Divine, nature as it stands for the world. The claim Surrealism makes is that the mind knows itself better, with the effect that external things – Thoreau's beans, for instance – are rendered less, not more, available to thought and language. Invigorating as it can be then, and significant as it no doubt was as a provocation to O'Hara, Breton's 'freedom' is secured at a cost; the cost being, as he elsewhere confesses, the arbitrariness of the word. Which is not to argue that O'Hara thinks of the word as not, in some sense, arbitrary – the word, for him, doesn't promise a correspondence – but that his enthusiasm, like Thoreau's, was for (and of) that which lies outside the imagination.

Enthusiasm, by this way of thinking, looks not to abandon reason, but to supplement it precisely where it must acknowledge itself – from a Kantian point of view – to be deficient, looking to step just so far into the world as to become acquainted with things. In this respect one aspect of Surrealist practice was crucial to O'Hara's innovation in writing, Surrealism having injected into literary expression an unprecedented speed. Thus Breton aimed for a 'monologue spoken as rapidly as possible ... which was, as closely as possible, akin to spoken thought'. Breton, in other words, wants to speak, or write, as quickly as thought. O'Hara, glad, no doubt of the Surrealist example of speed, and not least because speed, in conversation and writing, came very naturally to him, wants to go even quicker. The impression, in early O'Hara in particular, is that poetry is moving faster than thought. Thus as 'Second Avenue begins it *is* possible to hear an argument taking shape:

> Quips and players, seeming to vend astringency off-hours
> celebrate diced excesses and sardonics, mixing pleasures,
> as if proximity were staring at the margin of a plea ...
>
> This thoroughness whose traditions have become so reflective,
> your distinction is merely a quill at the bottom of the sea
> tracing forever the fabulous alarms of the mute
> so that in the limpid tosses of your violet dinginess
> a puss appears and lingers like a groan from the collar
> of a reproachful tree whose needles are tired of howling.
>
> (CP, 139)

I think I know what is being contested here. I think I know that the traditions the poem mentions, in their tendency to reflection, have ceased to be intimate with something, have lost 'proximity' or nearness. I know also, however, that if I carry on thinking like this the poem will run away from me, that the poem has thinking in it, but that it outpaces thought; and this is reasonable, because if reflection has a tendency to alienate writing, or the mind, from things, then one response would be to move so quickly from thing to thing that reflection cannot take hold. It would be good to think that this is what O'Hara means when, in the first of his poems 'On Rachmaninoff's Birthday', he shouts:

> Quick! a last poem before I go
> off my rocker.
>
> (CP, 159)

Going off his rocker would imply not knowing the world; by way of an alternative, the poem is his way of knowing, 'My pocket / of rhinestone, yoyo, carpenter's pencil, / amethyst, hypo, campaign button' (CP, 159). Whether or not this is right, certainly it is true that as he reconfigured the act of writing he considered it necessary for poetry to be quick, 'Dashing

the poems off,' as Ashbery puts it, 'at odd moments – in his office at the Museum of Modern Art, in the street at lunchtime or even in a room full of people' (CP, vii).

'On Rachmaninoff's Birthday' points towards a more direct sense in which O'Hara's object, as he experimented, was to evolve a way of expressing his enthusiasms; his enthusiasm in that poem (for Rachmaninoff) being the substance of the poem. If the question is 'What fuels poetry?', then in that case the answer is Rachmaninoff, O'Hara's enthusiasm for whom fuelled, through his lifetime, seven birthday poems. He created in this way from very early in his career. 'Memorial Day 1950', for instance, his first poem in *The Collected Poems* to name names, does what many New York School poems do in telling the history of its own coming into being. 'Picasso,' the poem begins, 'made me tough and quick, and the world', the ambiguity making it uncertain whether the world also made O'Hara, or whether Picasso made the world. Either way, the poem goes on to mention numerous other figures who have been significant in O'Hara's development: Gertrude Stein, Max Ernst, Paul Klee, Auden, Rimbaud, Pasternak, Apollinaire. You could call these figures influences, but that implies mysterious, only partly conscious mental processes, and O'Hara's way of dealing with them is much more direct than that. To put it simply, he enthuses:

> O Boris Pasternak, it may be silly
> to call to you, so tall in the Urals, but your voice
> clears our world, clearer to us than the hospital:
> you sound above the factory's ambitious gargle.
>   (CP, 18)

Enthusiasm, as 'Memorial Day 1950' tells it, and as it records the history of its own coming into being, is the stuff of poetry. And it explicitly remained so for O'Hara. Any number of poems are acts of homage – to Wyatt, to Schoenberg, to Mondrian, to name but three. Many are expressly 'To' friends: Jane, John Ashbery, Larry Rivers, John Wieners. Sometimes the object of his affection – Edwin Denby, Elaine de Kooning – is built into the fabric of the poem in the manner of an acrostic. Many times the poem gives voice to the enthusiasm of an occasion, 'John Button Birthday', for instance, or 'Poem Read at Joan Mitchell's'. Then there are the *Odes*, to people, objects and ideas. And then there were the *Lunch Poems*, lunch, as the dust-jacket had it, being the poet's 'favourite meal ...'. In all of these cases a formal decision is at stake, and in some cases – as in the occasional poems, poems to friends that were incorporated into letters, and especially the *Lunch Poems* – what is also at issue is the act of writing. In all cases the poem has the form and mode of production that it does because O'Hara is trying to catch or articulate an enthusiasm.

Chiefly, however, and much more broadly than all of this, what O'Hara was enthusiastic for was life itself – which would sound an impossibly vague and naive claim were it not that so many people who knew him and observed him working stated it to be the case. Thus as Joe LeSueur puts it towards the end of *Digressions on Some Poems by Frank O'Hara*, commenting on O'Hara's indifference – which I will come on to – to publication: 'As to his being indifferent about publication, it made perfect sense: it allowed him to embrace life, not careerist concerns, and it was through his everyday experiences that a poem might come to him'.[10] What I want to suggest in response to this remark is that 'life' – that which was going on around him – operated as a formal principle in and for his writing. Or rather that the form his writing often and most characteristically took, owed to the enthusiasm with which O'Hara's poetry disposed itself towards life; where 'life' has a quite specific value – a value as specific as 'nature' had for the Romantics – and where the claim can best be understood with reference to O'Hara's reading of Pasternak.

Among the prose pieces O'Hara wrote in the late 1950s and early 1960s, and in particular among the pieces he wrote in the period 1958–59, when critically he seemed especially certain of what poetically he had discovered, 'Zhivago and his Poems' is the only piece about a writer. As such, and as a piece about a figure he admired just as intensely as he admired Pollock, the review is unique in articulating what enthusiasm might mean for a writer, as opposed to a painter or the artist in general. In his writing on Pasternak, in other words, O'Hara conducts the enthusiasm which was his critical response to, and assessment of, painting into a statement of its value for, and operability in the medium of, the written word. The review articulates two aspects of the Russian writer's – and also O'Hara's – manner that can be thought of as enthusiastic. The first is identifiable in Zhivago's reflection, quoted by O'Hara, that:

> However far you go back in your memory, it is always in some external, active manifestation of yourself that you come across your identity – in the work of your hands, in your family, in other people. And now listen carefully. You in others – this is your soul. This is what you are. This is what your consciousness has breathed and lived on and enjoyed throughout your life – your soul, your immortality, your life in others. (SS, 102)

This remark catches O'Hara's enthusiasm in action: being and becoming himself when in circulation, inspiring others such that – though this is not the calculation – they enthuse about him; setting, as he said of Morton Feldman's music, 'the sprit in motion'; disseminating his values through his friends and contemporaries; passing things on, keeping life in motion. This, then, is O'Hara's enthusiasm as it acts in his social existence, as the mechanism by which he becomes intimate with others.

More intriguing, however, is O'Hara's presentation of Pasternak's relation with the external world. The discussion follows a consideration of Pasternak's assessment of Mayakovsky, the central thrust of which is that Mayakovsky misconstrued his relation to life: that as an avant-garde artist in the Romantic mode he took life to be a background to his actions, as the mediocrity against which his purpose was formed. This, of course, is a common artistic myth. Pound, for instance, too often fell victim to an image of life which counterposed it to the artist and which, as a consequence, alienated the one from the other. Pasternak, by contrast like O'Hara, has as his ambition an integrated art. Hence O'Hara's question:

> What, then, after rejecting the concept of the Romantic 'pose' in relation to his own life and art, does Pasternak's position become? He had already moved towards this decision in the poems written previous to 1917 and in a later volume he chooses the title from a poem, 'My Sister Life'. This expresses very clearly his position: the poet and life herself walk hand in hand. Life is not a landscape before which the poet postures, but the very condition of his inspiration in a deeply personal way: 'My sister, life, is in flood today ...' This is not the nineteenth-century Romantic identification, but a recognition. (SS, 102)

This 'recognition' imposes a burden on the poet, because as O'Hara sees it:

> In the post-epilogue book of poems we find that Zhivago has not written the poems he wanted to; nor the poems we expected ... in the course of creating the poems he has become not the mirror of the life we know, but the instrument of its perceptions, hitherto veiled. (SS, 106)

We can see O'Hara in this, I think, in the image of poet and life walking hand in hand, but also in the suggestion that 'life is ... the very condition of his inspiration', O'Hara's object, as he reconfigured the act of writing, being precisely to get as close to the 'condition of his inspiration' as possible. Hence the fact that he would type out a poem in the middle of a party, or on an aeroplane, or mid-conversation, or at work in the Museum of Modern Art. What O'Hara's enthusiasm disposed itself towards above all, in other words, was the life going on around him, and his way of expressing that enthusiasm was to position himself (and his typewriter) amidst its flow. Numerous friends and colleagues have pictured him working in this way, and Joe LeSueur remarks upon it frequently, as for instance when he observes, evocatively, how

> our presence ... must have inspired and galvanized him. This had less to do with his ability to concentrate than it did with the *way* he concentrated, for whatever happened around him often became part of the creative act in progress. The radio could be blaring, the phone could be jangling, people could be dropping by, someone could be in the same room with him (*talking* to

him); and when we lived in East Ninth Street, in a second-floor apartment so close to the street that it seemed an extension of it, a cacophonous symphony of ugly urban sounds played fortissimo outside our window, punctuated regularly by the sound of the Ninth Street crosstown bus making its stop next to the downstairs doorway – incredibly, these distractions not only failed to impede but seemed to spur the steady stream of words rushing from his teeming brain to his two nimble index fingers that decisively, at full tilt, struck the keys of his trusty, overburdened Royal portable. (D, 82)

It is important to be clear, through O'Hara's account of Pasternak, what this image of the poet at work should be taken to imply. The intimacy O'Hara identifies in Pasternak – walking hand in hand with life, and not as in 'identification' but as in 'recognition' – and which O'Hara so memorably achieved in a poem such as 'A Step Away From Them', but also in the totality of *The Collected Poems*, is like the nearness or nextness Cavell identifies Thoreau as achieving in *Walden*. New York –with its 'cacophonous symphony of ugly urban sounds', and for which O'Hara, at his typewriter, aimed to make himself the measure – was, for him, what Walden Pond was to Thoreau. And the claim is similar to, but crucially is not the same as, Pollock's famous claim that 'I am Nature'; and perhaps in the differences in the two media there is a justification for this, the pure physicality of action painting constituting an immediacy of sorts. The word, on the other hand, does not permit this, and Thoreau's more tempered claim, instead, was that he felt 'nearer to the vitals of the globe'. O'Hara reorientated the act of writing poetry by situating himself and his typewriter amid the flow, and so could justly claim an intimacy with life which we can well call nearness, the 'I do this, I do that' poems in particular making themselves, as he said of Pasternak, intimate with their condition of inspiration.

Knowing

O'Hara was an epistemological poet. The question of how art can be thought to know the world, and how its media can be turned towards life, was given repeated, careful and quite technical consideration in his criticism. Thus in 'Porter Paints a Picture', 'Composition' is described as 'a function of the sensibility: it is the personal statement of the insight which observation and insight afford' (SS, 55). It is not, he goes on,

an illusion as is the expression of an appearance, as is the representation of observation … Fairfield Porter's paintings stand or fall by their composition: it is the literal meaning of his perceptions and he will do any number of versions of a motif to perfect its utterance. (SS, 55)

Remarking on O'Hara's compositional practice, LeSueur observed that it was not his capacity to concentrate, but 'the *way* he concentrated' that permitted his intimate relation with the world. O'Hara, very deliberately, is observing a similar thing in Porter. Privileging the statement of what he calls 'composition', O'Hara identifies in Porter's best work an ideal interplay between 'insight and observation', between the operations of mind and its capacity for receiving things. What should be noticed in particular, here, is the attention given to what Kant would have termed faculties. Like Thoreau, in other words, O'Hara is engaged quite consciously in the problem of how people know things.

Elaine de Kooning is presented in similarly considered, semi-philosophical terms. Speaking generally of the new painters, under the heading 'Nature and the New American Painting', O'Hara finds them to be 'Turning away from styles whose perceptions and knowledge are not their own occasion', and that instead, 'these painters seek their own perceptions and in doing so have turned, voluntarily or involuntarily, to nature' (SS, 43). It is worth noticing here the balance of style and perception which is, historically, a starting point for the enthusiast, the painters seeking their own perceptions at the point at which 'style' had come to obscure 'knowledge'. Only here, as has been the case since Romanticism, the turn is not to God, but to nature. De Kooning, in this context, is more radically exposed than Porter: 'What she experiences seems to go straight to the canvas, partially due to her adroitness as a draughtsman in capturing physical movement; the force of her perceptions obliterates stylistic effects and sets free a plastic vitality' (SS, 44). Experience, in de Kooning, obliterates style, and so her work, crucially, 'does not refer back to the artist … but forward to life'. Art, then, in its composition, takes on the task that Kantian philosophy left over, referring the mind – Olson termed this capacity 'projective' – forward towards life. Pollock, of course, for O'Hara, positions himself uniquely in this respect, differing from Porter in the matter of insight. Thus in Pollock's act of concentration, which is not composition but 'a state of spiritual clarity', 'the artist has reached a limitless space of air and light in which the spirit can act freely and with unpremeditated knowledge' (AC, 26). There is a state of mind in art, in other words, whether identified in the quite different practices of Porter, de Kooning or Pollock, that enables an acquaintance with things in the world, O'Hara thus approaching questions of composition and creativity very largely as matters of epistemology.

His contemporaries identified this in him. Ashbery's portrait of O'Hara in action, in his introduction to *The Collected Poems*, several times tries to catch his mental process. Noting how O'Hara 'ignored the rules for Modern American poetry … drawn up from Pound and Eliot down to the academic establishment of the 1940s', Ashbery finds in the early poems something 'unlike poetry' and more like 'the inspired ramblings of a mind open to the point of distraction'. The interesting implication is that O'Hara's early work finds the poet in his most purely enthusiastic phase. A necessary phase, as Ashbery tells it, that permitted the less rambling later poems, work which seems 'entirely natural and available to the multitude of big and little phenomena which combine to make that almost unknowable substance that is our experience' (CP, vii, xi, xi). But Koch got closer, perhaps, to the nature of O'Hara's sensibility in his 1972 review of *The Collected Poems*, observing in his work, as he had observed in the actual writing of it, 'the immediacy of the relationship of what is happening outside to what happens in the poem' (H, 206). This consists, as Koch has it, of the same sort of combination of operations Ashbery describes, though in Koch they seem less chronological and the expression is more technical. Thus on the one hand, as one reads, 'One's feeling of being overwhelmed gives way to a happy awareness of expanded powers of perceiving and holding in mind' (H, 207). This, it should be noticed, is the Kantian sublime by any other name. It is also, quite precisely, the enthusiast's mode of knowledge; a mode of knowledge perhaps qualified by, or perhaps subsumed in, Koch's other image of O'Hara composing:

> It was always an emergency because one's life had to be experienced and reflected on at the same time, and that is just about impossible. He does it in his poems. (H, 206–7)

In the act of writing, as Koch would have it, O'Hara arrived at 'expanded powers' of holding in mind, where the greater capacity can be thought to consist of the ability, in composition, to experience and reflect at the same time. Which implies not, as Breton sought, a complete disabling of the critical faculties, but rather a state – call it writing – in which the manifold of experience can be held as such while at the same time subject to the operations of reflection. Quite how this was achieved is, obviously, difficult to say, involving as it ultimately would a report on O'Hara's experience. But then, of course, he provided just such a report – the poems – and so if it is not, naturally, possible to verbalize O'Hara's concentration, it is possible, as he did with Porter and with Pollock, to identify elements of O'Hara's way of knowing.

The first of these is a disposition toward categories. 'Grace / to be born,' O'Hara wrote in 'In Memory of My Feelings', 'and live as variously as possible'. The line is his epitaph, and in every aspect of his life, as consistently as if it were an ethic, O'Hara declined to deal with the world through the medium of categories. Feldman recalls that he was 'able to love and accept more difficult kinds of work than one would have thought possible', remarking how it was 'possible for him, without ever being merely eclectic, to write so beautifully about both Pollock and Pasternak' and 'to dedicate a poem to Larry Rivers one day and to Philip Guston the next'. It was a disregard for categories O'Hara himself identified with enthusiasm. Witness how, in his commentary on Robert Motherwell, he observed the artist's great good fortune to have first shown at Peggy Guggenheim's Art of this Century Gallery, where curatorial taste outwitted categories. Motherwell thus found himself:

> in a milieu where simultaneous passions for the work of Mondrian, Max Ernst, de Chirico, Léger, and Joseph Cornell were enriching rather than confusing, joined together in time, place, and enthusiasm rather than compartmentalized and classified as they would have been in most art schools of the time. (AC, 71)

Compartmentalization and classification were for second-rate artists and bureaucrats, and O'Hara, as an enthusiast, had a horror of both. 'My Heart' sets the position out:

> I'm not going to cry all the time
> nor shall I laugh all the time,
> I don't prefer one 'strain' to another.
> I'd have the immediacy of a bad movie,
> not just a sleeper, but also the big,
> overproduced first-run kind. I want to be
> at least as alive as the vulgar. And if
> some aficionado of my mess says, 'That's
> not like Frank!', all to the good! I
> don't wear brown and grey suits all the time,
> do I? No. I wear workshirts to the opera,
> often. I want my feet to be bare,
> I want my face to be shaven, and my heart –
> you can't plan on the heart, but
> the better part of it, my poetry, is open.
>   (CP, 231)

This is plain enough to speak for itself, but it is also pointed enough for certain details to be drawn from it: the desire for the 'immediacy' of a bad movie, for instance; O'Hara's opposition to the aficionado; the rhyming, and equal validation of, 'vulgar' and 'opera'; the fact that his feet are bare, ready to step naked into the world; the fact that his poetry, enthusiastically, 'is open'.

'My Heart' mixes categories up. Elsewhere the category is outwitted and outpaced, as in his epistemological masterpiece 'In Memory of My Feelings', where famously the self is quick, taking on and casting off guises faster than it is possible to make sense of:

I am a dictator looking at his wife I am a doctor eating a child
and the child's mother smiling I am a Chinaman climbing a mountain
I am a child smelling his father's underwear I am an Indian
sleeping on a scalp
          and my pony is stamping in the birches,
   and I've just caught sight of the *Nina*, the *Pinta*, and the *Santa Maria*.
          What land is this, so free?

                             (CP, 256)

This makes a point about poetry – O'Hara is writing in the spirit of Whitman, and also after Pound, injecting velocity into the idea of personae – but the passage makes a point about experience as well, about the relation between people and things. The point is that experience is not susceptible to a mind conducting itself in terms of categories. The whole poem is a consideration of this point, and an account also of what state of mind might be the alternative, one version of which makes O'Hara sound like Pollock in the grip of his enthusiasm:

                       as runners arrive from the mountains
   bearing snow, proof that the mind's obsolescence is still capable
   of intimacy

                             (CP, 255)

This formulation would seem to be clear: intimacy with things, snow in this case, is the object state, and what this entails, or requires, is obsolescence of mind. As in Pollock, then, 'the spirit can act freely and with unpremeditated knowledge'. This is not, however, by any means the whole of what 'In Memory of My Feelings' has to communicate about knowledge, because the mind of the poem, and the mind described by the poem, are far from obsolete. The mind of 'In Memory of My Feelings' has, rather, become capable of a remarkably agile double operation.

   This double operation is the substance of the poem's opening:

          My quietness has a man in it, he is transparent
          and he carries me quietly, like a gondola, through the streets
                         (CP, 252)

The image here, I think, is of a person beside himself, observing himself and also observing the state in which he observes himself. The image seems true as an account of numerous O'Hara poems, of the relation his poems often establish between poet and life, that relation consisting of a carefully presented double state: one aspect of self, a man, venturing after intimacy with the world, another aspect of self, his quietness, watching on. As when later in the poem, following the Whitmanesque celebration of a life lived variously, O'Hara watches on quietly in the midst of his experience:

> I watch
> the sea at the back of my eyes, near the spot where I think
> in solitude as pine trees groan and support the enormous winds
> (CP, 256)

Colloquially, being beside oneself would seem to imply distraction or madness. Here, though, it implies knowledge. It is this state Koch has in mind when he speaks of O'Hara's capacity to reflect on life and to experience it at the same time. It is this state, also, Cavell wants to ascribe to Thoreau when he presents him as 'next' to Walden Pond. The precondition of such a state of existence for Thoreau was 'supernatural serenity', *Walden* being an account, to borrow O'Hara's description of Pollock at work, of the numerous decisions necessary to achieve the state in which an intimacy with life might be composed. O'Hara, likewise, for all his activity, identifies a measure of quietness as the state of mind in which it is possible to know oneself as being intimate with the world. All of which is to present 'In Memory of My Feelings' as O'Hara's portrait of his own act of composition, as his self-revealing equivalent of 'Porter Paints a Picture', as 'Frank O'Hara Writes a Poem'.

The poem was, as Joe LeSueur observes, one of the first O'Hara wrote after his unhappy and poetically unproductive fellowship at the Writer's Theater in Cambridge. Perhaps it was for this reason that 'In Memory of My Feelings' becomes a recollection, as far as that is possible, of how he writes a poem, of the state of mind and self in which composition is possible. But also of how it had become possible in the first place, the poem, in its mix of autobiographical, historical and mythic modes, offering an account of the various processes and decisions through which the poet – as himself, but also as a figure through history – has arrived at a state of mind capable of intimacy with experience. An intimacy through which it is possible to record stillness, as when,

> At 7, before Jane
> was up, the copper lake stirred against the sides
> of a Norwegian freighter; on the deck a few dirty men,
> tired of night, watched themselves in the water
> as years before the German prisoners on the *Prinz Eugen*
> dappled the Pacific with their sores, painted purple
> by a Naval doctor.
> (CP, 255)

But if 'In Memory of My Feelings' is a recollection of how it is possible to write, of the state of mind in which experience can both be had and reflected upon, then as a recollection it is necessarily at a remove from the act itself, a watching of the watching through which composition can be achieved. Not that it is merely a proposal to write, just that it does not quite go on its nerve either. It is an account of composition rather than, in the purest sense, an act of composition. To catch O'Hara in the act one should read the poem he wrote next, 'A Step Away from Them'.

'A Step Away from Them', written on 16 August 1956 – The first great 'I do this, I do that' poem, as LeSueur puts it – stands, in this book's account of literary enthusiasm, as a major moment in the development of America's written consciousness; of the consciousness made possible by American writing. When he removed himself to Walden Pond, one of the networks that Thoreau distanced himself from was that of the transcendental self. In a fully dramatized sense his gesture was profoundly philosophical, an attempt to reacquaint the mind with things-in-themselves. Finding himself in the middle of the twentieth century, where the things of the world are as much urban and manmade as they are natural, and in which the environment is characterized by new kinds and degrees of flux, O'Hara's decision is that if a state of mind capable of intimacy with the world is to be viable, it must be achievable instantaneously, not through an act of prolonged separation: in a word, only a step away. What he achieves in the poem, in other words, is a state of mind equivalent to Thoreau's at Walden Pond, but where Walden is mid-town Manhattan and where the necessary quietness (of mind not environment) is achievable at a moment's notice. What I am interested in, in other words, is the poem's act of composition, where composition, following O'Hara's own critical sense of it, is taken to be the state of mind in which life can be known.

Not the least significant element of the poem's moment is the fact that it was written the day after Jackson Pollock's funeral, a day when, O'Hara not being prone to odes to dejection, he would have wanted to write a poem full of life; as full of life, perhaps, as he had ever written, requiring of him a special act of concentration. The poem is the record of that act, which is partly to make the simple but necessary observation that the poem itself is *not* O'Hara's lunch hour, or not in the sense he implies it is; not the part of his lunch hour when he is going for a walk. The poem, in other words, is written not quite in the present, but the moment after, when he is back at the museum. We find O'Hara, as we read the poem, not in the street but in the equivalent of the studio, *in* the act of composition. Crucially, however, what we are invited to imagine is that the act of composition is continuous with the experience which fuels it. His quietness, we are to understand – the quietness of composition – has a man in it. So while it is in his quietness that he writes the poem – being the way, as LeSueur puts it, that he concentrates – it is his quietness, also, that carries him through the streets: the man in the quietness venturing out, experiencing 'cats in saw dust'; the quietness, the mood of composition, dwelling on the experience such that it can enter the poem. The poem is thus a true account of what has just passed. The state in which the poem is composed being the state in which the life the poem presents was experienced – O'Hara watching on as he has reflected, and reflects upon, what he encounters: 'It is *my* lunch hour', '*I* look at bargains in wristwatches'.

The poem is therefore the equivalent, say, of Elaine de Kooning at work, when, as O'Hara said (as was mentioned earlier) 'what she experiences goes straight to the canvas, partially due to her adroitness as a draughtsman in capturing physical movement' with 'the force of her perceptions obliterating stylistic effects'. In O'Hara's poem the equivalent of this draughtsmanship is, in part, what one can call the poem's measure, the line taking its shape from the thing or event experienced: 'The sun is hot, but / cabs stir up the air'. It is also, in part, its rhythm, the pace with which, paratactically, the poem moves from one thing to another. There is a draughtsmanship, also, of sorts – if what draughtsmanship means is the capturing of movement – in the fluency with which the poem dissolves categories. Social categories – race, gender – are confused and pitched against one another. More fundamentally, space and time are characterized not by stability but by flux. Temporally this poem operates between the present moment and the eternity of death. Spatially it is poised between the construction of a building and the anticipation of a building being torn down. Outwitting categories throughout, in his experiencing and his writing, O'Hara has developed a way of holding things in mind. And it is easy to forget, O'Hara's poem being fifty years old now, and given how influential its mode has been, just how lacking in life, as it was handed down from Eliot to the New Criticism, Modern American poetry had become. Against that background, O'Hara evolved a way of writing that would permit an intimacy with New York, where life is not a backdrop but the condition of inspiration, and where the object of composition was to be as close to that condition as possible. 'A Step Away from Them' is thus an inspired poem, a poem written not in an elegiac mood but in a state of enthusiasm, fuelled by and directly communicating life in the New York street, where the poet's technical achievement is to let that life through.

Calling

O'Hara's relation to the world has been presented in terms of intimacy, the poet having reconfigured the act of writing and developed a way of concentrating which would permit the closest possible relationship with his condition of inspiration. His relationship to other people, where other people are readers, but where readers might equally be friends and colleagues as people he has never met, can be similarly understood. Intimacy with his interlocutor was quite as important to O'Hara as intimacy with things. As an interlocutor O'Hara is quite often described as an enthusiast. Introducing *The Collected Poems* Ashbery cites Schuyler's description of O'Hara's address as his 'intimate yell'. Schuyler himself recalls:

> His conversation was self-propelling and one idea, or anecdote, or *bon mot* was fuel to his own fire, inspiring him verbally to blaze ahead, that curious voice rising and falling, full of invisible italics, the strong pianist's hands gesturing with the invariable cigarette. (H, 82)

This is straight out of the enthusiast's handbook, or at least, straight out of the *Encyclopédie*, where Diderot defined enthusiasm as

> a living fire which prevails by degrees, which feeds from its own flames, and which, far from becoming feebler as it expands, acquires new strength in proportion to the extent that it spreads and communicates itself.[11]

O'Hara's own picture of himself talking is very much like Schuyler's, his memoir of 'Bunny' Lang catching the two of them in the act, the discovery of a shared admiration for Rimbaud and Auden leading to what O'Hara termed

> our 'coffee talks' which were to go on for years, sometimes long distance. At 11 each morning we called each other and discussed everything we had thought of since we had parted the night before, including any dreams we may have had in the meantime. And once we were going to write a modern Coffee Cantata together, but never did. (SS, 86)

This is conversation as intimate yell, as, perhaps, the inspired ramblings of a mind open to the point of distraction, and where sometimes, as in the case of the conversation with Lang, the immediate mediating device was the telephone.

Direct address – as in conversation – was always, for O'Hara, integral to the creative act. In various ways, at different moments in his career, he envisaged the poem as an act of intimate communication, as if in order to write there had to be a tangible structure of address. Much more than most Modern poets O'Hara invoked the figure of the muse. Early on the muse was typically a woman painter friend, Jane Freilicher, or Grace Hartigan (for whom he wrote 'In Memory of My Feelings'). Later it was Vincent Warren (for whom he wrote *Love Poems (Tentative Title)*), or sometimes Joe LeSueur, or Bill Berkson; and sometimes it would be one among his pantheon of heroes. Inevitaby, though, there was a figure in mind who inspired the poem by supplying O'Hara with somebody he wanted to talk with. And sometimes, crucially, the source of inspiration would be at the other end of the line, as when, as Koch reports it, he and O'Hara were writing their respective long poems 'When the Sun Tries to Go On' and 'Second Avenue', and when at the end of each day they would read their results to each other over the phone. For Ashbery the phone call has become one of the ways other voices are filtered into the poem, the work in progress, as Ashbery tells it, sometimes changing shape and direction when interrupted by a call. O'Hara, as his colleagues at MOMA remember it, was always on the phone, and in 'Personism', when he described his poetry's direct mode of address, it was in terms of the call:

> to give you a vague idea, one of its minimal aspects is to address itself to one person (other than the poet himself). ... That's part of Personism. It was founded by me after lunch with LeRoi Jones on August 27, 1959, a day in which I was in love with someone (not Roi, by the way, a blond). I went back to work and wrote a poem for this person. While I was writing it I was realizing that if I wanted to I could use the telephone instead of writing the poem and so Personism was born. It's a very exciting movement which will undoubtedly have lots of adherents. It puts the poem squarely between the poet and the person Lucky Pierre style, and the poem is correspondingly gratified. The poem is at last between two persons instead of two pages. In all modesty, I confess that it may be the death of literature as we know it. (SS, 111)

There is something very appealing, from the point of view of enthusiasm, of O'Hara's positioning of the telephone at the heart of his aesthetic, as if the 'call for' – what calls for poetry – can be found in the 'call to', where what the 'call to' stands for is a closeness of community in an otherwise technologically alienating world. But there is more, I think, to the connection of O'Hara's enthusiasm and his calling than such a play on words describes – even allowing for the fact that O'Hara was looking in every way to modernize the poet's vocation – and not least because as he downgrades the book in his mock manifesto, he is deeply serious.

Ashbery registers this seriousness in his Introduction to *The Collected Poems* when he remarks on Donald Allen's achievement in bringing the book together, given O'Hara's indifference to keeping, let alone publishing, his work. 'Given the instantaneous quality of the poems,' Ashbery judges, 'their problematical life seems only natural: poetry was what finally mattered to Frank, and even the poems themselves, like the experiences and personal relationships that went into them, were important but somehow secondary. His career stands as an unrevised work-in-progress' (CP, vii). LeSueur, it will be recalled, puts the point slightly differently, suggesting not that the experience was secondary to poetry but that his 'being indifferent about publication ... allowed him to embrace life, not careerist concerns, and it was through his everyday experiences that a poem might come to him' (D, 276). Either way, O'Hara is serious when in his manifesto he declares Personism's intention to put the poem between two persons instead of two pages. Thus, not only are the pages a matter of some indifference to him, they and the book they feature in are an intrusion between persons, the effect of the book being to distance the reader from the poem and the poet: hence the call. What O'Hara wants of and for poetry is the most immediate communication and community possible, and what he is all but proposing – witness the ambition to effect the death of literature – is the de- or un- or non-textualised poem. As an act of knowing, the poem barely requires preservation, the composition involved in writing having become, simply, part of the poet's way of being in the world. But since it is to be preserved, and as the state of knowledge is to be passed on, the poem must be as free of textual constraint as possible. This is why he thinks of the poem as a telephone call. It is a way of thinking about the poem that puts it squarely between two persons, and a way of thinking about texts which, in turn, puts O'Hara squarely in the publishing traditions of enthusiasm.

Enthusiasm, religiously speaking, is precisely a downgrading of the book, at least where the book is understood as a final authority mediating between the individual and his God. Enthusiasm, by contrast, places the religious *experience* between God and the individual, and considers that experience to be, in one sense, sufficient in itself. In so far, however, as the enthusiast wanted to issue a written report on the experience, the preferred mode of publication – for economic, but also for religious reasons – was typically the pamphlet.[12] The pamphlet is a text, of course, but a text which acknowledges its own lack of authority or incompletion; which recognizes the experience in question to be a work in progress, an ongoing experiment. Likewise, then, O'Hara's poems *were* written down, though often in the most ephemeral, least durable of formats: in letters and as single copies (often mislaid). Ashbery recalled in his 'Introduction' how 'Memorial Day 1950' survived only because he copied it out in a letter to Kenneth Koch. And yet, if often after much cajoling, some of the poems *were* published in his lifetime, even then his strong preference, as with the City Lights Pocket Books Series, was for the small-press, ephemeral-looking, pamphlet-like book. This was, as O'Hara must have understood it, the closest thing he might get to the call as book (the book as call), the small press being a version of enthusiastic dissemination.

Which is not to argue that the mode of publication of *Lunch Poems* guarantees intimacy between poet and reader. The small-press publication, in its typically limited availability, can quickly acquire a distracting aura all of its own. Equally, the City Lights pocket format in particular – in its portability and general un-onerousness – does mitigate the distancing nature of the orthodox book. Even so, the choice of format, from the point of view of Personism, is at best perhaps a damage limitation, with the intimacy of the poems, their hoped-for relation between persons, being secured not, in any unproblematic sense, by their mode of publication, but by the manner of the writing itself. As in 'The Day Lady Died', where the desire for closeness is inscribed into every line of the poem, the opening, for instance, establishing an intimacy with time and place:

> It is 12.20 in New York a Friday
> three days after Bastille day, yes
> it is 1959 and I go get a shoeshine.
> (CP, 325)

12.20 on 17 July 1959 is an abstraction, so this opening suggests, unless the individual can strike up an association with the moment, unless it is understood as a moment lived, hence the fact that O'Hara reports going to get a shoeshine. Which he does because, as the poem says, he does not know 'the people who will feed him', and so presumably he would like to make a good impression. He buys 'an ugly *New World Writing*', in the hope of getting to know what the poets, whom he doesn't know, in Ghana are doing. He goes to the bank, where Miss Stillwagon, whom he doesn't know, recognizes him sufficiently not to look up his balance 'for once in her life'. Then he chooses gifts, for Patsy Southgate and Mike Goldberg, demonstrating his fondness for each by, respectively, first agonizing over what best to give, and then knowing exactly what – a bottle of Strega – will be appropriate:

> then I go back where I came from to 6th Avenue
> and the tobacconist in the Ziegfeld Theatre and
> casually ask for a carton of Gauloises and a carton
> of Picayunes, and a NEW YORK POST with her face on it
>
> and I am sweating a lot by now and thinking of
> leaning on the john door in the 5 SPOT
> while she whispered a song along the keyboard
> to Mal Waldron and everyone and I stopped breathing.[13]

LeSueur suggests why this particular moment should have come to O'Hara's mind. Quite possibly the occasion in question was Holiday's last live performance. It was also an illicit appearance in that, having recently been convicted of dope offences, she was banned from singing anywhere where liquor was served. What O'Hara dwells on, however, what makes the poem, is Holiday's delivery, which is weakened, now, towards the end of her life, but which preserves the halting, breathy quality that was her signature: 'she whispered a song along the keyboard / to Mal Waldron and everyone and I stopped breathing'. The beauty of Holiday lies largely in her address, which O'Hara catches in his phrase 'everyone and I', and which means that what marked Holiday out as a performer was her ability to put the song between two persons: between her and everyone, between her and I. Holiday's delivery is, in Personism's sense of it, a call, and what her premature death calls for is an act of homage, and the poem offers this by presenting a secret, breathless moment.

Love

This has been an essay about a state of mind. I have argued that for O'Hara the act of composition was, quite self-consciously, a mode of knowledge; that he evolved a way of concentrating such that there might be an immediacy of relation between 'what is happening outside' and 'what happens in the poem'; that he reconfigured the practice of writing in order better to become acquainted with things. One word for this state of mind, following O'Hara's own discussion of composition, is enthusiasm, a condition O'Hara in his person, but also in his poetry, passed on: hence Koch's sense, on reading O'Hara, that 'One's feeling of being overwhelmed gives way to a happy awareness of expanded powers of perceiving and holding in mind' (H, 207). I have also argued that the state of composition, or creation, invariably required intimacy, that the rhetorical structure of an O'Hara poem invariably consists in a direct address, the poem, as Personism puts it, existing between two persons. Another word, I want to end by suggesting, for this knowing, enthusiastic, intimate state, is love. Witness, for example, Joe LeSueur's description of the effect of Vincent Warren on O'Hara's poetry:

> The deluge began immediately after 'Joe's Jacket'. Which is to say, right after Frank spent the weekend with Vincent. 'You are gorgeous and I'm coming,' 'Saint', 'Poem' ('Hate is only one of many responses'), 'Poem' ('I don't know what D. H. Lawrence is driving at'), 'Personal Poem', 'Post the Lake Poets Ballad', and 'Naphtha' were written in the subsequent three weeks, and that was only the beginning. For over the course of the next twenty-one months, Frank's output continued apace, steady and unbroken ... These marvelous poems testify to what finally came together for Frank, what he at long last experienced, love and the reciprocation of love – physical, sexual, romantic love, fully and deeply realized. (D, 223–4)

O'Hara met and fell in love with Warren, a dancer with the New York Ballet, in August 1959. The series of poems he wrote for and to him, many of which were published in *Love Poems (Tentative Title)*, are a sonnet sequence by any other name, reproducing in their structure of address, and in the way they dwell on presence, absence, secrecy and openness, the devices and themes that characterize Shakespeare's Sonnets. And as LeSueur says, what distinguishes the poems within O'Hara's body of work is the way, as he wrote them, everything seemed finally to come together. Which is to say, from the point of view of this essay, that the love poems he wrote between 1959 and 1961 are among the clearest, fullest, expressions of his enthusiasm.

The best commentator on the relation of love to enthusiasm is St Paul, his most famous treatise on love, 1 Corinthians 13, being also a treatise on enthusiasm. 'Though,' Paul writes, 'I speak with the tongues of men and of angels, and have not charity [by which, as modern translators understand it, he means love], I am become *as* sounding brass, or a tinkling cymbal'. And though, he goes on, 'I have the gift of prophecy and understand all mysteries, and all knowledge; and though I have all faith; so that I could remove mountains, and have not charity, I am nothing.' Love 'suffereth long … seeketh not her own … rejoiceth not in iniquity, but rejoiceth in the truth'. Love 'beareth all things, believeth all things, hopeth all things, endureth all things'. And so, of course, while, 'now we see through a glass, darkly … but then shall I know even as also I am known'. Thus love, as Paul presents it, acts like enthusiasm: it operates on the individual to animate and enhance the voice. It also acts as enthusiasm: it goes outwards, it seeks not itself, it permits knowledge and enables the knower to be known. It is also more than enthusiasm in that, for instance, it beareth and endureth, but then since, as Paul would have it, God is love, and since enthusiasm is, at its origin, a way of acquainting oneself with God, of breathing the god in, then there is, undeniably, an enthusiasm in love.

O'Hara's poems to Vincent present the enthusiasm of love. One might quote any number to demonstrate this, but one short lyric perhaps makes the point.

> Light   clarity   avocado salad in the morning
> after all the terrible things I do how amazing it is
> to find forgiveness and love, not even forgiveness
> since what is done is done and forgiveness isn't love
> and love is love nothing can ever go wrong
> though things can get irritating boring and dispensable
> (in the imagination) but not really for love
> though a block away you feel distant the mere presence
> changes everything like a chemical dropped on paper
> and all thoughts disappear in a strange quiet excitement
> I am sure of nothing but this, intensified by breathing
>
> (CP, 350)

This, I want to suggest, is one of those poems – it was written in the first flush of the Vincent period, in December 1959 – in which, for O'Hara, everything came together. What I want to suggest also, with the right degree of lightness and deadly seriousness, is that in this poem O'Hara rewrites 1 Corinthians 13. This second claim can only be a speculation, but I think one can hear Paul coming through, in the comic triad with which the poem opens, but also in the poem's rhetorical arrangement, in its repetitions and its diction:

> since what is done is done and forgiveness isn't love
> and love is love nothing can ever go wrong

This is unmistakably an O'Hara poem, but these lines have a sonority and an insistence that comes from elsewhere: O'Hara doesn't, typically, repeat for effect like that, his diction tending to alter as rapidly as it presses on. In this, and in the sentiment of forgiveness, there is, I think, a deliberate echoing of Paul.

The other claim, that this is one of those O'Hara poems in which everything comes together, in which he manages, in one brief utterance, to communicate the values which variously informed his writing, is less difficult to establish. In its basic mechanism, in its account of its compositional state, the poem is quite explicitly enthusiastic. Something overwhelming happens – here it is the presence of Vincent, acting on O'Hara's sensibility like a chemical reaction – from which follows a mood Thoreau would have recognized, 'a strange quiet excitement', out of which emerges the possibility of intimate speech. Thus that triad at the beginning is comic, but it is also in earnest. Love, in O'Hara, seeks not itself, but invariably finds its articulation in things, actions and events, being a state of mind, like enthusiasm, in which nearness to life is possible. 'Light clarity avocado salad in the morning': the effect of love, O'Hara asserts, is to make details noticeable. So similarly, at the end of 'Steps', the balance is of excess and detail, intimacy with the world made possible by love:

> and the little box is out on the sidewalk
> next to the delicatessen
> so the old man can sit on it and drink beer
> and get knocked off it by his wife later in the day
> while the sun is still shining
>
> oh god it's wonderful
> to get out of bed
> and drink too much coffee
> and smoke too many cigarettes
> and love you so much

(CP, 371)

'Steps' is an entirely characteristic O'Hara love poem. It is 'for' Vincent but it is not about him, it is about what he makes possible. And what he makes possible, in the love he enables, is a closeness to life, to life's incidental and contributory details: the box 'out on the sidewalk / next to the delicatessen'. It is in his love poems, in other words, that enthusiasm is most obviously integral to his way of concentrating. Witness the end of the earlier 'Poem', in which in the act of love (which is the act of writing), O'Hara asserts that 'I am sure of nothing but this, intensified by breathing'. What he is sure of ('this') is love, but what he is also sure of in the poem ('this') is his relation with life. It is a poem of 'light' and 'clarity' made possible by 'strange quiet excitement'. O'Hara wrote as an enthusiast, and the fullest expression of his enthusiasm is to be found in the writing of his love poems – composition, as he has it, 'intensified by breathing'.

Notes

1 Bill Berkson and Joe LeSueur (eds), *Homage to Frank O'Hara*, Bolinas, Calif., Big Sky, 1978, p. 139; hereafter referred to in the text as H.

2 Frank O'Hara, *Standing Still and Walking in New York*, ed. Donald Allen, Bolinas, Calif., Grey Fox Press, p. 147; hereafter referred to in the text as SS.

3 Frank O'Hara, *The Collected Poems of Frank O'Hara*, ed. Donald Allen, Berkeley and London, University of California Press, 1995, p. 234; hereafter referred to in the text as CP.

4 Ralph Waldo Emerson, 'Inspiration', *Letters and Social Aims*, London, George Routledge and Sons, 1883, pp. 260; Immanuel Kant, *The Critique of Judgement*, tr. James Creed Meredith, Oxford, Clarendon Press, 1952, p. 124.

5 Susan Sontag, *Against Interpretation*, New York, Farrar, Strauss, 1966, p. 14.

6 Frank O'Hara, *Art Chronicles 1954–1966*, New York, George Braziller, 1975, pp. 25–6; hereafter referred to in the text as AC.

7 See Geoff Ward, *Statutes of Liberty: The New York School of Poets*, London, Macmillan, 1993, pp. 260–82.

8 André Breton, *Manifestoes of Surrealism*, tr. Richard Seaver and Helen R. Lane, Ann Arbor, Ann Arbor Paperbacks, University of Michigan Press, 2000, pp. 22–3.

9 Ibid., p. 4.

10 Joe LeSueur, *Digressions on Some Poems by Frank O'Hara*, New York, Farrar, Straus and Giroux, p. 276; hereafter referred to in the text as D.

11 'Enthousiamse', in *Encyclopédie ou Dictionnaire Raisonée des Sciences, des Arts et des Métiers*, Paris, 1755, cited in Timothy Clark, *The Theory of Inspiration: Composition as a Crisis of Subjectivity in Romantic and Post-Romantic Writing*, Manchester, Manchester University Press, 1997, pp. 63–4.

12 Jon Mee provides an excellent discussion of the historic relation between enthusiasm and print culture, observing that 'Swift and Pope' associated 'the proliferation of print' (which very largely meant pamphleteering) 'with

religious non-conformity'. 'A large quantity of the eighteenth-century's print production,' he observes, 'was taken up with religious disputation or ... accounts of conversion experience'. See Jon Mee, *Romanticism, Enthusiasm and Regulation: Poetics and the Policing of Culture in the Romantic Period*, Oxford, Oxford University Press, 2003, pp. 58–63.

13 Frank O'Hara, *Lunch Poems*, San Francisco, City Lights Books, 1964, p. 26.

6

Relishing: James Schuyler

More than any other writer discussed in this book – more, even, than Thoreau – James Schuyler's enthusiasm is to be found in his language. So while there are ways in which this closing discussion could be front-loaded – through Schuyler's art criticism or his consistently exuberant correspondence, with a consideration of his more manic episodes, or in terms of the traditions he managed so gracefully to absorb – the place to start is among the words themselves: in his poems, but also in *The Diary*, a work of exceptional quality in its own right and in a very rich sense a continuation of his poetry. In presenting his enthusiasm I want to show how, in the process and experience of composing, Schuyler opened his writing up: to other voices, but also, as he was able confidently to put it in 'Slowly' (a poem which originated in *The Diary*) to 'the what of which you are a part'; where 'the what' was, as Schuyler called it, 'life' – as distinct from a Romantic 'nature', or, say, from a Heideggerean sense of 'being' – and with which he understood himself to be continuous.

What an enthusiastic reading of Schuyler should also bring to the fore, however, is pleasure, the sheer pleasure that can come of combining, or mouthing, or transcribing, words; a pleasure of which criticism is currently well advised not to speak. It is difficult to think of a word more alien to the current British Higher Education learning environment than pleasure: Aims and objectives? Pleasure; Transferable skills? Joy. Clearly what we are talking about here is a different language. A language, importantly, with which Schuyler understood himself to be, if not vociferously, perhaps, then subtly, combatively, in dispute. 'Think of the people,' he says in his *Diary* entry of 3 January 1968, 'who do the counting: would you want your son to marry one of them?'[1]

Thoreau-like in certain of the writing situations in which he found himself – he spent long, productive periods of his life on Fairfield Porter's island off the coast of Maine – and also in his general disposition towards his environment, what Schuyler wanted to determine in his poetry was how that environment might be known through language, how language can be made capable of showing the world.[2] His enthusiasm consists in that attempted showing, and in the perpetual reacquaintance with the environment it entailed. But it consisted also in pleasure, Schuyler taking an exquisite pleasure both in the sound of words – his own and other people's – and in the intensified relationship with the world that words can effect. His poems are acts of disclosure, where the disclosure is founded on an intimacy with both language and the world: an intimacy thwarted by the abstractions of administration.

'Freely Espousing'

Schuyler was 43 when, in 1969, he published his beautifully entitled book *Freely Espousing*. Prior to that he had published a novel, *Alfred and Guinevere*, with Harcourt Brace in 1958, and two volumes of poems, *Salute* (carrying screen prints by Grace Hartigan) with the Tiber Press in 1960, and *May 24th or So* with Tibor de Nagy Gallery Editions in 1965. *Freely Espousing*, published by Doubleday, was thus Schuyler's first generally available book of poems. The title poem was the first in the book, as it is now in the *Collected Poems*, and for this reason of presentation, but also because of the poem's air of purpose – it offers up for consideration (and delight) ways of handling the language which are, one way or another, characteristic of Schuyler's work as a whole – 'Freely Espousing' is inescapably a statement of poetic intent. Which is not to say that the poem is typical, being more loosely strung than is usually (though not always) the case. It acts as an introduction to Schuyler by dramatizing elements of the work as a whole, at the risk of overemphasis, but in the interests of clarity.

Unmistakably, what 'Freely Espousing' introduces is a poetry of quotation. Any number of the poem's lines and fragments might be quotations, and most of the poem has the air of something that originated somewhere else. This, for instance, is characteristic:

> "What is that gold-green tetrahedron down the river?"
> "You are experiencing a new sensation."

> *if the touch-me-knots*
> *are not in bloom*
> *neither are the chrysanthemums*[3]

Schuyler had various reasons for quoting in his poetry, but one of them, unquestionably, was pleasure. His *Diary* quite often consists, as Nathan Kernan, its editor, points out, of 'fragments of conversation that Schuyler reports because he enjoys the way something is expressed' (D, 13). Kernan cites a remark by Fairfield Porter, '"A dozen pair of your socks are vying with the hawkweed"', but he might have cited any number, *The Diary* being, among other things, a repository of lumps of language enjoyed – as is the poetry, some of which is made up of remarks that first appeared in *The Diary*. The elements of 'Freely Espousing' are not lifted from *The Diary*, but the same impulse is at work. To *get* the poem, in other words, one has to appreciate that lines exist in large part, sometimes exclusively, for the pleasure of their being uttered. Witness the opening, which includes the title:

> Freely Espousing
>
> a commingling sky
>
>> a semi-tropic night
>> that cast the blackest shadow
>> of the easily torn, untrembling banana leaf.
>>
>> (CP, 3)

To appreciate this beginning, one has to enjoy the way the phrases play on the inner ear, or the fact of rolling them quietly around one's mouth: or at very least one has to appreciate that Schuyler did.

In 'Freely Espousing', in other words, Schuyler might well be said to savour language, where 'savor' is a term from Stevens' essay 'The Noble Rider and the Sound of Words'. Stevens' argument in that essay is that little 'will appear to have suffered more from the passage of time than the music of poetry, and that has suffered less'. The point of the tricksy phrasing is to observe that, as the culture has grown to disregard the music of poetry, so that music has become all the more significant to the culture. With its neglect, Stevens argues, the need has deepened for the sound of words, for 'a finality, a perfection, an unalterable vibration, which it is only within the power of the acutest poet to give them'.[4] It is difficult to prove something as generalized as the cultural neglect of the music of poetry. Anecdotally, however, Stevens' argument would still seem to hold good. Recently I taught Schuyler to an otherwise informed and intelligent final-year class which was collectively incapable of naming 'alliteration'. It was a subject-specific term which had slipped from the vocabulary. This might not be thought to matter very much, though certainly such a slippage mattered to Stevens, hence the fact that in 'The Noble Rider and the Sound of Words', as in numerous other essays and in his poetry, he sets out to show that 'above everything else, poetry is words; and that words, above everything else, are, in poetry sounds'.[5] What other reason than that words in poetry are, above all, sounds, could one have given, for instance, for the existence of 'Bantams in Pine-Woods', where the central figure is 'Chieftain Iffucan of Azcan in caftan', and where the sound of the words acts to override everything, including the poem's ill-considered cultural politics. But if there is unquestionably something of Stevens' fondness for the pleasures of language in Schuyler, 'savouring' is not quite the word. As Stevens tells it, the poet, along with other artists, 'transforms us into epicures', implying, in the pleasure taken, a refinement that does not describe the way Schuyler handles language. Better, perhaps, to say that Schuyler relishes words – where relishing is a more lip-smacking response than savouring – and all words, or at least any kind of words, the way Marianne Moore did in her collage poems, and as she showed in her conversation notebooks; more organized repositories than Schuyler's *Diary*, but demonstrating a similar fondness for the language as it was uttered around her. Schuyler puts flesh on the bones of Stevens' argument. He quotes in his poetry in part simply because he relishes the sound of words, 'very directly / as in / bong. And tickle. Oh it is inescapable kiss.'

The act and significance of quotation has featured frequently in this book, being a mark, in various cases, of the writer's enthusiasm, of their work's willingness to give voice to words and meanings not their own. From *Walden* to *Lunch Poems* texts have been shown to open themselves to other expressions, where the changing nature of such openings through the course of Modern American literature has been understood as a gradual reconfiguration of writerly enthusiasm. No writer was more open, in this sense, than Schuyler, 'Freely Espousing' being a dramatization of that happy, sometimes ecstatic, condition. Reading Schuyler, however – his *Diary* in particular, but also those many poems which work like diary entries – is to be reminded how quotation comes about. Schuyler, in other words, doesn't so much quote as transcribe. This thought is not new; transcription is a word that has seemed, in general, well suited to Schuyler's writing. He suggested it himself in conversation with Jean W. Ross, observing that his work was 'concerned with looking at things and trying to transcribe them as painting is', a remark that Kernan takes to articulate a general quality in the poetry, where transcription fulfils something of the Emersonian ambition of finding poems in the world.[6] The *Diary*, however, demonstrates a less transcendent sense of transcription, numerous entries consisting of remarks copied out, or written across, as on 23 December 1968, where the whole entry consists of Schuyler having typed out:

– 'and possibly local slippery conditions' – the weather woman, 1 a.m. 12/23/68

Because it stands alone, because it isn't absorbed into any other text, what partly matters with an entry like this is the fact of it having been copied out; that Schuyler took the time on hearing the woman's remark to go to his typewriter and reproduce it on the page. And typically, when Schuyler quotes in his diary, the quote goes unglossed by commentary. It just stands there, perhaps alongside another unglossed quote, as for instance the entry for 17 August 1970, which consists simply of a quote from Harriet Beecher Stowe, and then this from the *Memoir* of the English engraver Thomas Bewick:

> From my sheep thus drawing into shelter, gave rise to an opinion I formed, and which has been confirmed by long reflection, that much may yet be done to protect the larger flocks from being overblown and lost on the bleak moors, in great snow-storms. Were long avenues made by double rows of whin hedges, planted parallel to each other at about six feet asunder, and continued in the form of two sides of a square, with the whins of each side drawn together, and to grow interplatted at the tops, so as to form an arched kind of roof, the sheep would, on instinctively [sic] seeing the coming storm, immediately avail themselves of such asylums, and particularly in the lambing season. (D, 84)

In *The Diary* the quote continues, heavy with the sound of detail – a whin is a form of 'furze or gorse' – Schuyler here, as elsewhere, demonstrating a fondness for the music of fact which led him, like Thoreau, to read extensively in natural history, in Gilbert White, for instance, and Charles Darwin.

Prior to the downloadable text, the easy cut-and-paste of which obviates the need of a physical relation with favoured or selected words, all writers who quote must have done something like this, copying words out onto some intermediary text – a notebook or file card – or sometimes directly into the work itself. A noticeable feature of Schuyler's copying out is that often he does it into his *Diary*, and that sometimes his *Diary* consists of that and nothing else. And while sometimes, as in Moore's notebooks, the *Diary* acts as an archive, Schuyler returning to it for resources for his poems, much more frequently the quoted remark has no existence in his body of work but there. *The Diary*, in other words, doubles as a commonplace book (as his poetry would from time to time, witness in particular 'The Fauré Ballade'), where remarks are quoted in large part simply because the pleasure of them is intensified in the act of transcription itself, because one way of really relishing an instance of language is to copy it out. More than that, to copy out another person's words is to develop a more intimate relation with them; not to make them one's own perhaps, but to take them into, to allow them to shape, one's sensibility; as – in the act of copying, as one becomes more familiar with the shape and rhythm of the sentences – they guide one's hand or one's fingers. Schuyler quoted, but in order to quote, as his *Diary* reminds us, he had first to transcribe, his transcriptions being a way of becoming intimate with utterances he relished.

There is relishing, also, in the manner of Schuyler's composition, in the way in which Schuyler would often collage a poem together. Many Schuyler poems are obviously collages ('Freely Espousing' is a case in point), but many that don't immediately look like collages are inconspicuously so, the transferable value and pleasure of the collage for Schuyler being the way it presented its various elements. Thus as he wrote to Miss Batie (a correspondent from Vancouver, who had written expressing an admiration for Schuyler's poem 'February' and with questions about the poet's practice):

> I know that I like an art where disparate elements form an entity. De Kooning's work, which I greatly admire, has less to do with it than that of Kurt Schwitters, whose collages are made of commercial bits and 'found' pieces but which always compose a whole striking for its completeness.[7]

It is clear how a poem like 'Freely Espousing' resembles Schwitters, or, for instance, Rauschenberg, in that the poem's snatches and fragments of language, while part of the whole, remain discrete elements, the effect of which can be to make the poem more thoroughly pleasurable in that each element can be enjoyed in and for itself. What Schuyler takes from the art of collage, however, is not simply a sense that, as Burroughs grasped it, language could be cut up and rearranged, spliced and respliced to stimulating effect; but, more like Moore, that language could (and should) be understood through collage, that it should be presented with the clarity with which collaging artists present their found materials. So it is not only, in 'Freely Espousing', quoted phrases one is invited to relish, but their constituent elements, as in

> the bales of pink cotton candy
> in the slanting light

– where the alliteration serves to hold the sounds apart. Or, for instance,

> Their scallop shell of quiet
> is the S.S. *United States*

– where the first line comes from Walter Ralegh's poem 'The Passionate Man's Pilgrimage', and where it is included very largely for its qualities of sound. Schuyler made collages in order that all the elements of the poem, written and voiced, its phonemes, syllables, vowels and consonants – the language in all its detail – might be understood as pleasurable.

Which view of the pleasures of Schuyler's poetry might seem to make it typically – and reductively – post-Modern, where the action of the writing is all in and between the words. And there *is* intensive action in and between Schuyler's words, and between the constitutive elements of those words, and this *is* integral to the pleasure and value of his work. You do want to get your tongue around the poems. You do want to have them on your ear. You do – I do anyway – while reading *The Diary*, find yourself copying large chunks of it out. Stevens' complaint that the music of poetry has suffered from the passage of time remains true, especially in British universities, where the pressure is constantly on to convert the experience of reading into something else, some other skill or outcome. In such an environment Schuyler's poetry exists as an education in the qualities and capacities of literary language. But there is more to the pleasure of uttering than the simple relishing of words, as a glance at another Schuyler collage, 'An East Window on Elizabeth Street', suggests.

'An East Window on Elizabeth Street' finds Schuyler in his most characteristic writing situation – the window in question looking out on part of lower Manhattan. The poem is vernacular in its quotation, in that much of the language that enters the poem comes up from the street. It is vernacular also in its music, which bears a trace of Stevens, but which has its source in the environment the poet looks out on to:

> burgeoning with stacks, pipes, ventilators, tensile antennae –
> that bristling gray bit is a part of a bridge.
>
> (CP, 85)

As with any number of Schuyler poems the extraordinary thing here, as he puts it in 'February', is that 'it all works in together', that the elements the poem presents – the constituents of its manifold – don't, in their individuality, exceed the sense of a whole. What holds this particular collage together, what makes its various elements compose a Schwitters-like entity, is the image of assemblage in the closing lines, where

> Out there
> a bird is building a nest out of torn up letters
> and the red cellophane off cigarette and gum packs.
>
> (CP, 85)

Not to labour the point, but the bird is up to what Schuyler is up to, making himself at home in his environment with the materials the environment provides, the scraps and fragments, the torn-up letters and gum packs. Or to change the metaphor slightly, Schuyler opens his writing up to the voices of his environment, makes a poetry of what he finds, in order to be at home in the world in which he finds himself.

Only the relationship is more physiological than that suggests. Thus while there is not a voice, as such, in this poem – Schuyler does show himself speaking at one point, but only so as to make his absence elsewhere more apparent – there is, nonetheless, a mouth in the poem. Or rather, the poem has a mouth, opened wide and made physiologically vivid:

> ("Rinse and spit"
> and blood stained sputum and big gritty bits
> are swirled away.)
>
> (CP, 84)

This image extends a metaphor Schuyler has just before introduced, the buildings he is looking at being thought of, in their alignment, as dental. But as the continuation of a metaphor the image of the mouth is gratuitous in that the scene does not require it to appear. Except that in another sense it does, because in this poem of quotation and vernacular music, the scene comes about through the implied mediation of the mouth, Schuyler composing the scene and, as he does so, relishing the way the words he utters play in and around his tongue. And again, it would be wrong to make too much of this, to fixate on a particular image, except that what Schuyler provides here is an image of the poem being mouthed, where mouthing is different from, or at least an inflection on, voicing. To set the argument out: Schuyler relishes words not simply as they afford pleasure, but because the words he finds – as with the bird and its torn-up letters – constitute, in some sense, a way of being at home in the world, and where the contact and continuity implied by that statement comes, naturally (which is to say physiologically) enough, to focus on the mouth – the opening from which the words flow. Which brings one back to 'Freely Espousing', which has its own vivid mouth action: 'bong. And tickle. Oh it is inescapable kiss.' To understand the full enthusiasm of Schuyler's writing, one has to register the kinds of intimacy he thinks words are capable of; and to understand that intimacy one has to appreciate the intercessions of his mouth.

Kissing

Like another Schuyler collage, '"The Elizabethans Called It Dying"', 'Freely Espousing' is, in one sense, a love poem. '"The Elizabethans Called It Dying"' is a poem of the upper East Side, in particular the stretch of Manhattan that looks across the East River to Welfare Island, now called Roosevelt Island. Digressing through the expressions, spoken or written, that emerge from that location – its capacity for acquaintance with the neighbourhood extending with each new incorporated detail – the poem concludes by announcing itself a love poem:

> not to be in love with you
> I can't remember what it was like
> it must've been lousy
> (CP, 11)

This comes as a surprise, because nothing that went before seemed to speak of love, except that on reflection love was the condition of the poem's writing, the state in which the generous intimacy of the collage was made possible. 'Freely Espousing' wraps up in a similar fashion:

It is not so quiet and they
are a medium-size couple who
when they fold each other up
well, thrill. That's their story.

(CP, 4)

Here the concluding lines are more of a piece with the whole poem – one can think of the couple as freely espoused, as each retaining their individual identities even as they 'fold each other up'. Which happy image of a relationship replicates the relations the poem identifies in language, disparate elements existing independently and within a whole. 'Freely Espousing', in other words, also has as its condition of composition a particular intimacy, between the 'medium size couple', an intimacy brought to the fore earlier in the poem by the expression, 'Oh it is inescapable kiss'. But it isn't the couple in 'Freely Espousing' who kiss. The statement arises as Schuyler is reflecting on language, on words which 'echo the act described'. 'Oh it is inescapable kiss', in other words, is trying to say something about language, something that seems central to Schuyler's poetry.

It seems central partly because there is a good deal of kissing in Schuyler.[8] To press the point, because it is important to register the frequency of the image and the consistency of its use, in 'In January'

a leafless beech stands wrinkled, gray and sexless – all bone
and loosened sinew – in silver glory

And the sun falls on all one side of it in a running glance, a
licking gaze, an eye-kiss.

(CP, 81)

'The Crystal Lithium' records

A promise, late on a broiling day in late September, of the cold kiss
Of marble sheets to one who goes barefoot quickly in the snow

(CP, 116)

'Await' thinks of time as

hours compressed into
a kiss, a lick, or
stretched out by a
train into an endless
rubber band.

(CP, 133)

'So Good' – an elegy for Schuyler's Grandmother, who taught him the names of flowers and birds – kisses twice, the second time presenting snow and rain going

as Granny went
embanked in flowers
so long ago, so
cold a cheek to
ask a child
to kiss.

(CP, 180)

While early in 'Hymn to Life' a 'Gull coasts by, unexpected as a kiss on the nape of the neck', the poem later remarking how

'"When I
was born, death kissed me. I kissed it back."
(CP, 216, 220–1)

The most significant kiss poem in Schuyler, however, is 'Going', the kiss there clearly aiming to articulate something about the way Schuyler's poetry disposes itself towards words. 'Going' consists of five sentences, the first and fifth being quite exhilarating presentations of phenomena that exemplify 'October', their detail equalling anything one might find in Thoreau. Thus, to hear the first, which runs across eleven lines, and builds powerfully through its syntax:

In the month when the Kamchatka bugbane
finally turns its strung-out hard pellets white
and a sudden drench flattens the fugitive
meadow saffron to tissue-paper scraps
and winds follow that crack and bend without breaking
the woody stems of chrysanthemums so the good of not disbudding
shows in smaller flights of metallic pungency,
a clear zenith looks lightly dusted and fades to nothing
at the skyline, shadows float up to lighted surfaces
as though they and only they kept on the leaves
that hide their color in a glassy shine.

(CP, 32–3)

Compelling as it is, as it presses towards its conclusion, a sentence such as this deserves a commentary. Happily, the poem itself proceeds to provide one, the second, third and fourth sentences each, separately and more or less figuratively, articulating the relation to the world that the opening sentence stands to exemplify. Thus the second sentence presents an instance of limited but fervent communication, as 'A garnering squirrel makes a frantic chatter at a posse of cats/ that sit and stare while their coats thicken'. The fourth sentence presents a more successful transmission, though again it is wordless, as

the light slants
into rooms that face southwest: into this room
across a bookcase so the dead-brown gold-stamped
spines look to be those to take down now.

The cats don't *get* the squirrel's chatter, but here the light stamps itself decisively onto the books, as if the world could make its way directly onto the page. The poem doesn't believe this exactly, but it does want to assert an intimacy of sorts between language and the world, and the intimacy it has in mind is that proposed by the third sentence, where

Days
are shorter, more limpid, are like a kiss
neither dry nor wet nor on the lips
that sends a light shock in rings
through all the surface of the skin.

We have come across part of this metaphor before, the light shock in rings being how, in *Ion*, Plato presented inspiration, and how Melville recapitulated it when presenting the relation between major writers. The question is, how does Schuyler's 'kiss' supplement the metaphor, and how is this poem's relation to the moment it presents explicable as such?

What we are invited to think by the poem is that language, or at least, language used as well as Schuyler can use it, is capable of taking the impression of a day, is capable of being kissed. But what does this mean? One way to answer this question is to think again of how Stevens thought of the sounds of words. Thus, while lamenting in 'The Noble Rider and the Sound of Words' that the music of poetry has suffered greatly from the passage of time, Stevens makes the case for such music beyond the pleasures inherent to it: 'I repeat that [the poet's] role is to help people live their lives. He has had immensely to do with giving life whatever savor it possesses. He has had to do with whatever the imagination and senses have made of the world.'[9] The argument as to how the poet gives life its 'savor', how he or she helps 'people live their lives', unfolds across the essays, lectures and academic pieces of *The Necessary Angel*. What Stevens wants to establish there is a relation of 'intensification' between the poet's handling of the sound of words and the lives people live. One word for that relation is analogy – analogy, as Stevens argues it, being central to poetry, or rather, as he puts it: 'Poetry is almost incredibly one of the effects of analogy'. There is, he suggests, 'always an analogy between nature and the imagination', and poetry is 'the outcome of the operation of one imagination on another through the instrumentality of the figure'. Or to put the sentiment at its most enthusiastic, analogy is 'a rhetoric in which the feeling of one man is communicated to another in words of the exquisite appositeness that takes away all their verbality'.

Stevens' quasi-historical discussion of analogy is, for the most part, concerned with the poet's use of figure. Crucially, though, as he brings the idea up to date, he reverts from figure in language to the music of language, asking the question, 'What has this music to do with analogy?' The answer he offers is that the sound of words 'carries us on and through every winding, once more to the world outside of the music at its conclusion'.[10] This is suggestive, but doesn't quite nail the point. Where Stevens nails it instead, where he gets to the crux of the proposition that there is analogy in the sound of words, is in 'The Figure of the Youth as Virile Poet':

> The pleasure that the poet has … is a pleasure of agreement with the radiant and productive world in which he lives. It is an agreement that Mallarmé found in the sound of
> > *Le vierge, la vivace et le bel aujourd'hui.*[11]

There is, Stevens argues here, and as he wants to demonstrate in a late poem such as 'Extracts from Addresses to the Academy of Fine Ideas' (a poem written after he had ceased to relate to the world according to the mechanisms of Kant) there is an agreement with the world to be had in the sound of words. Language used with due attention to the sound of words is not so much a medium in which analogies with the world might be made, but an analogy itself. In the sound of words, to say it again, as Stevens suggests, there can be an agreement with the world.

Schuyler is a maker of analogies, numerous major poems proceeding through what one might call an analogical enquiry. Persistently he asks how one thing can be put in terms of another – how the squirrels' chatter might be rendered by the cats. 'A Man in Blue' works like this: the November afternoon being presented in terms of the Brahms Schuyler listens to as he looks out on to it; Brahms telling Bruno Walter to think of his second symphony 'as a family / planning where to go next summer / in terms of other summers' (CP, 16–17). 'February' works in a similar way, Schuyler trying to get at the day's defining quality through a series of likenings: 'like the UN Building on big evenings', 'like grass light on flesh' (CP, 4). The moments of real agreement in Schuyler, however, occur when the poetry's sound is most clearly to the fore, as in the opening sentence of 'Going', where October – in 'its strung-out hard pellets', and 'meadow saffron' flattened to 'tissue-paper scraps', and the 'crack and bend' of 'the woody stems of chrysanthemums' – finds its expression, and agreement, in Schuyler's extraordinarily supple and extended handling of sound.

One way, then, Schuyler wants us to think about the relation the poem has to the environment it presents is in terms of the impression promised by a kiss. This takes us back to collage. The object of Schuyler's various poetry – where the variousness lies largely in the writing's brilliantly fluent separation of sounds – was, as he put it in the poem with which, late in life, he always began his readings, to 'salute' the 'various field' which was invariably, as he looked out on it, his subject. So likewise in 'Going', where the sounds of Schuyler's composition are held apart and heard in order that the scene they present can be apprehended in terms of its constitutive elements. In Schuyler names don't agree with things in any simple way, but language, in its internal relations, can resemble, or, rather disclose, arrangements of things. Or so Schuyler thought. As he wrote to the painter John Button: 'one important reason for making drawings, I imagine, is not to draw a likeness of what one sees but to find out what it is one sees' (SL, 33). Schuyler finds out what he sees in 'Going', his emphasis on the sound of words at the beginning and the end of that poem allowing him to see better the elements of his environment.

Likewise in 'Light from Canada', where the light is

> scoured and Nova
> Scotian and of a clarity that
> opens up the huddled masses
> of the stolid spruce so you
> see them in their bristling
> individuality.
>
> (CP, 100)

The light opens the spruce up, but so does Schuyler's language, which in its facility for sound, in its free-verse, alliterative attention to each of its elements, provides an analogue for, or achieves an agreement with, 'the stolid spruce … in their bristling individuality'. Which means that, as Schuyler understands it, language is capable of intimacy with the world, that the page is capable of presenting the world's impression; where the impression is to be found not in language's figures and representations, but in the arrangements of its elements, imprinted in the distribution of its various parts: 'Oh it is inescapable kiss'.

Voicing

Although when finally he performed his work he was a 'fucking sensation' – Schuyler's own, uncharacteristically immodest words, but a judgement shared by many who heard him – for most of his life he declined to do so. A reason he gave for this, over and above terror at the prospect, was a suspicion of the effect the intervention of his voice would have on the sound of the poems. As he told Robert Thompson: 'Very often, if you hear a person read a poem, you don't hear what the poem sounds like at all. It goes by too quickly, and their voice distracts you from all the inner sounds of a poem.'[12] What is obscured in the poetry reading, in other words, is, as he puts it, 'the voice of the poem'.

He expressed such a dissatisfaction with voice on a number of occasions. In his *Diary* entry for Thursday 8 December 1988, he reports on the

> *not*-fun of having one's words yelled at one, in duet with the clanging of a Steinway. Poems, for the most part, meant to be read at a glance, journal jottings, almost unsingable, and certainly not like this. If the voice is treated as another instrument, then it must sound as well played as the piano (or whatever): and it did not, oh no, not either of them. (D, 244)

The unhappy event in question was a performance of two song-cycle settings of Schuyler's poems by the composer Gerald Busby. In part his complaint is against the particular singers – hence the suggestion that if the voice is to be treated as an instrument it must sound as well played as any other. The meat of the complaint, though, is against the idea of the poems being sung at all, and so quite likely no rendition could have satisfied Schuyler, for whom the best kind of voice was not, in fact, one played like an instrument, but one, as it were, that knew how to efface itself. Thus in the entry of a few days before, Monday 5 December 1988, Schuyler reports attending the Church of the Incarnation, at Madison Avenue and 35th Street, remarking that 'Father Ousley (the Rev J. Douglas, that is) has a fine voice which he uses with equally fine lack of affectation – no Episcopal throat there, (D, 243). It is intriguing to contemplate the Episcopal throat in the context of a discussion of Schuyler's enthusiasm, the implication being that an Episcopal voice would too thickly overlay and intervene on its text; which would seem to imply in turn that Schuyler preferred the unintrusive voice, the voice which gave itself over to another's agency.

I will come on to the religious aspect of Schuyler's enthusiasm at the end of this essay. What I want to concentrate on here is the suggestion Schuyler gives of the relative voicelessness of his writing, where voice, in that sense, means the voice of the poet, the poet's voice. *In* that sense, Schuyler's writing barely has a voice, doesn't conform to the imagined contours of the speaking voice, but is, as he puts it, unsingable. The writing does, however, so he suggests, have a voice of its own, being the 'voice of the poem' that the reading obscures. This would seem true, in that there are relations internal to a Schuyler poem that are available to the silent listening of the inner ear, but which a reading would, however sensational, fail to bring out. Still, though, to speak of the voice of the poem is to place a certain construction upon it, as if the point of reading were to identify that mediating tone. What I want to suggest, instead, taking on board Schuyler's own suspicion, is that his best writing doesn't so much have voice but that it voices, that what one hears is not voice but a voicing.

Some of Schuyler's best work – some of the later poems of *Freely Espousing*, and the environmental lyrics, including the title poem, of *The Crystal Lithium* – are without voice in the explicit sense that there is not, in the poem, an 'I' speaking. His most voiceless writing, however – and therefore, as he points out, his most unsingable – is to be found in his *Diary*. There are, roughly speaking, three phases to Schuyler's *Diary*. He started to keep it – a single entry in 1967 notwithstanding – at the suggestion of Fairfield Porter on 1 January 1968, writing it more or less regularly until the summer of 1971. Then, after a handful of entries in 1981, he took it up again in October 1984 – when he and the artist Darragh Park decided to collaborate on a diary of words and pictures for publication – stopping in December 1985. He then resumed the diary in June 1987, keeping it up sporadically until near the end of his life, in February 1991. The three sections of the diary differ in various ways – in terms of preoccupation (mortality towards the end), setting (Long Island and Maine, where Schuyler lived with the Porters through the 1960s and early 1970s, and Manhattan where he lived through the 1980s until his death), but also address. Written with publication explicitly in mind, the middle section of the diary clearly has a voice: Schuyler engages in exchanges with the diary itself, with future readers, and sometimes stages rhetorical banter between a private and a soon-to-be-public self. All of which is something of a shock when one comes upon it, the clarifying virtue of the shock being to show just how peculiarly without voice had been the early phase of *The Diary:*

November 29, 1969, Amherst

> Morning. There's half a moon a quarter ways up the clear faded sky. In the shadows the fallen leaves are pale with frost and those in the light look toasted. Inside the woods, behind the wild white scratches of the bare branches, there is a dark warm green of a single pine: a homely, inviting glow.

August 17, 1970

> The rain falls in rods, pinning everything in place.

September 1, 1970

> A wonderful freshness, the air billowing like sheets on a line, and the light with a clarity that opens up the huddled masses of the spruce and you can see their bristling individuality.

There are three things one might notice in entries such as these. The first is that, really to enjoy Schuyler's *Diary* one has to enjoy weather, or writing about weather, which is to say writing constantly attuned to change. The second thing to acknowledge straight away is that, obviously, there is a consciousness at work in such diary entries. There is a composing self and, plain as the writing can be, it does run, quite freely at times, to analogy and metaphor. But the third thing to notice is Schuyler's intention in writing. 'Some days,' he wrote on 27 April 1971, 'I have an almost irresistible urge to write.' The diary itself was conducive, instrumental even, to that urge. The keeping of it would seem to have enabled him to become more of a writer, in that judging by his publication history he wrote more continuously after he had started it. *The Diary*, that is, facilitates the urge to write, giving Schuyler a form in which he might always be composing, which would always be readily available for his writing. To put this another way, the urge to write invariably amounted to an urge simply to get things down, where things are not aspects of the reflective self – Schuyler's *Diary* is almost never a vehicle for self-expression – but things of the world, where the object in writing was to get some aspect of the world onto the page.

Once started, *The Diary* quickly became integral to Schuyler's whole writing practice. *The Crystal Lithium*, published in 1972, and the book that emerged through the most vigilant period of Schuyler's diary-keeping, is a markedly different book from *Freely Espousing*. There are various reasons for this, including the differing nature of the two books' composition: *Freely Espousing* gathered together work dating from the1950s to the late 1960s; *The Crystal Lithium* showed the overall cogency of work produced in a quite concentrated burst. Which is not to say that the latter book diverges radically from the former, continuing, as it does, Schuyler's twin habits of observation and collage. The difference, felt in the longer title poem of *The Crystal Lithium*, but apparent also in a number of the book's shorter pieces, lay rather in the intensification of the writing in response to environment, and – because it is only partly true to call that writing observational – in the shifting relation it presented between the self and the world. These differences, it seems safe to say, were to do with the writing of *The Diary*, the effect of which was to permit in Schuyler a new intimacy with the conditions of his inspiration.

Partly this is true in that certain poems, or lines from poems, come directly through or out of *The Diary*. Schuyler demonstrated this by publishing a section of his diary as such – he called it 'A Vermont Diary' – in *The Crystal Lithium*, where the poems 'Slowly', 'A Gray Thought' and 'Verge' are shown to have had their first existence as diary entries. Better instances than these, though – because 'A Vermont Diary' might possibly have been written with publication expressly in mind – are the cases where unversified lines in *The Diary* become parts of poems. As Kernan notes, the opening of 'Light Blue Above' has its first existence as part of a diary entry, as do the defining phrases of 'Light from Canada'. To take this kind of effect as an instance of Schuyler becoming intimate, through the *Diary*, with the condition of his inspiration is to say that through writing in the journal he arrived at – or located, or found – poetry; *The Diary* being a medium through which Schuyler could access a quality of language which became the sound of his new poems. Not to over-egg this, but in the quietness and relative unselfconsciousness of the early phase of *The Diary* he found a means of producing – one might say catching the sound of – what he termed 'the voice of the poem'.

There is another sense, however, in which *The Diary* permitted in Schuyler an intimacy with the condition of his inspiration, where what is at issue is not the voice of the poem, even in the sense Schuyler means it, but its own relative voicelessness, where the writing is given over to a voicing of things in the world. Thus the urge to write which often defines the diary – the urge, simply, to get things down on paper – is apparent in a number of poems in *The Crystal Lithium*. But what also shows in those poems is the consequence of the continuous recording *The Diary* consists of. Schuyler grew more closely acquainted with his environments – Maine in particular, but also Long Island and Vermont – through the act of writing them down; thus the poems of *The Crystal Lithium* pay a still more local and particular attention than anything in *Freely Espousing*. The poems vary in the degree of authority they want to attribute to the relation they have with the environments that give rise to them. Thus in 'Verge', written in Vermont, Schuyler all but ascribes words to the world:

> An unseen
> something stirs
> and says: No
> snow yet but
> it will snow.
> The trees sneeze:
> You bet it
> will, compiling
> a white and wordless
> dictionary
> in which brush
> cut, piled and
> roofed with glitter
> will catch and burn
> transparently
> bright in white
> defining "flame."
>   (CP, 111)

Schuyler is fond of the Emersonian illusion – though it is only ever used for rhetorical effect – that nature supplies words (or at least meanings). 'Hymn to Life' ends in a similar fashion, the poem, having dwelt beautifully on the phenomena of May, giving itself over, in the last lines, to the month's own voice: 'May mutters, "Why ask questions?" or, "What are the questions you wish to ask?"' Elsewhere the poetry is less rhetorically confident, not finding its words in the world, but, as in 'A Gray Thought', discriminating between similar things in a way that is possible because, through the keeping of his *Diary*, he has arrived at a language capable of registering the finest of distinctions.

Most striking, though, in respect of the intimacy Schuyler achieves through his diary, with the environments that are the conditions of his inspiration, are the poems that catch and voice process. As in 'Evening Wind', which first describes wind as an effect in trees, and which concludes by presenting it as an effect in language:

> Wind, you don't
> blow hard enough, though
> rising, in the smoky blue
> of evening, mindless and in love.
> Or would be if the wind
> were not above such thoughts,
> above thought in fact
> of course, though coursing,
> cool as water, through it.
>
> (CP, 103)

Wind won't be caught by thought, this poem suggests, not as thought characteristically voices itself, won't respond to thought's address. Rather, language must somehow be given over to wind, to its coursing through. The sound of its coursing runs through thought and its locutions, through 'though' and 'of course', until what one hears is 'coursing' 'through' . Where the assonance is not the sound of the wind exactly, but sound is the overwhelming effect, language having made itself available to what is heard.

A better example still is the title poem itself, whose object is not to present a particular phenomenon, but to catch, in its extraordinarily extended sentences, the multiplicity of phenomena. The self is not an observer of these phenomena, but it is buffeted by and circulates among them, and all the power of the poetry is in its carrying on, and on:

> Where kids in kapok ice-skate and play at Secret City as the sun
> Sets before dinner, the snow on fields turns pink and under the hatched
>   ice

The water slides darkly and over it a never before seen liquefaction of
    the sun
In a chemical yellow greener than sulphur a flash of petroleum by-product
Unbelievable, unwanted and as lovely as though someone you knew all
    your life
Said the one inconceivable thing and then went on washing dishes …

                                         (CP, 118)

Schuyler was an avid reader of diaries. He mentioned in interview, and in *The Diary* itself, the diaries of, among others, Francis Kilvert, George Templeton Strong, Gilbert White and Virginia Woolf. But he also mentioned Thoreau, whose diaries, as he told Carl Little, he was 'always reading in', and whose *Week on the Concord and Merrimack Rivers* he finds – as he reports, late in his own diary, when he turns up a yellowed scrap of paper – he once transcribed from in the early 1950s. What his own *Diary* most resembles, however, in the extended intimacy of its meditation, is *Walden* itself. Except that in *Walden*, given Thoreau's polemical gesture – the gesture of setting up house by the pond in the first place, but also the political gesture implicit in his writing – the voice of the author is more to the fore. Thoreau was there by design, and he had a design on the reader, and his relation with the world is inevitably mediated as such. Schuyler's acquaintance with the environments of Maine and Long Island was, by contrast, accidental, and his writing of them was, relative to Thoreau, un-rhetorical. His urge, as often as not, seems to have been simply to get the world down. Which is not to say that Schuyler's environments speak through his *Diary*. Rather, *The Diary* takes great pains to voice its world, where what is meant by such a voicing is not direct transmission, but that, to echo a Schuyler phrase, he gave a shape in language to that of which he was a part.

One can think of Schuyler's *Diary*, therefore, as in some sense equivalent to O'Hara's reconfiguration of the act of writing, of his situating the typewriter in the middle of the conversation. It was a relation with environment Schuyler himself thought of enthusiastically, hence the entry for 22 February 1971, which reads as follows:

Creepily misty morning, dank, dark, disheveled and rather ominous, like a destroyer just gone into dry dock. But how beautiful it was at the first light to hear the repetitious song of a cardinal – my pleasure in it is more than just that I can recognize it: it is not unlike that which someone who doesn't 'know' music takes in the songs he does know. Simple and right from the heart to the heart – or perhaps from the throat to the ear is enough, but in that way in which hearing is itself suddenly a kind of singing. (D, 109)

The claim, as in Thoreau, is not to immediacy, but to nearness, to the proximity to things achievable in the act of voicing. In Thoreau the effect was crowing; here, that which Schuyler hears is suddenly a kind of singing, words forming in the act of listening. In his *Diary*, this is to say, Schuyler understood himself, sometimes, as arriving at a form of writing only minimally intervened upon by voice and its effects. Or to put it another way, he approaches, in the growing absence of his voice, a voicing of other agencies, a precarious mode of utterance given the name, historically, of enthusiasm.

Showing

In Schuyler's 1950s poem 'April and its Forsythia', published in *Freely Espousing*, the census taker turns up. 'She had on', the poem reports, 'transparent overshoes, coat and / hat' and, naturally, had a few questions she needed to ask. Schuyler doesn't report the conversation, but some of its content is made apparent. 'That census taker,' he observes, a few lines after having introduced and then seemingly forgotten about her – 'I'm the head of a household. / I am also my household. Not bad' (CP, 23). But not, as the poem doesn't overlook to imply, good either. Schuyler doesn't make too much of it, but what sense can it really make to designate him the head of something which consists only of him? That would be to make him the head of himself, which is a nonsensical proposition, and a conclusion, so the poem allows one to think, that could only arise out of bureaucratic stupidity. Whatever it was the census was designed to establish, it hasn't done an effective job in Schuyler's case, its mode of questioning garbling the situation of the single, one might say – because what this poem of 1950s New York partly has in mind is homosexuality – unmarried man.

But the woman does show something. She shows, by her clothing – those transparent overshoes, coat and hat (are they all transparent? Schuyler declines to determine that implicitly comic detail) – that outside, in the world, it is snowing. Which is what the poem means to show also; not that it *is* snowing – he could just tell us that – but what this particular snowfall is like. This is not, as the poem is careful to observe, something we can take for granted:

> What variety snow falls with and has: this kind lays like wet sheets
> or soaked opaque blotting paper: where a surface makes
> a natural puddle, its own melting darkens it, as though it had lain
> all winter and the thaw is come. (CP, 23)

This description distinguishes it from the snowfall Schuyler observes in 'Empathy and New Year', where it 'isn't raining, snowing, sleeting, slushing' but is, in fact, 'raining snow'. 'Raining snow' is quite a good description, but is also deficient in the way description is, the words failing, quite, to make clear what the snow is like, which is why in 'April and its

Forsythia' the emphasis is firmly on 'showing', on the fact that, as the poem says, 'Snow isn't secret, showing further aspects, how small / cast lions would look if they grew maned'. Only even as he makes this point, quietly establishing that it isn't by describing a thing that one brings it into view, he seems already to have moved away from his subject, not showing snow, but indicating what snow shows. Except that actually that is his subject. Thus, it is not clear from 'April and its Forsythia' whether the census taker established what she needed to – though the suspicion freely offered is that her bureaucratic approach to the world is hardly likely to issue in anything of worth. Despite herself, however, she does help to establish that it is snowing. 'April and its Forsythia', in other words, is a gentle comedy of knowledge, where the butt of the joke is administration.

How things can be known, how they show themselves, was an ongoing question for Schuyler. Quite often, as in 'April and its Forsythia', what results is comedy, a burlesque on the way things are thought to be known but, as he wants very much to assert, aren't. As in 'Sorting, wrapping, packing, stuffing', where the joke is in the present participles which name ways of containing and organizing the world, but which in their ongoing grammatical nature show that such organization is a hopeless pursuit. Thus in the poem nothing will stay packed, like, for example, the 'blue fire escape' Schuyler notices as he fills up his suitcase:

> But how do you pack a blue fire escape – even if the man
> got off it out of the 97 degree sun
> and blizzards, then sullied snow that left
> disclosing no car where one was.
>
> (CP, 27)

This looks like a conceptual error, in that nobody, surely, would want to pack a blue fire escape, except that what is at issue in the poem is not a category mistake, but the mistakes categorical thinking – with its inclination to sort, wrap, pack and stuff – makes. Here, then, the butt of the joke is Kant, as Schuyler concludes the poem with a list of books he can't, in his packing, contain:

> *My Heart Is like a Green Canoe*
> *The World Is a Long Engagement Party*
> *The Great Divorce Has Been Annulled*
> *Romance of Serge Eisenstein*
> *Immanuel Kant, Boy Detective*
> *Emma Kant, Mother of Men*
> *Judy Kant, R.N.*

> The great spruce have stopped shrinking
> they never began and great hunks of the world will fit
>
> (CP, 26)

What prevents hunks of the world fitting, which is a nonsensical statement unless understood as an operation of mind – hunks of the world fit in the world, they just don't always fit points of view – is invariably, in Schuyler, the category. This is the gist of those many poems of his which take as their title or subject a month or a season, the names of which indicate knowledge on the part of the user, but where the point of the poem is always to establish that nothing is permanently known. What is necessary is an active knowing, a knowledge always going back into the world, revisiting its formulations and qualifying its findings, as in 'Standing and Watching', with its minimal but crucial variations between stanzas, and whose title implies passivity but whose tense is active.

But then the question is how, if not through the practice and nomenclature of the category, do things come to be known, how do they show themselves? In response to which fundamental enquiry, in his poetry and prose, Schuyler provides a rich and suggestive vocabulary of knowing. 'December', for instance, a poem which insists on reacquainting with that most clichéd of months, proposes a series of terms: 'Having and giving but also catching glimpses / hints that are revelations' (CP, 14). The poem doesn't settle for a single term, on the grounds, perhaps, that to do so would be to replicate the inactivity of the category, but in its sequence of suggested names it hones in on a recognizable epistemological relation. Another term to set against inadequate modes of knowledge, and which stands behind much of Schuyler's writing, is 'display', to the implications of which for poetry he gave careful thought. Reflecting in his *Diary* on the process of going back through his books to prepare his *Selected Poems*, he notes that 'a lot of thought and affection went not only into writing the damn poems, but also their, uh, display' (D, 191). The way work was displayed mattered to Schuyler in the sense that it matters how paintings are hung, the miscellaneous quality of a number of his books serving, in the spirit of collage, to show individual elements at their best. What he didn't do was just plonk a bunch of poems together, as if their arrangement didn't matter, as if the way items are displayed doesn't contribute to what they are capable of disclosing. Which term was, as 'Empathy and New Year' shows, another of Schuyler's words for the way things come to be known, all twigs after snow, as that poem has it, being 'emboldened to / make big disclosures' (CP, 79).

Such words – revelation, display, disclosure – steer us back into Heideggerean territory, though this time to 'The Origin of the Work of Art', where Heidegger asks, of the work in question 'What happens here? What is at work in the work? Van Gogh's painting is the disclosure of what the equipment, the pair of peasant shoes, *is* in truth. This being emerges into the unconcealment of its Being.'[13] And where in asking how things, in their being, might be known he asserts: 'Only, certainly, by granting the thing, as it were, a free field to display its thingly character directly. Everything that might interpose itself between the thing and us in apprehending and talking about it must be first set aside.'[14] It is foundational to the work of art that, as Heidegger asserts, it responds to a problem from Kant, where the problem is the idea we have, or have been given, of the thing, and where the world is understood as a set of such things. Thus: 'According to Kant, the whole of the world, for example, and even God himself, is a thing of this sort, a thing that does not itself appear, namely a "thing-in-itself"'.[15]

This non-appearing thing is a function of the thinking that produced it, man transposing 'his propositional way of understanding things into the structure of the thing itself'; where the propositional structure is deeply imbricated with conventional grammar, and what it says about things is that they are essences which bear attributes, and that the essences can't be known. For Heidegger the origin of the work of art – where work implies not an object but an activity; he is talking, crucially, about the *work* of art – lies in this flawed sense of things, it being art's function to 'open up in its own way the Being of beings'. 'This opening up, i.e., this revealing, i.e., the truth of beings, happens,' he asserts, 'in the work'. Just exactly *how* it happens he declines to say, partly because it is precisely the purpose and privilege of art to effect the revealing. Thus, when it comes to the essence of the work of art, 'Each answer remains in force as an answer only as long as it is rooted in questioning'. ('May mutters, "Why / Ask questions?" or, "What are the questions you wish to ask?"') Which can sound as if Heidegger is dodging the bullet, except that the seeming evasion is in accordance with the thinking of the piece, because what is at issue is not naming an essence but the work art does of showing things. From which it follows that art is known when it shows itself as such: shows itself, if one can say so, in the act of showing. In part this is a question of the work's own display, Heidegger noting that a work placed in a collection lacks the revelatory qualities of work set up in a situation – a temple, for instance – meant for consecration or praise. In part, also, the work of art's revelatory potential has to do with the nature of its relation to its truth; the way in which, in the work, truth happens. But crucially the *work* of art lies also in the sense of intimacy it must effect, such that poetry should be thought of as a 'projective saying', the object of which is 'unconcealment', the saying, as he puts it, of the 'nearness and remoteness of the gods'.[16]

All of which should, I hope, sound both quite like and quite unlike Schuyler. Thus when Schuyler wrote his letter to Miss Batie, he wanted to establish that in some sense the origin of the work had to do with the way it happens.

It seems to me that readers sometimes make the genesis of a poem more mysterious than it is (by that I perhaps mean, think of it as something outside of their own experience). Often a poem 'happens' to the writer in exactly the same way that it 'happens' to someone who reads it. (SL, 240)

Equally, though, Schuyler's writing is very largely unburdened – if not quite totally so – by any concept so total and overdetermining as Heidegger's idea of Being. Crucially, though, what Heidegger sketches is a relation between the work of art and the world which is rooted in showing, where the showing amounts to a kind of intrinsic allegory, and where allegory, it is worth recalling, derives from the Greek meaning 'other speaking'. Schuyler is always showing. Always in his writing – it is axiomatic – one thing is in the process of disclosing something else.

The Diary demonstrates this constantly. Thus, just as Thoreau was forever noting forms of circulation, so Schuyler is forever noting how things show themselves in and on and through one another.

January 2, 1969

A maple against the light has the dark thin substance of a shadow. …How well the grime on the windows shows up in this winter light.

March 4, 1971

The speed of the wind is seen more in the length of the stroke a branch makes than in the quickness with which it moves – how strong the wind must be that that tree moves at all!

Wednesday, July 20, 1988

Thunder and lightning last night, rather near at hand, but not right here – did it rain? Such heavy fog this morning, the universal wetness proved nothing: but the tall pale delicate cups of the hostas flattened (almost) on the ground do: it rained alright.

November 16, 1970

After a week of rain, late this afternoon the sun shone out under pigeon colored clouds and turned the elm twigs red, the last leaves on the plane tree glowed like dark red glass and the house, freshly painted white, became the color of the sun.

One might go on, and especially one might mention the fascination the late *Diary* has with the Empire State Building, which is shown repeatedly and beautifully taking the impression of something else. Or one might point to any number of poems whose dynamic consists in one thing showing up in another, sentences moving on as effect gives way and passes into further effect. The great statement of this, however, this proliferating showing of things showing things, is 'Hymn to Life'.

As with 'April and its Forsythia', the drama of 'Hymn to Life' has, in part, to do with administrative ways of knowing; against which bureaucratized view of the world – the poem is set in Washington and is punctuated by the to-ing and fro-ing of civil servants – Schuyler presents his own way of bringing the world into view. This amounts in the writing, as he puts it in the poem, to a constantly 'restless surface', in which sentence by sentence something is always happening. This being May, things are everywhere blooming and coming into display, and at every turn something is showing itself in and through something else. As when, in one of any number of shimmering passages:

> The sky
> Colors itself rosily behind gray-black and the rain falls through
> The basketball hoop on a garage, streaking its blackboard with further
> Trails of rust, a lovely color to set with periwinkle violet-blue.
> And the trees shiver and shudder in the light rain blasts from off
> The ocean. The street wet reflects the breakup of the clouds
> On its face, driving over sky with a hissing sound.
>
> (CP, 216)

Or as when, in what is perhaps the poem's emblematic passage:

> Far away
> In Washington, at the Reflecting Pool, the Japanese cherries
> Bust out into their dog mouth pink. Visitors gasp. The sun
> Drips, coats and smears, all that spring yellow under unending
> Blue.
>
> (CP, 222)

Which mouthing, producing a gasp, steers the attention back to the poet himself, who in showing things as always themselves showing things, presents himself at various points in the poem as crucial to the whole process. As when, for instance, he suggests that: 'Time brings us into bloom and we wait, busy, but wait / For the unforced flow of words'. Or: 'The day lives us and in exchange / we it' (CP, 215).

All of which amounts to what? What sense of knowledge does Schuyler present here? What I want to suggest is that there is in his poetry a quite unforced, undogmatic sense of 'showing', in which 'life' (in all its variety), not 'Being' (in its oppressive singularity), is understood to be in a constant state of revelation, things showing themselves in other things all of the time, one thing always being the medium for the disclosure of another. One such medium, though it has a special status – being the form of disclosure of all other disclosures – is the page, and especially the poet's page. Thus at the end of 'April and its Forsythia', the census taker having taken her leave, the poet takes his leave also:

> Ugh. The head of this household is going out in it.
> Willingly nor not, I'll check up on Central Park
> where branches of sunshine were in bloom on Monday.
>   (CP, 23–4)

According to this, and according to Schuyler's poetry as a whole, it is the poet's appointed task – not the bureaucrat's – to show things as they are; a task he is equal to by dint of the fact that he understands himself as continuous with things, with the 'what of which you are a part'. He is confident of this continuity because, in his writing, with its restless surface, its ceaselessly processive syntax, and its often voiceless subject position, the great divorce of self from world has, in a manner of speaking, been annulled. Which is to say that Schuyler's poetry can perform its function of showing because his language is premised not on what Heidegger called a propositional structure, but on a way of thinking about things which takes them always to be showing themselves. Not as themselves, as such, not in their essences, but in and on other things, and especially – through the intercession of the poet's language – on the page. As when, in the *Diary*, allegorically and suggestively:

> the house, freshly painted white, became the color of the sun.

Enthusing

There is an aspect of James Schuyler's enthusiasm it is sad to contemplate. On 23 October 1951, as Nathan Kernan puts it in his detailed chronology of the life:

> Schuyler visited his friends Donald Windham and Sandy Campbell in a manic and ecstatic state, claiming to have talked to the Virgin Mary who told him that Judgement Day was at hand. The next day Schuyler entered Bloomingdale mental hospital in White Plains, New York. (D, 283)

This was the first of numerous similar episodes in Schuyler's life. His mental health was quite frequently fragile, such that, as William Corbett observes in the *Selected Letters*, he was unable, after 1961, to hold down regular employment, and such that through the 1970s and the first half of the 1980s, he was several times hospitalised (SL, 135). During one such period of hospitalization in 1975, he wrote 'The Payne Whitney Poems', subsequently published in his 1980 collection *The Morning of the Poem*. In that short, deeply moving, diary-like cycle, Schuyler presents in miniature many aspects of his work: the importance of observation, a fascination with the vicissitudes of weather, a fondness for the collage-like list (as in 'Sleep'), and, throughout the cycle, a sense that in writing one might better make oneself at home in one's world. Also, though, not surprisingly, there is in the poems a more than usually urgent enthusiasm, as in 'Linen', when Schuyler presumes identity with the situation he is trying to present: 'Now, this moment / flows out of me / down the pen and / writes' (CP, 254). 'What', the last poem of the cycle, consists of a series of borderline paranoid questions: 'What's in those pills?', 'Why are they hammering / iron outside?' The last of which, 'What is a / poem anyway', prompts a statement likening poetry to madness:

> The daffodils, the heather
> and the freesias all
> speak to me. I speak
> back, like St. Francis
> and the wolf of Gubbio.
> (CP, 258)

I have no interest, in this essay, in pathologizing Schuyler's poetry. What he wrote when his mental health was robust is demonstrably different, in detail and quality, from the few works – often jottings – that survive from his periods of breakdown. Unquestionably, however, such that it would be false not to observe it, there was in Schuyler's structure of thought a propensity to externalize speech, such that agencies incapable of words were imagined to voice themselves. There is a tendency towards this, I think, in the last phase of *The Diary*, much of which dwells on Schuyler's conversion to Episcopalianism. Considered doctrinally, a turn to Episcopalianism does not, of course, show a propensity towards the more extreme implications of enthusiasm, as was indicated in the discussion of Evert Duyckinck's differences with Melville. In Schuyler's case, however, the religious turn in his thinking produced a certain simplification, not least in his positioning of voice. One hears this in part in the way the diary is given over, increasingly frequently, to passages transcribed from scripture, where as often as not the meaning is an uncomplicated discourse with the divine. As in, for instance, from Isaiah: 44, 'Sing, O heavens, for the Lord has done it; Shout, O depths, of the earth; break forth into singing, O mountains, O forest, and every tree in it!' (D, 248). Of a piece with this is a slide, from time to time, in the prose of the *Diary*, towards the transcendental, where what is being shown, as in Emerson and also Heidegger, is not life in its various effects, but the world as sign:

> After the days and days of heat going higher and higher, the torn and dirt-soaked gray pressing down and down into the streets, into rooms, in muggy, hugging haze ... an ascending depth into which to rise, infinity: and if that is

the look of the Infinite, the Creator, the Unseeable and Unknowable, who, indeed, would not love him? (D, 194)

And then finally, as Schuyler continues his practice of transcription in his *Diary*, cobbling bits and pieces from his reading together, the quotes start to lose something of their miscellaneous quality, and start instead to operate according to some kind of design, where the purpose seems to be to assert an easy interchange with things. Thus the entry for Monday, 23 November 1987 consists of a quotation from Pasternak's Memoir *Safe Conduct*: 'an indifference to the immediacy of truth, is what infuriates him. As though this is a slap in the face of humanity in his person' (D, 202). The entry for 4 July 1988, meanwhile, is a quote from Freud that Schuyler came across in the *New Yorker*: 'I learnt to restrain speculative tendencies and to follow the unforgotten advice of my master, Charcot: to look at the same things again and again until they themselves begin to speak (D, 228–9).

Schuyler's best writing steadfastly resists a drift towards the transcendental, whose simplifying of the world into signs is what, in many respects, his poetry exists to counteract. A voracious reader, capable of brilliant developments of major Modern writers – not least Thoreau, Stevens, Moore and Pound – Schuyler arrived at a poetry which, in its qualities of sound and syntax, constituted a constantly deft acknowledgement of the way things happen. At his best he achieved a language for the relation between the self and his or her environment, where the self could be appreciated as just another effect; an intimacy with the world in writing which understood itself as entirely provisional. One can well call this poetic enthusiasm, with all the tensions of experiment, mediation and immediacy that phrase implies, with its complications and richnesses of voice; but it is also well to identify it as 'Freely Espousing'; where what the phrase implies is an unfettered utterance, and where the cause is language and its capacity to disclose.

Notes

1 James Schuyler, *The Diary of James Schuyler*, ed. Nathan Kernan, Santa Rosa, Calif., Black Sparrow Press, 1997, p. 30; hereafter referred to in the text as D.

2 After a breakdown in 1961, Schuyler lived with Fairfield Porter's family for the best part of twelve years, spending his summers on Great Spruce Head Island, off the coast of Maine. Prior and subsequent to that he mostly lived in Manhattan.

3 James Schuyler, *Collected Poems*, New York, Farrar, Straus and Giroux, 1998, p. 3; hereafter referred to in the text as CP.

4 Wallace Stevens, *Collected Poetry and Prose*, New York, Library of America, 1997, pp. 662, 663.

5 Ibid., p. 663.

6 Jean W. Ross, 'CA interviews the author', *Contemporary Authors*, vol. 101, ed. Frances C. Locher, Detroit, Gale Research, 1981, p. 446.

7 James Schuyler, *Just the Thing: Selected Letters of James Schuyler*, ed. William Corbett, New York, Turtle Point Press, 2004, p. 239; hereafter referred to in the text as SL.

8 For another discussion of the figure of the kiss in Schuyler, see Gillian Conoley, 'The Inescapable Kiss', *Denver Quarterly*, 24.4, Spring 1990, pp. 42–8.

9 Stevens, *Collected*, p. 661.

10 Ibid. pp. 714, 720.

11 Ibid., p. 678.

12 Robert Thompson, 'An Interview with James Schuyler', *Denver Quarterly*, 26, Spring 1992, p. 111.

13 Martin Heidegger, *Basic Writings*, ed. David Farrell Krell, London, Routledge, 1993, p. 161.

14 Ibid., p. 151.

15 Ibid., p. 147.

16 Ibid., pp. 150, 165, 195, 197, 198.

Afterword: enthusiasm and audit

This book has been about the transmission of literature. It has shown various writers taking responsibility for that transmission, whether within their writing or in their cultural activism. The word for both kinds of action has been enthusiasm. Enthusiasm, it has been argued, is integral to what Modern American literature, in particular, knows; enthusiasm being, as each of the writers discussed here has one way or another understood it, the state of mind in which composition is possible. It is also integral to the circulation of literature, enthusiasm and enthusiasts having been, at various moments, crucial to the renovation and continuation of literary activity. What this implies, what a discussion of literary enthusiasm shows, is that there is inherent in literary understanding – in the way literature knows the world – what Shaftesbury called an 'itch to impart'. Which is to say that in some sense it is inherent in the structure of literary value that there is an impulse to keep discoveries in circulation. 'Some days,' Schuyler wrote on 27 April 1971, 'I have an almost irresistible urge to write.' 'There's no use,' Pound wrote,

> in a strong impulse if it is all or nearly all lost in bungling transmission and technique. This obnoxious word that I'm always brandishing about means nothing but a transmission of the impulse intact. It means that you not only get the thing off your chest, but that you get it into somebody else's.[1]

The word for both Schuyler's 'urge' and Pound's 'impulse', for the state of mind each associates with writing, has historically been enthusiasm. Enthusiasm fully understood, as an intense, sometimes ruinous relation of the mind to its object, is integral to the creation and the circulation of literature.

With the circulatory aspect of enthusiasm particularly in mind, and following Lewis Hyde, an analogy has been drawn with gift economics, where the gift is understood as a form of circulation relatively unencumbered by mediations (money); and where what matters is not, chiefly, what is returned, but that the thing in question has been passed on.

At its best, along the lines of the gift – though both circuits can quickly be corrupted by the will to dominate – literary enthusiasm stands for the ceaseless and unfettered circulation of works and their insights. It is, isn't it, the most natural thing in the world, when you have read a great work of literature, to want to pass it on; the reading is barely complete before that recirculation has happened. This is what each of the writers in this book believed, each building that insight into their writing practice. As Marianne Moore said, 'If you are charmed by an author, I think it's a very strange and invalid imagination that doesn't long to share it. Somebody else should read it, don't you think?'

Modern American writing, in so far as it can be understood to have its foundations in Emerson, had its origins, as he observed, in a fully developed, historically aware, enthusiastic view of the world; that enthusiastic point of departure being crucial, so it has been suggested, to the literature's mobility, form and subject matter. William Penn identified in George Fox's experimentalism a desire for 'nearness' with the condition of inspiration, the same 'nearness' that Stanley Cavell has described as American literature's preferred relation with things. It is a sense of nearness which folds the enthusiasm of religion back into the enthusiasm of aesthetic philosophy. There what it promised, after Kant in particular, in the moment of being out of one's senses, was a supplement to the processes of understanding and reason (an overcoming of the 'hindrance of sensibility'), whereby a closer acquaintance with the world is made possible. What enthusiasm thus wants to name is a state of mind in which it is possible to grasp, or to be grasped by, the things and ways of the world. Kant presented this state under the heading of aesthetics, and Heidegger in particular understood it as the work of poetic language. The writers I have discussed in this book have written in the conviction that, as O'Hara repeatedly asserted, composition is a mode of knowledge, that techniques can be arrived at (largely through the jettisoning of inappropriate techniques) whereby through language the world can be better known. *Walden*, according to this point of view, is what Thoreau knew. 'A Step Away from Them' is what in mid-town Manhattan, at 12.40 of a Thursday in August 1956, O'Hara knew. 'Critics and Connoisseurs' is Marianne Moore's statement of how things are known. 'Hymn to Life' is Schuyler's knowledge.

Precisely because of such religious and aesthetic origins, Modern American writing runs freely and readily into conflict with bureaucracy, as this book has several times shown. Which means that as this book has turned its head to the situation in which it is written, so an American literature born of an enthusiastic state of mind has once again been taken as a riposte to a British formalism. But this is not to make a national argument, not least because, as Emerson, Thoreau and Pound in turn did battle with the bureaucratic mindset, it was in American universities, quite as much as in some specious, generalized sense of British character, that they found their target. Not to mention the fact that now, above all, as America exports its religious-economic base across the world, there is nothing to endorse in its headline sense of national fundamentalism. Melville anticipated this – it is tempting in this context to say 'foretold' – and it is critical to *Moby-Dick* that he understood how deeply enthusiasm can corrupt. Hence Ahab, in whom Quaker peculiarities, though 'unoutgrown', were plainly distorted, and through whom an original impulse to permit general participation in spiritual experience became an urge to dominate, to exercise tyranny over others' minds. Yet to shy from enthusiasm because in every spiritual experimentalist there is an incipient antinomian would be, as it were, to throw Ishmael out with the saltwater. It would be to ignore in *Moby-Dick*, and the cultural possibilities it sets up, Ishmael's urge to see what whaling is, and once having seen it to pass it on in the form most appropriate to its transmission. It would be to ignore, also, the novel's generous and unforbidding circulation of other texts. And above all it would be to ignore the fact that in Ahab what Melville presents is an enthusiast who has become, among other things, a bureaucrat, who uses form and ritual as a mode of coercion, whose relation to things involves constantly converting them into what they are not. Ahab, as generations of commentators have rightly observed, is a proto-dictator, and unquestionably his status as such owes in part to his charisma, and so through a process of distortion to his enthusiastic origins. But that he can manage his mission owes to his readiness to mediate and manipulate knowledge, to operate according to the prescriptions of the bureaucratic mind.

In so far, then, as this book about American literature, written from and referring to a British university setting, makes an argument back and forth across the Atlantic, what is at issue is the form of literary knowledge. What the American writers I have been discussing variously present is an ongoing argument for forms of expression which follow writing's insights and imperatives. The currently coercive character of the forms and procedures of British university existence mean that what literature knows, and how it operates, is, on a routine basis, being lost from view. Bureaucracy, in its current British academic manifestation, has two general characteristics. The first is a tendency to subject non-specific, machine-readable language – the most graphic version of which is the projected star-rating system of the RAE – whereby in the process of valuation the terms of the work are so translated as radically to diminish its proposed content. The second and related general characteristic is a tendency to bring the circulation of literary work, understanding and values to a halt. What is required by the present bureaucracy are 'outputs', where outputs are endpoints, assessable products that can be assigned a numeric value, and where that value becomes the object – the work existing for the purpose of audit – and where the effect of audit is to foreclose the process of transmission; to bring it to a halt; to effect a STOP. It is in the nature of bureaucracy, this is to say, that it militates directly against the understanding of literature; that it works in opposition to the enthusiastic state of mind which, at some level or another, is vital to literary activity.

Such enthusiasm is difficult to sustain. Of the enthusiasts discussed in this book, only Moore lived out a long and relatively steady life. Thoreau died of tuberculosis at the age of forty-four. Melville died in obscurity, having long since retreated from the American literary scene, deeply despondent at the reception and commercial failure of *Moby-Dick*. Pound's cultural enthusiasm distorted into zealous anti-Semitism. Frank O'Hara died at the age of forty, in a state, so some have argued, of literary exhaustion. James Schuyler was periodically hospitalized throughout his life. Emerson had anticipated this. 'What is a man good for,' he asked, 'without enthusiasm? and what is enthusiasm without this daring of ruin for its object?' What he understood was that, difficult as it can be to sustain, and whether at the time people like it or not, literary culture requires enthusiasm. Which makes it all the more important that the writer as enthusiast should be recognized, that their terms should be understood, that the energies by which they circulate value should be appreciated and made known. And it makes it crucial that institutions professing a concern for literary culture, instead of operating procedures that militate daily against its dissemination, should permit the enthusiasms by which such culture is passed on.

Note

1 Ezra Pound, *Selected Letters: 1907-41*, ed. D. D. Paige, London, Faber and Faber, 1970, p 23.

Acknowledgements

I have long since been grateful whenever in my reading I have come across literary enthusiasts: writers and critics who as a principle of their thought and action have sought to pass work on. Several years ago now I was fortunate to spend a few months in the libraries of Harvard University, reading and rereading the work of people who have come for me to stand for enthusiasm. I am grateful to my colleagues in the School of English at the University of Kent, and to the Department of English at Harvard for making that preliminary reading possible. Then, as now, Frank O'Hara seemed an exemplary enthusiast, and not least for the idea of literary community he stimulated. It is a sense of community marked by great generosity, and it persists not least in Boston, where I was lucky enough to be at the receiving end of Bill Corbett and Ed Barrett's hospitality. It is a pleasure to thank them for that here.

For me, as for many people, the book which best conceptualizes the generosities of literature is Lewis Hyde's *The Gift*, and I am glad to be able to acknowledge it as a work which enabled me, at an early stage, to start to think about the possibilities of enthusiasm. Since then my thinking about poetry and enthusiasm has benefited greatly from conversations with a number of people. I am grateful to my colleagues on the MA in Modern Poetry at the University of Kent, David Ayers and Jan Montefiore, and also to the MA's students, for the free-flow of ideas that made the collective teaching of that course such a stimulating pleasure. I am grateful also to Robert Potts, with whom, as co-editor of *Poetry Review*, I spent many a long hour in happy and, for me, instructive discussion. It was a great pleasure to be holed up with him in Betterton Street for three years. The Philosophy Reading Group at the University of Kent has always offered the most welcoming of learning environments, and outside of that I have been glad to be able to bat ideas about with Murray Smith. I especially want to thank the following people who have helped me in one way or another with the preparation of the book: John Beck, Keith Carabine, Stephen James, Simon Malpas, Michael Schmidt, David Trotter, and Geoff Ward. The Enthusiast, as ever, knows who he is.

Initial research for this book was enabled by a British Academy Travel Grant. Completion was made possible by a grant from the Arts and Humanities Research Council. I am grateful to both organizations, and in particular to the AHRC's anonymous external assessors, for the care with which they considered the project and the timely encouragement they gave it. At various stages, elements of the book were presented as research papers, at the universities of Oxford, Cambridge, Reading and Newcastle. I am glad of the invitations to speak on these occasions, and for the questions and discussion they gave rise to. I am grateful again to Manchester University Press, to its readers, and especially to Matthew Frost, for his keen eye and his ceaselessly generous spirit. This book is for Eli and Nora, great enthusiasts both, and for Abi and Lily, with love and thanks.

The author and publisher wish to thank the following for permission to re-present the words of Ezra Pound, Marianne Moore, Frank O'Hara and James Schuyler: Faber, Carcanet, Alfred Knopf, and Farrar, Straus and Giroux. Every effort has been made to trace all copyright holders, but if any have been inadvertently overlooked the publishers will be happy to put matters right in any subsequent edition.

Bibliography

Andrews, Edward Deming, *The People Called Shakers: A Search for the Perfect Society*, New York, Dover, 1963

Berkson, Bill and LeSueur, Joe (eds.), *Homage to Frank O'Hara*, Berkeley, Calif., Big Sky, 1978

Bowra, C.M. *Inspiration and Poetry*, London, Macmillan, 1955

Breton, André, *Manifestoes of Surrealism*, tr. Richard Seaver and Helen R. Lane, Ann Arbor, Ann Arbor Paperbacks, University of Michigan Press, 2000

Brodhead, Richard H. (ed.), *New Essays on Moby-Dick*, Cambridge, Cambridge University Press, 1986

Buell, Lawrence, 'Moby-Dick as Sacred Text', in Richard H. Brodhead (ed.), *New Essays on Moby-Dick*, Cambridge, Cambridge University Press, 1986, pp. 53–72

Buell, Lawrence, *The Environmental Imagination: Thoreau, Nature Writing, and The Formation of American Culture*, Cambridge, Mass., Belknap Press of Harvard University Press, 1995

Cain, William E., *A Historical Guide to Henry David Thoreau*, Oxford, Oxford University Press, 2000

Carpenter, Humphrey, *A Serious Character: The Life of Ezra Pound*, London, Faber and Faber, 1988

Casaubon, Meric, *Treatise Concerning Enthusiasm* (1656), Scholars' Facsimiles and Reprints, 1970

Cavell, Stanley, *In Quest of the Ordinary: Lines of Skepticism and Romanticism*, Chicago and London, University of Chicago Press, 1988

Cavell, Stanley, *The Senses of Walden*, Chicago and London, University of Chicago Press, 1992

Clark, Timothy, *The Theory of Inspiration: Composition as a Crisis of Subjectivity in Romantic and Post-Romantic Writing*, Manchester and New York, Manchester University Press, 1997

Conoley, Gillian, 'The Inescapable Kiss', *Denver Quarterly*, 24.4, Spring 1990, pp. 42–8

Cookson, William, *A Guide to the Cantos of Ezra Pound*, London, Anvil Press Poetry, 2001

Derrida, Jacques, 'Che cos'è la poesia?', in Peggy Kamuf (ed.), *A Derrida Reader: Between the Blinds*, London and New York, Harvester Wheatsheaf, 1991, pp. 221–37

de Staël, Germaine, *Major Writings of Germaine de Staël*, tr. Vivian Folkenflik, New York, Columbia University Press, 1987, p. 321

Douglas, Major C.H., *Economic Democracy*, London, Cecil Palmer, 1920

Duff, William, *An Essay on Original Genius and its Various Modes of Exertion in Philosophy and the Fine Arts, Particularly Poetry* (1767), ed. John L. Mahoney, Delmar, New York, Scholars' Facsimiles, 1978

Ellmann, Maud, *The Poetics of Impersonality: T.S. Eliot and Ezra Pound*, Brighton, Harvester Press, 1987

Emerson, Ralph Waldo, *Letters and Social Aims*, London, George Routledge and Sons, 1883

Emerson, Ralph Waldo, *The Collected Works of Ralph Waldo Emerson*, Cambridge, Mass., Harvard University Press, 1971

Emerson, Ralph Waldo, *Essays and Lectures*, New York, Library of America, 1983

Emery, Clark, *Ideas into Action: A Study of Pound's Cantos*, Miami, Fla., University of Miami Press, 1958

Emmott, Elizabeth Braithwaite, *A Short History of Quakerism (Earlier Periods)*, London, Swarthmore Press, 1923

Fox, George, *Journal of George Fox, Seventh Edition in Two Volumes, with a Preface by William Penn*, London, W. and F. G. Cash, 1852

Fredricks, Nancy, *Melville's Art of Democracy*, Athens and London, University of Georgia Press, 1995

Garber, Frederick, *Thoreau's Redemptive Imagination*, New York, New York University Press, 1977

Hamm, Thomas D., *The Quakers in America*, New York, Columbia University Press, 2003

Heidegger, Martin, *Basic Writings*, rev. and expanded edn, ed. David Farrell Krell, London, Routledge, 1993

Holley, Margaret, *The Poetry of Marianne Moore: A Study in Voice and Value*, Cambridge, Cambridge University Press, 1987

Hume, David, *Essays Moral, Political and Literary*, Oxford, Oxford University Press, 1966

Hyde, Lewis, *The Gift: Imagination and the Erotic Life of Property*, London, Vintage, 1999

Kant, Immanuel, *The Critique of Judgement*, tr. James Creed Meredith, Oxford, Clarendon Press, 1952

Kant, Immanuel, *Critique of Pure Reason*, tr. Norman Kemp Smith, London, Macmillan, 1986

Kenner, Hugh, *The Poetry of Ezra Pound*, London, Faber and Faber, 1951

Knox, R. A., *Enthusiasm: A Chapter in the History of Religion*, Oxford, Oxford University Press, 1950

LeSueur, Joe, *Digressions on Some Poems by Frank O'Hara*, New York, Farrar, Straus and Giroux, 2004

Locke, John, *An Essay Concerning Human Understanding*, Oxford, Clarendon Press, 1985

Lovejoy, David S., *Religious Enthusiasm in the New World: Heresy to Revolution*, Cambridge, Mass. and London, Harvard University Press, 1985

Marx, Karl and Engels, Friedrich, *Selected Works in One Volume*, London, Lawrence and Wishart, 1980

Matthiessen, *American Renaissance: Art and Expression in the Age of Emerson and Whitman*, London, Oxford, New York, Oxford University Press, 1979

Mee, Jon, *Dangerous Enthusiasm: William Blake and the Culture of Radicalism in the 1970s*, Oxford, Clarendon Press, 1992

Mee, Jon, *Romanticism, Enthusiasm and Regulation: Poetics and the Policing of Culture in the Romantic Period*, Oxford, Oxford University Press, 2002

Melville, Herman, *Moby-Dick*, ed. Hershel Parker and Harrison Hayford, New York, W.W. Norton & Co., 1967

Melville, Herman, *Mardi and a Voyage Thither*, ed. Harrison Hayford, Hershel Parker G. Thomas Tanselle, Evanston and Chicago, Northwestern University Press and Newberry Library, 1970

Melville, Herman, *Pierre, or The Ambiguities*, Evanston and Chicago, Northwestern University Press, 1971

Melville, Herman, *Moby-Dick; or The Whale*, ed. Harold Beaver, Harmondsworth, Penguin, 1972

Melville, Herman, *The Confidence-Man: His Masquerade*, Evanston and Chicago, Northwestern University Press and Newberry Library, 1984

Melville, Herman, *Moby-Dick; or, The Whale*, ed. Harrison Hayford, Hershell Parker and G. Thomas Tanselle, Northwestern University Press and Newberry Library, 1988

Moore, Marianne, *The Complete Prose of Marianne Moore*, London, Faber and Faber, 1987

Moore, Marianne, 'The Art of Poetry: Marianne Moore', in George Plimpton (ed.), *Poets at Work: The Paris Review Interviews*, Harmondsworth, Penguin, 1989

Moore, Marianne, *Becoming Marianne Moore: The Early Poems, 1907–1924*, ed. Robin G. Schulze, Berkeley, University of California Press, 2002

Moore, Marianne, *The Poems of Marianne Moore*, ed. Grace Schulman, London, Faber and Faber, 2003

More, Henry, *Enthusiasmus Triumphatus*, London, 1656

Nietzsche, Friedrich, *On the Genealogy of Morality*, Cambridge, Cambridge University Press, 2003

O'Hara, Frank, *Lunch Poems*, San Francisco, City Lights Books, 1964

O'Hara, Frank, *Art Chronicles: 1954–1966*, New York, George Braziller, 1975

O'Hara, Frank, *Standing Still and Walking in New York*, ed. Donald Allen, Bolinas, California, Grey Fox Press, 1975

O'Hara, Frank, *The Collected Poems of Frank O'Hara*, ed. Donald Allen, intro. John Ashbery, Berkeley and London, University of California Press, 1995

Olson, Charles, *Call Me Ishmael*, Baltimore and London, Johns Hopkins University Press, 1997

Oppen, George, *New Collected Poems*, Manchester, Carcanet, 2003

Oxley, William, *The Cauldron of Inspiration*, Salzburg, Universität Salzburg, 1983

Parker, Hershel, *Herman Melville: A Biography, Vol. 1*, Baltimore and London, Johns Hopkins University Press, 1996

Parker, Hershel, *Herman Melville: A Biography, Vol. 2*, Baltimore and London, Johns Hopkins University Press, 2005

Pasternak, Boris, *Doctor Zhivago*, tr. Max Hayward and Manya Harari, London, Collins and Harvill Press, 1959

Pasternak, Boris, *Safe Conduct: An Early Autobiography and Other Works*, London, Elek Books, 1959

Penn, William, 'Preface' to George Fox, *Journal of George Fox*, London, W. and F. G. Cash, 1852

Plato, *The Dialogues of Plato*, tr. B. Jowett, Oxford, Clarendon Press, 1967

Pound, Ezra *The Spirit of Romance*, Norfolk, Conn., New Directions Books, 1929

Pound, Ezra, *Guide to Kulchur*, New York, New Directions, 1938

Pound, Ezra, *Literary Essays of Ezra Pound*, ed. T. S. Eliot, London, Faber and Faber, 1954

Pound, Ezra, *Gaudier-Brzeska: A Memoir*, Hessle, Marvell Press, 1966

Pound, Ezra, *Selected Letters: 1907–1941*, ed. D. D. Paige, London, Faber and Faber, 1970

Pound, Ezra, *Selected Prose 1909–1965*, ed. William Cookson, London, Faber and Faber, 1973

Pound, Ezra *The Cantos*, London, Faber and Faber, 1986

Pound, Ezra, *Personae: The Shorter Poems of Ezra Pound*, London, Faber and Faber, 1990

Richardson, Robert D. Jr, *Henry Thoreau: A Life of the Mind*, Berkeley, Los Angeles and London, University of California Press, 1986

Ross, Jean W., 'CA Interviews the Author', *Contemporary Authors*, vol. 101, ed. Frances C. Locher, Detroit, Gale Research, 1981, pp. 42–8

Schuyler, James, *The Diary of James Schuyler*, ed. Nathan Kernan, Santa Rosa, Calif., Black Sparrow Press, 1997

Schuyler, James, *Collected Poems*, New York, Farrar, Straus and Giroux, 1998

Schuyler, James, *Selected Art Writings*, ed. Simon Pettet, Santa Rosa, Calif., Black Sparrow Press, 1998

Schuyler, James, *Just the Thing: Selected Letters of James Schuyler, 1951–1991*, ed. William Corbett, New York, Turtle Point Press, 2004

Shaftesbury, Earl (Anthony Ashley Cooper), *Characteristicks of Men, Manners, Opinions, Times, in Three volumes*, London, John Darby, 1715

Smith, Nigel (ed.), *A Collection of Ranter Writings from the Seventeenth Century*, London, Junction Books, 1983

Sontag, Susan, *Against Interpretation*, New York, Farrar, Straus, 1966

Stammy, Cynthia, *Marianne Moore and China: Orientalism and a Writing of America*, Oxford, Oxford University Press, 1999

Stevens, Wallace, *Collected Poetry and Prose*, New York, Library of America, 1997

Thompson, Robert, 'An Interview with James Schuyler', *Denver Quarterly*, 26, Spring 1992, pp. 105–22

Thoreau, Henry David, *Excursions*, New York, Corinth Books, 1962

Thoreau, Henry David, *Early Essays and Miscellanies*, ed. Joseph J. Modenhauer, Edwin Mower and Alexandra C. Kern, Princeton, NJ., Princeton University Press, 1975

Thoreau, Henry David, *A Week on the Concord and Merrimack Rivers*, New York, Library of America, 1985

Thoreau, Henry David, *Walden*, ed. Stephen Fender, Oxford, Oxford University Press, 1997

Tomlinson, Charles (ed.), *Marianne Moore: A Collection of Critical Essays*, Englewood Cliffs, NJ., Prentice Hall, 1969

Tucker, Susie L., *Enthusiasm: A Study in Semantic Change*, Cambridge, Cambridge University Press, 1972

Ward, Geoff, *Statutes of Liberty: The New York School of Poets*, London, Macmillan, 1993

Wesley, John, *The Works of John Wesley, Volume V*, Grand Rapids, Mich., Zondervan Publishing House, 1872

Yeats, W. B. (ed.), *Oxford Book of Modern Verse, 1892–1935*, Oxford, Clarendon Press, 1936

Index